T0214922

The Adventurous and Practical Journey to a Large-Scale Enterprise Solution

The high failure rate of enterprise resource planning (ERP) projects is a pressing concern for both academic researchers and industrial practitioners. The challenges of an ERP implementation are particularly high when the project involves designing and developing a system from scratch. Organizations often turn to vendors and consultants for handling such projects, but every aspect of an ERP project is opaque for both customers and vendors.

Unlocking the mysteries of building a large-scale ERP system, **The Adventurous and Practical Journey to a Large-Scale Enterprise Solution** tells the story of implementing an applied enterprise solution. The book covers the field of enterprise resource planning by examining state-of-the-art concepts in software project management methodology, design and development integration policy, and deployment framework, including:

- A hybrid project management methodology using waterfall as well as a customized Scrum-based approach
- A novel multi-tiered software architecture featuring an enhanced flowable process engine
- A unique platform for coding business processes efficiently
- Integration to embed ERP modules in physical devices
- A heuristic-based framework to successfully step into the Go-live period

Written to help ERP project professionals, the book charts the path that they should travel from project ideation to system implementation. It presents a detailed, real-life case study of implementing a large-scale ERP and uses storytelling to demonstrate incorrect and correct decisions frequently made by vendors and customers. Filled with practical lessons learned, the book explains the ins and outs of adopting project methodologies. It weaves a tale that features real-world and scholarly aspects of an ERP implementation.

The Adventurous and Practical Journey to a Large-Scale Enterprise Solution
Threading the Way to Implementing an ERP through MIDRP Practice

FANAP Studies & Research Center

CRC Press
Taylor & Francis Group
Boca Raton London New York

CRC Press is an imprint of the
Taylor & Francis Group, an **informa** business
AN AUERBACH BOOK

First edition published 2023
by CRC Press
6000 Broken Sound Parkway NW, Suite 300, Boca Raton, FL 33487-2742

and by CRC Press
4 Park Square, Milton Park, Abingdon, Oxon, OX14 4RN

CRC Press is an imprint of Taylor & Francis Group, LLC

ISBN: 978-1-032-43993-8 (hbk)
ISBN: 978-1-032-41175-0 (pbk)
ISBN: 978-1-003-36980-6 (ebk)

DOI: 10.1201/9781003369806

Typeset in Garamond
by MPS Limited, Dehradun

Contents

Contents

Preface

Hedging against the high failure rate of enterprise resource planning (ERP) projects has been the main concern of both academic and industrial practitioners. The challenges of ERP implementation are exacerbated when it comes to its design and development from scratch. In this respect and according to a normal condition, the customer would appoint a well-experienced vendor to accomplish its requirements under the umbrella of an integrated enterprise solution. However, what would be happening if the previous experiences within the target region as well as the underlying limitations cast doubt about employing a popular ERP vendor? How could a fresh vendor surmount the challenges of the ERP implementation to satisfy the requirements of the customer with a large-scale business? In this circumstance, every aspect of an ERP accomplishment project is opaque for both customers and vendors. The related literature on the detailed and comprehensive procedure for conducting an ERP project is not significant since it is tied to commercial issues. Due to the fierce market competition, the websites of the popular ERP vendors avoid sharing the necessary data about the main issues and challenges and the way of coping with the problems. Meanwhile, what should be done by that fresh vendor in the significant lack of practical data? The corresponding fresh ERP vendor has to go through a broad spectrum of commercial and scientific documents in order to derive the appropriate methodology while using trial-and-error to put that methodology into practice. This can be a time-consuming and burdensome task for the involved parties.

To unlock the adventurous mysteries of running a large-scale ERP from A to Z, the current book articulates the story of implementing an applied enterprise solution with the cooperation of MIDHCO and FANAP companies. The book is designed in a way to meet the needs of ERP participants in practice by illuminating the whole path in the most digestible and comprehensive form. The book focuses on a real case study of implementing a large-scale ERP up to the smallest detail using a storytelling tone. Such a tone is to clearly reflect the influence of adopting wrong and right decisions that may be adopted by fresh vendors and customers in the context of an ERP. By gathering a package of practical lessons learned, a newcomer in the field of ERP implementation would probably adopt correct decisions instead of prohibitive wrong ones. Accordingly, the cost of trial-and-error would be reduced, and thereby the failure rate for the participants of these types of projects could be minimized. For instance, the current book implies how and why the ERP's participants should adopt an initial project methodology and then switch to a matured counterpart under certain circumstances. Notably, the book weaves a complicated plot that follows both adventurous and scholarly facets of being engaged with an ERP implementation project. The adventurous tone of the content is mainly employed in describing the onset involvement at the beginning involvement of the key story's characters with every new step towards completing the desired solution. Meanwhile, the rest of the content is to signal the adopted knowledge-based practices to resolve the real challenges being captured by the scholarly tone throughout the book.

Precisely, the book covers the field of enterprise resource planning by considering state-of-the-art concepts in terms of software project management methodology, design and development integration policy, and deployment framework. In the context of project management of enterprise solutions, our book involves a new applied hybrid methodology composed of the waterfall as well as a customized Scrum-based approach. Regarding the software architecture, the content of the current book provides a novel multi-tiered design being equipped with an enhanced flowable process engine. In case of the software development, the present book employs a unique platform for coding business processes in the most efficient manner. Additionally, the proposed integration innovatively embeds different modules of the ERP into the physical devices of the addressed case study. Finally, the new facet associated with the software deployment of this book can be attributed to the presence of a heuristic framework to successfully step into the Go-live period. This heuristic framework is very valuable since it has been derived through an excruciating trial-and-error in a real environment.

In terms of the potential audiences, the book fits well with the requirements of researchers and industrial practitioners, simultaneously. The researchers-based target audiences include undergraduates, post-graduates, and professors who are looking for a comprehensive source with practical implications in the courses associated with enterprise solutions. The industrial practitioners-based target audiences also involve both ERP customers and vendors who need managerial insight and technical information on directing such a project from scratch. All in all, the present hoped-for study can play a workable role in streamlining business and research-oriented activities.

Acknowledgments

Due to the case study-oriented subject of this book, it could not be prepared under the participation of only a handful number of individuals. Generally, this book is indebted to two groups of people: the professional practitioners who paved the way for providing the essence of the book's material and the intellectual ones who gathered that material on the basis of a scientific publication.

In detail, the material of this book is a direct outcome of implementing a large-scale software project through the active collaboration of MIDHCO and FANAP companies under the supportive umbrella of the Pasargad Financial Group. Accordingly, our sincere gratitude goes to Dr. Ali Asghar Pourmand and Dr. Shahab Javanmardi as the CEOs of MIDHCO and FANAP on the behalf of the corresponding staff, respectively. They succeeded in managing their resources in a way that the line-by-line facts of the book could be shaped. Furthermore, the exceptional performance of Dr. Mohammad Jafar Ekramjafari, the consultant of MIDHCO's CEO, is no mean feat owing to taking on the mantle of fruitfully advancing this complex project. Let's be thankful for the wise resourcefulness of Mr. Ramin Amrbar, Mr. Mohammad Emami, and Mr. Peiman Gholami, the project managers of MIDHCO Co. Their significant cooperation with the specialists of FANAP Co. resulted in the reflected achievements of the current study. The realization of the project also owed to the depth of experience of POSCO ICT Co. under the supervision of Mr. Jaewoo Lim. Besides, Dr. Majid Ghasemi, the CEO of the Pasargad Financial Group, is gratefully appreciated owing to his grand strategy in terms of underpinning the companies to get involved in a completely innovative and knowledge-based project. Indeed, such an outlined strategy in the project was the cornerstone of creating the present work.

Meanwhile, the commendable original plan behind documenting the engineering value of that project in a storytelling manner and thereby writing this book pertained to Mr. Hamidreza Amouzegar, the deputy of Development & Technology of FANAP Company. To properly fulfill such an idea, FANAP Studies & Research Center undertook the responsibility of brainstorming, plotting, and consequently writing this book via the significant engagement of its scholar members. In this regard, special thanks to the members of the Center, for their brilliant idea, knowledgeable leadership, and constant monitoring over the completion of this work. The Center's scholars did a great job in framing the skeleton of the book's content and handling the word-by-word documentation of each chapter. Hence, the deepest thanks are also expressed to Dr. Sajjad Jalali, Dr. Mohammad Amini, Dr. Ali Gharaei, and Mrs. Mona Chenani Saleh. In addition to playing a critical role in documenting Chapter 1, 3, and 4, Sajjad's contribution was indispensable in crafting an engaging storytelling tone and fitting it into the body of the book. Having a profound knowledge of computer science, Mohammad admirably carried out the documentation of the software development-oriented content of Chapter 5, 6, 7, 8, and 10. Ali has a pervasive influence in enriching different parts of this book, particularly, by establishing the thorough review of Chapter 2 and showcasing the project's launching process of Chapter 9. No one could also neglect the added value of the book that was gained from the superb and delicate English language editing practice of Mona.

Additionally, FANAP Studies & Research Center had in-depth interviews with the elites and key influencers of the project in order to extract workable data and useful insight for writing the book's chapters. Among the others, Mr. Mohammad Bastam, Mr. Hamed Mehrara, Mr. Masoud Maghsoudlou, and Mr. Alireza Kazerani deserved a genuine appreciation for describing the technical terms associated with the designed software architecture and development. The practical guidance of Mr. Mohsen Ghasemi, Mr. Mohammad Saeed Gholami, and Mr. Amir Arsalan Safari was highly prized for covering one of the main scopes of the book, namely the business analysis. Furthermore, thanks to Mr. Mohammad Saeidi, Mr. Amir Mastali, and Mr. Mohammad Hamidi for giving detailed information related to the project management methodology of the case study. Thanks to Mr. Hojatollah Badrlou, Mr. Mansour Shiani, and Mr. Ali Adineh for meticulously narrating the ups and downs of the deployment experience and devising the underlying methodology.

Apart from the above-mentioned contributors, the commitment of Mr. John Wayzalek and Mrs. Randi Cohen from the editorial office of Taylor & Francis is enormously admired. They professionally and patiently came up with different issues and challenges that were caused from the initial negation to the publication point. Last but not least, the unique role of Dr. Adel Hatamimarbini is widely acknowledged as the facilitator of proceeding the publication process.

Vahid Hajipour
Head of FANAP Studies & Research Center

Contributor Biography

FANAP Studies & Research Center serves as the knowledge preservation and dissemination headquarters of the FANAP Co., a giant information and communications technology (ICT) solution provider. To align with the devised mission, the divisional structure of the center encompasses four departments of scientific research, market research, scientific publication, and scientific events. The scientific research department spotlights and documents the groundwork of the valuable applied maneuvers of the company in dealing with real-world business challenges. The market research department puts knowledge-based ideas into practice by directing the development of high-tech services such as a data annotation platform and an AI-enabled robotic system in the banking sector. The division of the scientific publication also hosts the editorial office of the *Journal of Applied Intelligent Systems & Information Sciences (JAISIS)* through embracing practical studies on different streams of ICT. Furthermore, the center looks for designing scientific events to learn the target audiences how to cope with novel technological concepts/tools using innovative educational methods like gamified ones. Currently, 15 full-time specialists and a broad network of experts in ICT projects with profound academic and seasoned business backgrounds are interactively pursuing the Center's mission.

Despite being founded recently (i.e., in 2020), several research works are conducted under the supervision and affiliation of the center (i.e., *Research Center, FANAP Co., Tehran, Iran*). Notably, the senior scholars of the center who contributes to the present book, i.e., Vahid Hajipour, Sajjad Jalali, Mohammad Amini, and Ali Gharaei have successfully published prolific papers in a significant number of prestigious journals such as *Safety Science, Computers & Operations Research, Knowledge-based Systems, Expert Systems with Applications, Computer and Industrial Engineering, IEEE Transaction of Engineering Management, Journal of Intelligent Manufacturing, Applied Soft Computing, International Journal of System Science, Engineering Optimization, Measurement, Journal of Computational Design and Engineering, Reliability Engineering and System Safety, International Journal of Advanced Manufacturing Technology*, among others. To expand interprofessional collaborations, FANAP Studies & Research Center welcomes joint research programs with active scholarly parties all around the globe in the context of cutting-edge topics, including but not limited to, enterprise solutions, artificial intelligence, data science, Internet of Things, cloud computing, blockchain, and robotics.

Chapter 1

Introduction

"To reach a robust economy that remains effective under variable market conditions, you should be the technology provider."

—**Hamidreza Amouzegar**, *Deputy of Development & Technology of FANAP Co.*

The highest decision-making body of a large-scale steel-making company sets an ambitious target for a 4.2 million tones spike in annual production. To this end, the company probably needs to efficiently use its resources which leads to a significant decrease in product cost. Despite possessing high-tech machinery, the most disrupting barrier is related to the inefficient functionality and intractable monitoring of the day-to-day business processes. Soon, the managers figure out that the underlying problem could be handled by employing information technology in terms of a framework called enterprise resource planning (ERP). However, the realization of such a remedy occupies their mind. What is the best way of implementing an ERP system that optimizes the utilization of the company's resources and leads to a decrease in the prime cost? An informed and critical choice is now supposed to be made by the decision-makers: the choice between either purchasing an ERP product from popular vendors or ordering a newcomer to develop the product from scratch. Meanwhile, both options are accompanied by certain risks. The former is hardly consistent with the existing trading problems and cultural conditions. The latter is also prone to failure since there is almost no previous experience with promising results in the target region. This poses a real dilemma for that company: should it neglect the pre-specified target, i.e., a significant increase in annual production? In case of implementing ERP, which choice is the most feasible and efficient one to be adopted? Apart from the financial problems, can the international products satisfy all the needs of the company? In

DOI: 10.1201/9781003369806-1

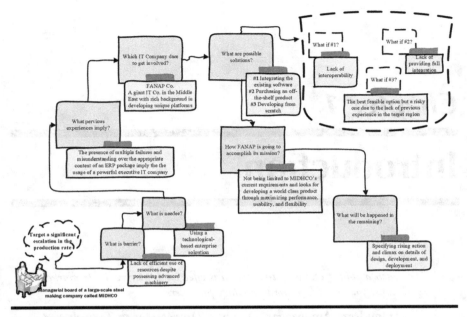

Figure 1.1 Story configuration.

case of adopting a newcomer, is there any reliable yet eligible IT company which dares to undertake such a project from scratch?

This book is intended to narrate an adventurous yet scholarly story about the formation of an ERP product. The main characters are a steel-making company and an IT one as the buyer and vendor, respectively. The story is adventurous since it does not follow a straightforward plot. By unfolding the plot, it would be revealed how the role of that IT company changes from facilitating the deployment of an off-the-shelf ERP to developing a tailor-made solution from the scratch. At the same time, the book also follows a scholarly context to delicately devise the magnitude, complexity, and engineering value of such a project. In the rest of this chapter, the key concepts associated with the story are briefly discussed which are also schematically illustrated in Fig. 1.1.

1.1 Exposition

When we talk about a large-scale industrial business, it means that we are referring to a company with a distributed network of business units, a complex hierarchy, and a massive volume of communications. Aimed at creating value, large companies frequently seek technological tools to capture the inherent complexities of their structures. Herein, there is a large-scale steel-making company, called MIDHCO (Middle East Mines & Mineral Industries Development Co.). The company is made up of multiple business units that are dispersed over a wide geographical region. To gain a competitive edge, MIDHCO's managers set an ambitious target to boom their business. To do so, the number of MIDHCO's business units has gradually expanded. However, such an expansion brings new challenges due to the lack of coordination across its multiple units which interrupts monitoring and decision-making. They are aware that without the presence of an integrated system, the whole hope of hitting the target would be abandoned. Thus, in order to prevent from simply leaving the competition arena, the company has to engage with technological solutions.

Needless to say, technology has entered human life since the origin of the universe with the aim of accelerating and changing the way in which evolution happens (Mishakov et al., 2018). With the advent of information and communication technologies (ICT) and its gradual evolution, the world is continually entering new eras, often referred to as the "Fourth Industrial Revolution," "Information or Digital Age," and so on (Mayer & Oosthuizen, 2020; Polizzi & Harrison, 2022). In fact, industry and technology are two pieces of a puzzle that should be set next to each other in order to create a complete and impeccable image of today's business across the globe. Then, it becomes evident that without technology the image is incomplete and thus productivity will decrease.

Any industry that can take advantage of existing opportunities based on its long-term goals will capture future markets. There are typical instances showing the upshot of the popular companies' strategies toward coping with technology and fierce competition. Among the others, Nokia and Kodak are two companies that have succumbed to the pressures arising from the technological revolution and simply left the competition arena. In contrast, Fujifilm and Samsung which produce the same products and face the same pressures from digital technologies are still in the vanguard of the related industries and have survived throughout the global competition. Actually, MIDHCO Company is not isolated from such a fact and the managers have readily accepted the necessity of utilizing new technologies in spite of existing exogenous limitations.

Meanwhile, enterprise solutions (synonymously called ERPs) are the embodiment of technological advancement in the industrial context (Silva et al., 2022). By virtue of enterprise solutions, the organizational processes are harmonized in a structured manner and many redundant activities are eliminated. Decision-makers are seamlessly provided with sufficient integrated information to monitor the correct direction of the organization's progress (Almajali et al., 2022). With the promising outcomes thereof, why not MIDHCO managers invest in acquiring a total enterprise solution for their large-scale steel-making industry to achieve the ambitious goal? Actually, the story of this book is broken when MIDHCO sets out to have an ERP solution for its business units.

1.2 Challenges

The managers of MIDHCO decide to do the necessary preliminary actions toward gearing up for a perfect enterprise solution to maximize the company's utility. Concerning different organizational cultures, it is a known fact that ERP implementation differs from region to region (Spano et al., 2009). Accordingly, the corresponding managers start reviewing the previous experiences in the same geographical region of MIDHCO. The results reveal the high rate of failures and potential difficulties in ERP implementation projects. As prime instances, Amid et al. (2012), Babaei et al. (2015), and Nikookar et al. (2010) were almost unanimous in specific dilemmas of large-scale companies for ERP implementation. The managerial instability and myopic presupposition of observing ERP's benefits in a short period besides the too bureaucratic structure of the large-scaled companies were deemed as detrimental factors.

The high frequency of the failures also stemmed from the lack of significant organizational maturity level. In this case, the business processes could not be aligned with the best practices since the adaptation needed a higher maturity level than the potency of the organizations. Furthermore, the companies in the target region could not legally benefit from the products of the leading off-the-shelf ERP vendors owing to the lack of supportive services as a result of trading difficulties. In the meantime, Asl et al. (2012) overemphasized the relationship between a successful ERP project and the accessibility of the vendors' supportive services.

The managers also discern that there is a common misunderstanding in the industrial community of considering enterprise solutions as simple software, being also emphasized by previous studies such as Wallace and Kremzar (2002). Precisely, there exists even some vendors which sell enterprise transactional software or supply chain management software as an ERP (Duguay et al., 1997). Furthermore, in many organizations, there were different software solutions available distinctively. Apart from ERP systems, there are many business solutions such as supply chain management, customer relationship management, business intelligence application, payroll, and human resource systems, each of which deals with its own specialized aspect. Sometimes these solutions are designed by different vendors, which makes the transfer of information more complicated. For this reason, such solutions are called isolated systems, automation islands, or information silos. This lack of communication hedges against automating even simple processes to be proceeded.

These ramifications, in fact, cause MIDHCO's managers to be distrustful and surge them to advance such a challenging project with caution. The managers are aware that under any possible ERP implementation scenario, an eligible yet reliable IT company is required to supervise the project. In terms of eligibility, that company needs to possess enough level of expertise and technical knowledge to undertake such a complicated project. The reliability of that company is also a must due to the two facts. First, the corresponding IT Company would probably deal with the detailed data and information of MIDHCO. Thus, the prospect of a security breach should be avoided by adopting a trustful company. Second, the prior experiences indicate that the ERP implementation entails a long-range nature and subsequently the contribution of the IT company along this tough horizon should be considered in advance. In fact, the nominated company should tolerate the rough accomplishment framework of satisfying the high-level expectation of MIDHCO. But which company would dare to endanger its reputation on such a risky project?

1.3 Major event

To adopt the desired IT Company, MIDHCO has to consult with its main shareholder, namely, Pasargad Financial Group (PFG) and get the necessary allowance. Considering the aforementioned criteria, PFG recommends its own IT sector subsidiary, called FANAP Company. Actually, in January 2006, PFG in cooperation with a number of elites and entrepreneurs in the ICT industry established FANAP Company. FANAP is currently one of the largest private ICT companies in Iran with more than 4,000 employees. The company is working in multiple categories such as payment and e-commerce, telecommunications services, financial services (stock exchange, bank, and insurance), smart health and public services, and enterprise solution.

The participation of FANAP is the major event of the story owing to the fact that its subsequent performance and role would definitely influence the project's outcomes. In the meantime, how FANAP is going to get engaged with surmounting MIDHCO's request? In response, FANAP and MIDHCO need to negotiate on the possible ways of fulfilling the corresponding expectations, trying to find a solution and thereby finalizing the type of their cooperation.

1.4 Solution

Now, MIDHCO and FANAP review the possible scenarios for solving the problem based on the recommendations of the previous scholarly studies. In fact, according to Kurbel (2013), there are three alternatives for companies to achieve an integrated enterprise solution. The alternatives include interconnecting the existing separated software, purchasing besides embedding the required modules of a popular vendor, and applying a tailor-made product under the presence of a professional consultant. By analyzing the options, it has been revealed that the current software of MIDHCO lacks the interoperability to be synched with each other. The second choice may be subjected to failure since it would be so excruciating for MIDHCO's managers to surmount the trading dilemmas with the popular vendors. The third choice is also a challenging one.

Although FANAP possesses the necessary resources and manpower for developing that product, the sheer novelty of the project and possible unforeseen issues make the process of decision-making complicated. Since both second and third choices seem to be controversial decisions, FANAP and MIDHCO agree on employing a professional consulting company to provide them with the necessary insight. TEC Company has been selected among all the candidates and after visiting MIDHCO's business units as well as conducting research field, the company has released its comment. Apart from trading problems, it has been stated that even the closest ERP solution in the international market would not technically cover all the requirements of MIDHCO. For instance, the regional law and regulation of work demand the joint integration among a specific number of modules such as human resource, financial, and health, safety, and environment (HSE) modules. Such a feature does not exist in popular off-the-shelf products.

Therefore, the consultant's comment makes the second-choice undesirable while the first choice has been already put aside. For this reason, MIDHCO has focused on the third choice, which is developing a tailor-made ERP based on its unique requirements. FANAP has now got involved literally in a large-scale risky IT project and consequently should consider appropriate rising actions to fulfill MIDHCO's expectations. Hence, FANAP decided to invest in this area that has been previously experienced by none of the existing vendors in the target region. FANAP's managers are determined to solve this problem once forever and produce a completely indigenous ERP for MIDHCO, called MIDRP. Of course, the same decision had already been made in PFG on the core banking and core insurance solutions, which led to the production of indigenous solutions for the Iranian bank and insurance by FANAP. Considering previous experiences, a separate unit is formed in FANAP Company by hiring more than 200 analysts and software developers to implement the ERP based on global standards. The production of this solution is considered to be the largest software development project in the target region. But, how FANAP is going to accomplish such a mission? And what are different perspectives on the mission?

1.5 Mission

FANAP is now appointed as the main executive responsible for developing and deploying the MIDRP project. Subsequently, FANAP's managers need to define a strategic mission with strong principles for the MIDRP product. Is the product going to either follow the theme of the classical ERPs or offer a world class one being equipped with up-to-date technologies? The basic analyses indicate that the classical ERP could satisfy the current MIDHCO's requirements. But what about the prospective future modifications and evolutions in MIDHCO's business process. Is the classic version consistent with MIDHCO's motto, i.e., "entering into a world-class context"? FANAP decides to go beyond the classical version and invest in designing a highly applicable and modern platform to fulfill MIDHCO's needs during a long planning horizon.

FANAP's experts on the mission to realize a world-class enterprise product concentrate on building a perfect platform to accomplish a set of goals, i.e., maximizing the system's flexibility, performance, and usability. The flexibility of a system implies its capability to easily adjust to the business' changes, keep pace with the scalability, and update the transactional process without stopping the applications (Abd Elmonem et al., 2016). FANAP is dedicated to developing a flowable process engine to fulfill the flexibility goal of the mission that also facilitates the system's supportability and scalability facets. In terms of maximizing performance, FANAP also aims at mapping out a fully integrated framework to ease the resource monitoring of all business units in real time. Indeed, integration means the use of specific technological tools throughout the organization to communicate and connect software applications and hardware systems owned by an organization (Kähkönen et al., 2017). The proposed integrated enterprise system has to embody all the needs of MIDHCO in an exhaustive package. So, there should be no need for MIDHCO to buy a separate solution for being merged with MIDRP. To further enhance the system performance, another advanced mission associated with MIDRP is to be equipped with optimizing tools such as artificial intelligence and information filtering systems.

Finally, FANAP looks for maximizing the usability of MIDRP by considering the capability of being synched with the hybrid cloud platform, mobile-based applications, and web monitoring systems. Such options, in fact, will enable the end users of MIDHCO to easily access easily to the system anywhere anytime. To heighten the usability, FANAP seeks to utilize three-dimensional web-monitoring systems to assist in the visual controlling of the business units. Therefore, using the knowledge of its experts, FANAP Company is to present a distinguished product that can be a competing product on a global scale. The subsequent complete descriptions of the details of the design, development, and deployment of the proposed mission are discussed in the upcoming chapters. Notably, for the sake of smoothing the FANAP mission accomplishment, MIDHCO employs a professional consultant called POSCO ICT that significantly contributes to the project, being demonstrated later.

1.6 Remaining

In this book, we intend to present a comprehensive enterprise solution to showcase the efforts made by the story's characters to realize the required ERP solution. It, in fact, threads the tortuous way of implementing an ERP through the MIDRP practice. This book tries to explain how to construct an enterprise solution from A to Z. The book is neither a tutorial for specific software, nor talking about how to choose and install it. Instead, this book discusses a story about how to implement a successful enterprise solution with all underlying challenges in a particular industry. Moreover, it can be used to understand how to design, develop, set up, and deploy a software system in a large organization. This book can be the right guide for those who want to get acquainted with organizational software and ERP products. Solution providers as well as ERP users can also take advantage of the valuable experience gained during this project. Throughout the book, the reader finds out the successes, pitfalls, and lessons learned from this project. The remainder of this book is as follows.

In Chapter 2, we answer the questions about what an ERP really is, what features it has, and how it works. This chapter outlines the components of the ERP system and how it is designed and deployed in a general way. In Chapter 3, the business scale of the steel-making case study MIDHCO is introduced. Afterward, we elaborate on the specification of the developed product, i.e., the MIDRP solution. The structure, methodology, and life cycle of the MIDRP project are discussed in Chapter 4. Chapter 5 discusses the system architecture and its components. In Chapter 6, all business processes used in the MIDRP solution are analyzed. Chapter 7 explains the whole story of design and development in producing such a solution. The integration framework is one of the most important chapters of the book that will demonstrate how the components of the system come together and communicate with each other. This part is discussed in Chapter 8. Chapter 9 demonstrates how to install and deploy the MIDRP solution in the hosting company. Finally, in the last chapter, the system intelligence and cutting-edge utilities of MIDRP are demonstrated. In all chapters, we will discuss the issues and challenges that arise during the design, implementation, and deployment of this adventurous journey.

References

Abd Elmonem, M. A., Nasr, E. S., & Geith, M. H. (2016). Benefits and challenges of cloud ERP systems – A systematic literature review. *Future Computing and Informatics Journal*, *1*(1), 1–9. doi: 10.1016/j.fcij.2017.03.003

Almajali, D. A., Omar, F., Alsokkar, A., Alsherideh, A. A. S., Masa'Deh, R. E., & Dahalin, Z. (2022). Enterprise resource planning success in Jordan from the perspective of IT-business strategic alignment. *Cogent Social Sciences*, *8*(1), 2062095. doi: 10.1080/23311886.2022.2062095

Amid, A., Moalagh, M., & Zare Ravasan, A. (2012). Identification and classification of ERP critical failure factors in Iranian industries. *Information Systems*, *37*(3), 227–237. doi: 10.1016/j.is.2011.10.010

Asl, M. B., Khalilzadeh, A., Youshanlouei, H. R., & Mood, M. M. (2012). Identifying and ranking the effective factors on selecting Enterprise Resource Planning (ERP) system using the combined Delphi and Shannon Entropy approach. *Procedia – Social and Behavioral Sciences*, *41*, 513–520. doi: 10.1016/j.sbspro.2012.04.063

Babaei, M., Gholami, Z., & Altafi, S. (2015). Challenges of enterprise resource planning implementation in Iran large organizations. *Information Systems, 54*, 15–27. doi:10. 1016/j.is.2015.05.003

Duguay, C. R., Landry, S., & Pasin, F. (1997). From mass production to flexible/agile production. *International Journal of Operations & Production Management, 17*(12), 1183–1195. doi:10.1108/01443579710182936

Kähkönen, T., Smolander, K., & Maglyas, A. (2017). Lack of integration governance in ERP development: A case study on causes and effects. *Enterprise Information Systems, 11*(8), 1173–1206. doi:10.1080/17517575.2016.1179347

Kurbel, K. E. (2013). *Enterprise resource planning and supply chain management: Functions, business processes and software for manufacturing companies.* Springer. https://books. google.com/books?id=rRp_AAAAQBAJ

Mayer, C.-H., & Oosthuizen, R. M. (2020). Positive transformation towards the Fourth Industrial Revolution: Empirical evidence from a technology company. *International Review of Psychiatry, 32*(7–8), 659–672. doi:10.1080/09540261.2020.1763927

Mishakov, V. Y., Beketova, O. N., Bykov, V. M., Krasnyaskaya, O. V., & Vitushkina, M. G. (2018). Management technologies to adapt modern principles of industrial enterprise' management. *Journal of Advanced Research in Law and Economics, 9*(4), 1377–1381. doi:10.14505//jarle.v9.4(34).25

Nikookar, G., Yahya Safavi, S., Hakim, A., & Homayoun, A. (2010). Competitive advantage of enterprise resource planning vendors in Iran. *Information Systems, 35*(3), 271–277. doi:10.1016/j.is.2009.09.002

Polizzi, G., & Harrison, T. (2022). Wisdom in the digital age: A conceptual and practical framework for understanding and cultivating cyber-wisdom. *Ethics and Information Technology, 24*(1), 16. doi:10.1007/s10676-022-09640-3

Silva, J. P., & Gonçalves, J. (2022, June 6–7). Process standardization: The driving factor for bringing artificial intelligence and management analytics to SMEs. *2022 10th International Symposium on Digital Forensics and Security (ISDFS).*

Spano, A., Carta, D., & Mascia, P. (2009). The impact of introducing an ERP system on organizational processes and individual employees of an Italian regional government organization. *Public Management Review, 11*(6), 791–809. doi:10.1080/1471903 0903318954

Wallace, T. F., & Kremzar, M. H. (2002). *ERP: Making it happen: The implementers' guide to success with enterprise resource planning.* Wiley. https://books.google.com/books?id= 3j86qt9VQ2kC

Chapter 2

ERP Systems

"Prior to diminishing the enterprise solutions' upshot at the level of automating the organizational activities, notice that the principles of an ERP are strictly interconnected with technology, process-oriented thinking, and cultural terms."

—Mohammad Saeed Gholami, *Member of Integration Committee of*
MIDRP

FANAP on the proposed mission to offer a world-class product is now supposed to review the different perspectives of ERP systems. This is a basic yet crucial activity since providing an innovative ERP product entails assessing the previous background of similar systems. To get acquainted with the new trends of ERP, one first needs to grasp the main concept of enterprise solutions and then figures out its gradual development throughout the years. Subsequently, it seems substantial to gain knowledge on the content of an ERP package as well as the details of different implementation approaches. Moreover, one cannot get involved with an ERP project while ignoring the underlying financial aspects. The global market for enterprise resource planning (ERP) is projected to rise to $78.4 billion by 2026 while it is currently estimated to be $40 billion (Allied Market Research, 2019). Additionally, working isolated from the rest of the main competitors makes nonsense when an ERP vendor is going to deliver a top-level product. Accordingly, it would be prudent to analyze the product of the leading companies. Afterward, the new trend of ERP needs to be studied while the existing state of similar products in the target region can be regarded as the final primitive assessment step. As a result, the rest of this chapter is to follow such a thread.

2.1 ERP: Issues and Challenges

By definition, ERP is a solution that includes diverse software modules and integrates all the processes of an organization into a single centralized system to provide visibility, productivity, and intelligence. The purpose of this solution is to incorporate all the activities of an enterprise into a single software package instead of having various software that applies to different areas of the enterprise. This means that all sectors of an organization use a common solution that fully satisfies the organization's needs. The whole information about the organization is also stored in a single database and there is no longer any concern about the transfer of information. Conceptually, ERP is a set of modules which are connected to a database with a user interface and has several functional features supported by different business units. Since ERP modules use a single database, employees in different departments (e.g., accounting and sales) can access the required information for their specific needs without any delay (Ganesh et al., 2014). Based on the definition of APICS,[1]

> ERP is a framework for planning all the resources of a business, from strategic planning through execution. Information technology tools and software can automate process links, share information across functional areas, and process business transactions efficiently. Real-time sharing of data is enabled by using a common database across these modules.
>
> (Cox & Blackstone, 2002)

Using a centralized enterprise system in all parts of an organization derives a plethora of benefits, according to Magal and Word (2011). Among the others, it can be referred to as increasing the accuracy of the information, determining strategies based on previous data analysis, standardizing the business processes, and offering more efficient supply chain and inventory management. Despite offering the chance for significant improvements to businesses, the design and implementation of enterprise solutions are accompanied by challenges and obstacles (Grossman & Walsh, 2004). In fact, running an ERP is challenging since it demands major changes in the business process of the organization. Next, it is the matter of cost. If an organization wishes to procure an ERP from a reputable vendor, it should cost hundreds of millions of dollars. Furthermore, designing and implementing this solution is complicated, and there is usually not enough skilled manpower in organizations to maintain such systems.

Meanwhile, worldwide statistical research has shown that nearly 70% of ERP deployment projects have failed. For example, the failure of the SAP ERP project at Hershey's Chocolate Company made a loss of almost $100 million in 1999. Nike Company also suffered a loss of 400 million euros from the failure of the ERP project (Grossman & Walsh, 2004). This indicates that if the reasons for the failure of ERP projects are thoroughly investigated and the results are properly exploited, the likelihood of success in such projects can increase. Al-Mashari et al. (2003)

enumerated the most important reason for failure. Not recognizing the well-fitted solution for the organization in terms of cultural and technical performance besides choosing an inappropriate vendor can be regarded as prime causes. Undermining the training practice of the workforce, neglecting the continuous change management, the absence of close collaboration between the executive team and the employer, and underestimating the implementation were also detrimental factors.

2.2 ERP Evolution

It may be better to trace the history of ERP back to the time when it was pioneered and when the concept of integrated systems emerged. Although integration may be a general concept, it is a perfect starting point for the emergence of ERPs. Simply, the cornerstone of integrated solutions is the information systems that can track and monitor business processes. Manufacturing environments were the first place where the integrated systems were formed. Initially, the inventory management system was a partial embodiment of integrated solutions by combining information technology and business processes to maintain an appropriate level of stock in the organization. Then, MRP-I was used in manufacturing organizations between 1960 and 1970. In fact, the software system was used to plan production and inventory control so that all processes would work seamlessly (Sancar Gozukara et al., 2022).

From the manufacturing standpoint, the ERP onset goes back more than 100 years. In 1913, an engineer named *Ford Whitman Harris* developed the Economic Order Quantity (EOQ) Model, a non-computerized system for production planning (Kumar & Paikray, 2022). For decades, EOQ has been the standard tool for production management. But in 1964, *Black & Decker* became the first company to introduce a Material Requirements Planning (MRP) solution that computerized the EOQ concept. In 1983, MRP-I was substituted with MRP-II (Manufacturing Resource Planning). MRP-II provided modules as a core component of software architecture and offered key functions of integrated manufacturing, including purchasing, bill of material, scheduling, and contract management (Sahoo & Lo, 2022).

For the first time, various manufacturing tasks were integrated into a common system. MRP-II was also a novel framework in which organizations could contribute to better production planning, inventory reduction, and less waste by sharing and integrating organizational data and increasing operational efficiency. With the advent of computer technology in the 1970s and 1980s, concepts similar to MRP II were created to handle business activities beyond production, including finance, customer relationship management, and human resource data. By 1990, Gartner technology corporation named "enterprise resource planning" for this new category of business management software (Jacobs, 2007). In the beginning, these systems were sophisticated and expensive. In many cases, ERP vendors force companies to re-engineer their business processes to yield a smooth flow of information across the organization by following software module logic. The rapid

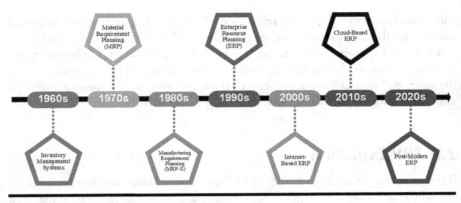

Figure 2.1 Timeline history of ERP.

growth of computing power and the Internet pose more challenges for ERP vendors encouraging them to redesign ERP products in a customized way and offer add-on modules. To cope with the cumbersome activity of upgrading a specific version associated with an on-premise ERP, the cloud-based solution was a game-changer by introducing software as a server (SaaS) model (Ahn & Ahn, 2020). Fig. 2.1 shows the timeline evolution of the main branches of ERP.

2.3 ERP Modules

Needless to say, every organization has multiple and complex processes whose proper, smooth, and seamless operation can be the most substantial requirement in accomplishing the business's goals. The processes can be categorized as a set of units called modules. A total enterprise solution consists of several modules that manage the organization's processes and are core components of the ERP system. There are three main types of ERP modules, including functional modules, technical modules, and application suites (Bradford, 2015). The functional modules are to guide the core processes of the organization. According to Fig. 2.2, they include but are not restricted to the financial, human resource, production, purchasing, inventory, and sale module.

The technical modules are completely incorporated into the functional modules. They help to integrate different functional modules and application packages. Technical components of ERP systems are illustrated in Fig. 2.3 by embracing basic components, security module, network and user interface, management information system, software programming module, analysis module, and open APIs for external use.

Besides, an application suite encompasses a set of information systems that are interconnected and divided into inter-company and intra-company systems. The typical example of inter-company systems involves supply chain management and

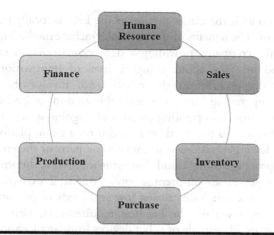

Figure 2.2 ERP functional modules.

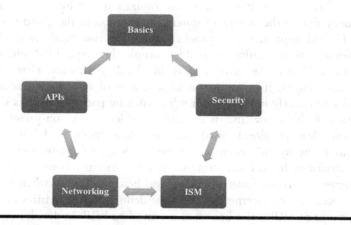

Figure 2.3 ERP technical modules.

supplier relationship management while customer relationship management and product lifecycle management can be categorized as intra-company ones.

2.4 ERP Deployment Models

Since organizations are different in scope and are unable to make the same changes, different methods have been proposed for deploying ERP systems, each of which has its own merits related to the structure of the organization. There are three main types of deployment models in the ERP market (Jagoda & Samaranayake, 2017).

On-premise model is the classic version of the ERP is locally installed in a corporate environment. The benefits of this approach include modifying applications to fit the needs of the company, providing a significant degree of data control and management, and bringing about a higher level of information security. The downsides of this approach, on the other hand, involve the long-term implementation, the upgrading issues, a considerable amount of investment costs (the cloud environment only has operating costs), and ongoing system maintenance.

Another ERP system is provided by a vendor on a cloud platform. One of the major challenges for organizations is to move some parts or the entire information of their business processes to the cloud. For some industries, the amount of security and control they get in an on-premise environment is extremely crucial. The benefits of this approach include causing low and predictable costs, choosing and purchasing modules based on the business requirements, bearing no hardware costs, providing access via mobile or other devices from any location, and enjoying performance stability because of the constant updating of the software by the vendor. However, there are some disadvantages, including the lack of complete control over the ERP system for customization and integration, and the lack of security due to the storage of system information in the cloud environment.

Hybrid approach is a combination of the two previous models that utilize different vendor solutions to build a completely unique ERP solution. In fact, the hybrid ERP is cost-effective just as the cloud systems are. However, like the on-premise system, it guarantees a high degree of information security. Also, the ability to quickly integrate with other software packages such as CRM is another feature of this model that is difficult to achieve in the on-premise system. If the organization has already used the on-premise system and intends to add cloud features, the hybrid system is the best option. Hybrid systems make it easy for organizations to add new features to their systems. Lower implementation and maintenance costs, easier upgrades, and better flexibility when the system is not connected to the Internet are the most defining characteristics of hybrid systems. This type of ERP is also known as postmodern ERP. In detail, postmodern ERP is to streamline the integration of the administrative and operational layers of organizations (Katuu, 2020). The administrative ERP addresses official processes such as financial management, human capital management, and procurement. Many industries only need the capabilities of the administrative layer, so their strategy is entirely focused on this type of ERP. These industries may complement their ERP capabilities by means of industry-specific modules. However, sometimes organizations have to perform other tasks like order management, workflow management, supply chain management, and production management where the use of an operational ERP strategy is needed. In the case of businesses that need to combine their activities with asset management, alignment between administrative and operational ERPs allows organizations to streamline the process (Gartner Glossary, 2016). A well-known example of this type of ERP is to order a car. Traditional ERP systems are like purchasing a new car that is limited to choosing the color of the car or its interior fabric. Post-modern ERP, on the other hand, is like designing a car as you prefer to be. After a while, you can add other components to this car. Therefore, Post-modern ERP is a core ERP with almost unlimited flexibility.

2.5 ERP Development

The development of each product encompasses phases such as identifying requirements, producing designs and prototypes, conducting tests and quality assurance, and ultimately producing the final product. Development of information systems such as ERP, which is a complicated software project, requires a high degree of coding skills and in-depth specialist knowledge. As depicted in Fig. 2.4, ERP system development is an iterative process that is constantly evolving as companies continually need new modules and features (O'Leary, 2000). ERP development is a continuous process that the stages are briefly described here.

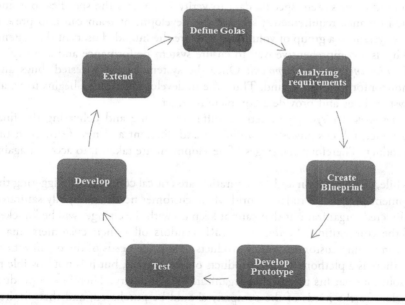

Figure 2.4   Development procedure of ERP software.

- *Defining goals*: That is, the customer must determine what the system developer should deliver at the end of the development process. In other words, the customer and IT experts must agree on what the performance and features of the final product should be by analyzing the requirements.
- *Providing blueprint*: Like all manufactured products, an initial design acts as the basis for the whole process, which must be described in detail. This

system layout contains complete information about the development process, the timeframe, and the resources that should be used.

■ *Developing prototype*: Here, developers begin their work, which involves decisions on the database, back end, front end, and the entire technical aspects of developing ERP software. The choice of developing frameworks such as Java, Python, or NET should be specified according to the system requirements. However, at this stage, it is determined whether the system is hosted on the local servers or the cloud. This is mostly related to the system costs, but the growing trend of developing ERP systems tends to utilize the cloud feature due to its many benefits described later. Transfer and integration of previous system data to the current system should also be conducted here. The integration of other legacy software such as CRM, Accounting, etc. should also be considered. Designing a UX/UI to show the system to the end users is also an important step in this step.

■ *Conducting test*: This is where developers test the system to verify whether the requirements are met or not. This phase entails two steps: first, developers should enter system-specific data to verify if it meets the specifications and performance requirements; second, the development team can also present the system to a group of volunteers who are the intended users of the system. This is a comprehensive way to ensure system performance and security.

■ *Conducting final development*: Once the system has been tested, bugs and nonconformities are found. Thus, the re-development phase begins to fix all system bugs and provide a complete product.

■ *Upgrading the system*: Sometimes, after producing and delivering the final product, the customers are willing to add different and new features in the product. Therefore, the stages of development are taken into account again.

Meanwhile, customization and configuration are critical concepts for triggering the development process. In today's world where customer needs are rapidly saturated and redirected, organizations that cannot keep up with the changes will be knocked out of the competition. In this way, ERP vendors offer their customers, many options, including customization of products to suit the needs of the organization. In fact, there is a plethora of ERP products on the market, but it is not possible to find a solution that fits the specific organization or industry. Therefore, a product that is close to the needs of the company should be purchased, and then limited customization should be carried out. An important point to keep in mind during customization is that you should not change all system functions. Clearly, such solutions receive numerous updates that may interfere with many of the software functions due to customization. Hence, most companies try to make limited cases to customize (Parthasarathy & Sharma, 2016).

Another important point is the configuration of the system, which is sometimes confused with customization. Both concepts are used to integrate an ERP solution with the business environment. These two concepts work together to make ERP perform optimally, so understanding the key differences between them is essential. In fact, to implement an ERP system, the business needs must be specified. To meet customers' needs, you can either configure the current system or customize a new system. In other words, customizing a feature is an extension or modification that requires separate coding or separate forms. Nevertheless, configuration occurs when you use the existing organization's tools in the system to change its behavior or features.

Customizing an ERP system means adding functional features to the software that do not exist in the generic version. In fact, ignoring the customization by the vendor incurs additional time and complexity to the organization which requires seasoned human resources. The following are some customizations cases in an organization:

- Modifying or enhancing the existing features
- Adding new features and options not available in the original version
- Supporting third-party vendor applications
- Adding task management processes.

However, system configuration means setting up an ERP system based on the specifications of the target organization. In other words, configuring an ERP software involves optimizing the core functions and components of the system so that it can integrate with the existing system environment. Solution providers usually have enough experience to connect your business needs to the system configuration. The following are some examples of features offered by configuration:

- Setting language, currency, and timezone
- Adjusting the page layout and standard options
- Setting up email clients
- Customizing objects and fields' setting
- Defining security parameters
- Defining roles, hierarchies, and access levels.

2.6 ERP Costs

The total ERP cost includes the expenditure of packaged software, hardware, additional services, and support. There are several factors to consider before purchasing and implementing an ERP system. Here are some key factors influencing the cost of an ERP system (Lindley 2008):

- *Number of users*: the cost-effectiveness of an ERP can be explored in relation to the number of users who will access it. The number of users needs to be estimated, and naturally, the more users you have, the more cost the vendor will charge you. Of course, new users who may be added to the system in the future should be considered as well.

- *Add-ons/customization*: Appending add-ons, customizing or configuring an application is not inexpensive option. In fact, it is necessary to select a solution for your organization that will meet most of your core needs through the built-in capabilities.
- *Implementation strategy*: Depending on the experience of the organization's staff, you may decide to employ an ERP consultant to make the ERP system implementation process smoother. Most vendors are getting involved with the installation and training of employees by incurring additional expenses to the customer. In addition, some vendors offer a higher number of consulting assistance options that also bring about extra costs.
- *Cost per module*: With respect to the analysis and development of each module, the related costs are influenced by front-end and back-end development, quality control, project management, and product management, which are calculated depending on the complexity of the module itself.
- *System integration*: Depending on the information structures, databases, and APIs, the cost of interconnecting the modules is calculated.
- *Data migration and validation*: Transmitting old data into the new ERP system and validating data must be categorized as the underlying cost.
- *Testing procedure*: Numerous modifications may be required during each test phase that should be enumerated in the cost estimation.
- *Deployment method*: It is more expensive to deploy an on-premise ERP solution than a cloud-based one. Moreover, taking into account other factors such as training, maintenance, and customization costs, the overall cost of on-premise deployment becomes even more costly. Both methods of deployment have many advantages and disadvantages; however, the low initial cost is the major benefit of cloud deployment which makes it attractive to some companies. Yet it should be remembered that, in the long run, businesses choosing cloud ERP software would ultimately pay the cost equal to on-premise solution prices.
- *Customer training and support*: Support and maintenance costs make up an average of 15–20% of the software budget. There are two types of training methods. Some vendors offer virtual training through videos and online courses. On the other hand, some vendors offer advanced training options including in-person courses, which typically cost more than virtual courses.
- *Software maintenance and updates*: The ERP solution requires periodic updates that may not be included in the basic setting of software costs. Particularly, an on-premise system needs regular and timely maintenance before switching to a cloud-based ERP solution to ensure that the solution satisfies the expectation.
- Estimating each of the aforementioned measures will help the company determine how much it costs for acquiring an ERP solution.

2.7 Top ERP Leaders

Nowadays, many companies are working on producing enterprise solutions. Here, the pioneers of the ERP as well as the most reputable ones with significant large market share.

2.7.1 SAP

SAP is a German software company that owes much of its reputation for producing enterprise solutions for managing business operations and customer relationships. The company was founded in June 1972 by five former IBM engineers working in the artificial intelligence (AI) department. In fact, after the failure of IBM's integrated systems project, they decided to leave and establish a separate company. In 1973, SAP launched its first commercial product, a financial accounting system called SAP R/1. In 1979, the SAP R/2 model was released, introducing additional capabilities to the previous version, including material management and production planning. SAP S/4 HANA is the latest version of SAP's enterprise software kit introduced in 2015. The company's forward-looking approach is to concentrate primarily on cloud-based technology such as blockchain, the Internet of Things (IoT), AI, machine learning, and quantum computing (Magal, & Word, 2011).

Currently, the organization has more than 440,000 clients in over 180 countries. The organization has staffed more than 100,000 people worldwide (until December 2019). In addition to the four main multinational service delivery networks, SAP also includes a network of 115 branches and numerous research and development institutes in different countries around the world. The company spent 4.3 billion euros on R&D in 2019. SAP-affiliated R&D institutes have chosen a specific area of expertise to work. For example, SAP laboratories in Bulgaria specialize in developing software under the Java platform. In addition to running independent research institutes, the company has also collaborated extensively with prestigious universities around the world. SAP partnered with several universities in 1988 to launch a system called the University Alliance Program (SAP UAP). Currently, over 250,000 students at universities around the world have access to SAP through this system.

SAP became the world's third largest software and programming company in 2016. It, in fact, focuses on 25 industries in six industrial sectors, namely process, discrete, consumer, and service-based categories besides financial and public-oriented applications. It also offers integrated products for large, medium, and small-sized companies. Almost 80% of its clients are small- and medium-sized companies. In 2019, the company's total revenue stood at around €27.5 billion, of which €7 billion was for cloud-based products and is projected to triple over the next three years.

2.7.2 Oracle

Oracle is one of the giant worldwide information technology companies, founded in 1977. This American company is known not only for computer software development, but also for advanced equipment. Also, the company's database system is one of the world's most successful ones. The Oracle Applications division was launched in 1987 and began developing business management software that is closely integrated with Oracle database software. The company launched its first ERP product in 1988 entitled Accounting Systems. In 2005, the company acquired PeopleSoft, a company offering enterprise solutions, and subsequently marketed its products as Oracle PeopleSoft. In 2019, the company became the world's second largest software product company. It has a long history of producing enterprise software and has marketed a variety of products (Jacobs, 2007).

As one of Oracle ERP's solution providers, NetSuite can cover a wide range of industries to automate and centralize processes across different sectors. The solution includes modules such as financial management, distribution, CRM, and supply chain management. NetSuite ERP represents more than 16,000 clients in more than 200 countries. The solution extends to a wide range of industries, including retail, education, energy, food and beverage, healthcare, manufacturing, and distribution. NetSuite ERP is cloud based and uses a subscription-based pricing model.

2.7.3 PeopleSoft

PeopleSoft is an American company founded in 1987 to provide enterprise software solutions. Its common solutions include Human Resource Management Systems (HRMS), Financial Management Solutions (FMS), Supply Chain Management (SCM), Customer Relationship Management (CRM), and Enterprise Performance Management (EPM). The company released its first ERP software in 1996, PeopleSoft 6, which included the manufacturing module. It has also purchased JD Edwards, one of 2003's most prominent ERP software firms. The company was acquired by Oracle in 2005 (Anderson et al., 2006).

2.7.4 Microsoft

Microsoft is one of the most prestigious and popular IT companies in the world. This company is one of the largest tech corporations by market capitalization for many years. Their ERP solution, called Microsoft Dynamics ERP, includes five packages that are focused on medium-sized organizations, subsidiaries, and the small divisions of larger organizations. Microsoft Dynamics ERP focuses on special industries including financial services, manufacturing, public sector, as well as retail and service sectors. Each of these products has special capabilities that serve a specific scope of business (Elbahri et al., 2019).

- *Microsoft Dynamics AX*: Through standardizing processes and helping to simplify compliance, this software is designed to help companies do business across locations and countries. AX edition is the only ERP system designed for organizations of large scale.
- *Microsoft Dynamics GP*: By managing the market changes, enabling unique business requirements, and linking business processes around the enterprise, the solution will help businesses respond to new opportunities.
- *Microsoft Dynamics NAV*: This approach is intended to assist companies in streamlining industry-specific business processes.
- *Microsoft Dynamics SL*: The emphasis is on project-driven organizations to offer reports and business analysis and automate projects across company divisions in different locations.
- *Microsoft Dynamics C5*: It can assist with finance, manufacturing, supply chains, analytics, and electronic commerce for small- and medium-sized enterprises.

2.7.5 Epicor

Epicor is an American software company founded in 1972. The company is known for producing ERP solutions for small and mid-sized businesses. Manufacturing, retail, timber and building materials, automotive, distribution, and services are the specific industries for which EPICOR provides its solutions. Their first solution was released in 1984 with financial and accounting functionalities under the name Platinum Software. In 1999, the name Platinum changed to Epicor Software. The latest version, Epicor 10, is available on the cloud or on-premise platform. They are also known to supply enterprise products for the steel and mineral industries (Xu et al., 2011).

2.7.6 Sage

Sage Group is a British software company that designs and builds organizational software such as customer relationship management, ERP, accounting, and banking software. Sage was launched in 1981 and their ERP solution, called Sage X3, was initially released in 2000. This solution is designed for medium-to-large national and global manufacturers focusing on chemical, distribution, equipment, fashion, food, and beverage sectors, as well as the industrial manufacturing industries. Sage ERP X3 is a web-based and cost-effective ERP solution which includes supply chain, production, and financial management (Intelligence 2014).

2.8 New Trends in ERPs

As ERP's past is full of major changes, its future will be also dynamic due to the advancement in novel technologies. Owing to higher computational speed and data storage, more data can be collected and analyzed with higher precision and quickness.

In this regard, numerous new intelligent tools are available for rapid and accurate decision-making. For example, with the aid of machine learning, it is possible to achieve better results in performing the desired task. AI can automate and simplify data-driven decision-making. IoT can be used to exchange information between humans to machines and machine to machine. Smartphones with 5G technology are able to control and monitor anything at any time. Virtual reality omits the burdensome collection of data. Data integration using blockchain technology can be accomplished for cross-party trade exchanges. With SaaS-based ERP cloud systems, more and more businesses can use ERP solutions in their business operations because of their cost-effectiveness and performance. Technology advances have always been in the history of ERPs, and this trend continues to grow. Here are some ERP trends.

2.8.1 Two-Tier ERP

Historically, most ERPs have been used as a unified system for large company activities and all subsidiaries. It means that a common solution is used for all organizational processes. But sometimes this led to failure to deploy ERP systems since it wasn't a workable and customizable solution for all business entities. A separate version of ERP may need to be considered for each subsidiary. One of the emerging topics in the field of ERP, which will be one of the most controversial trends in the 2020s, is the introduction of two-tier models based on the lessons learned from the failed efforts of some companies (Bahssas et al., 2015). The two-tier ERP model involves the twice implementation of ERP solutions in a company. The first-tier ERP system is implemented at the enterprise level, also known as the "legacy application." The second tier of the ERP system is implemented separately in the subsidiaries of the company. A two-tier ERP can be useful for the organization in the following situations:

- When you have a subsidiary that is large and has grown well enough to require ERP system features.
- When you have purchased another company that does not have an ERP system or has an ERP solution that is outdated or no longer supported.
- When you have a subsidiary that operates in a separate industry from your parent company.

A two-tier ERP model allows the subsidiaries to customize their second-tier ERP solution and optimizes their unique business needs. At the same time, the IT infrastructure of the subsidiary can remain seamlessly integrated with the core business through a two-tier ERP, so you can completely ascertain that data from your subsidiary can be exchanged. But the key argument is that the two-tier ERP model requires the double effort of the employees in the core company and the subsidiaries. It is also vulnerable to user interventions, for example, essential data such as customer orders and financial information can be removed by an employee at the subsidiaries.

2.8.2 Cloud and Edge Computing in ERPs

Cloud computing is undoubtedly one of the greatest technological advancements that have influenced ERP in the past two decades. That has contributed to the implementation of cloud-based ERP solutions, providing several benefits over conventional ERP. ERP has long been recognized as a costly business solution and is therefore not affordable for small- and medium-sized businesses (SMEs). It is subjected to high expenses, such as licensing, infrastructure, and maintenance costs. On the other hand, On-premise ERPs face limitations, such as lack of growth in line with corporate growth and lack of integration with novel technologies. But with the introduction of cloud ERPs, many of these barriers have disappeared.

Cloud ERPs are cost-effective for small- and medium-sized companies, so consumers can only pick the modules they need in their businesses. Since the information is stored in the cloud, it has a low maintenance cost. With the ability to update continuously, the cloud solution can be updated with the latest features and higher security. Noteworthy, there are also other interesting features, such as business-to-business (B2B) electronic invoicing, real-time data processing, a ledger system for safe data exchange, and integration with blockchain technology. However, due to hosting on vendor servers, built-in AI can be used to analyze and optimize the business process rather than purchasing a separate AI solution (Lenart, 2011).

But today, the cloud solution alone is not enough to quickly process and analyze the data generated by IoT devices, connected facilities, and other digital platforms. Edge computing is another approach we can expect over the next decade. In this novel approach, the calculation and processing of data are carried out where the data are produced. Such technology can be installed on the device itself (i.e., sensors) or close to the device and can be used to transfer data to a centralized server for analysis. In fact, instead of providing a cloud network and remote control, everything is logged in and analyzed via locally connected devices (Peng & Gala, 2014).

The procedure of cloud computing requires significant bandwidth and a fast data transferring method to exchange real-time data. In edge computing, each connected device returns operational data to the on-premise server to be recorded and analyzed. In fact, the edge-computing provides an internal network without continuous data transmission to the cloud. Since all data are collected and processed locally, these reports are real time. As a result, edge computing has led to lower costs, lower network traffic, and improved solution performance.

2.8.3 ERP-II

ERP is a software solution that manages and controls business processes through covering financial, manufacturing, distribution, sales, and other business areas. ERP-II or extended ERP is usually referred to as another stage or next-generation ERP that incorporates other applications and business processes. Integration with ERP is required to eliminate redundant information and processes. ERP-II can result from improved technology, functionality, or user access improvements (Koh et al., 2008). Today, a concept has emerged in which traditional ERP is seen as the backbone of the organization and fully integrated with other operating systems such as SCM and CRM. Since these systems are beyond the boundaries of organizations, their integration poses new challenges. Therefore, the access of customers to organizational data through web pages and mobile has been facilitated, regardless of location.

Some specifications of ERP-II are introduced as follows:

■ *Functionality*: the functionality of the modules such as supply chain management, supplier relationship management, and customer relationship management has been enhanced. This attribute strengthens cooperation with external organizations or businesses.

■ *External access*: ERP-II may allow access to the organizational information of external entities. For instance, a factory allows another plant or its customer to have access to planning information. Solutions with such a feature have more stringent security issues that prohibit access to sensitive company information. The exchange of information with supply chain partners is the most critical feature of ERP-II.

■ *Web or Internet based*: ERP generally refers to a software system that is hosted on and accessed via a secured company network. ERP II can allow users to access all their applications through a web browser; this approach allows external users to access ERP's information.

■ *SaaS*: SaaS typically refers to a data hosting system where the latest and updated version of the software is used by all clients. In fact, ERP has recently been introduced on a SaaS basis that is available on the vendor servers. Companies pay the subscription fee and receive it as a service over the web or cloud platforms.

2.8.4 AI in ERPs

Nowadays, add-ons are being used to incorporate AI capabilities into business systems. However, the future trend for renowned ERP vendors considers the introduction of these capabilities as a built-in feature. It stems from the fact that the amount of data produced in various organizational processes is growing dramatically and there is an urgent need for tools that can process and analyze data. For example, through AI tools such as machine learning (ML) and natural language processing (NLP), the ERP solution can recognize patterns and trends in generated data and provide a higher level of insight into business processes (Software Advice, 2018). This can simplify routine processes and eliminate human error. Furthermore, it ensures that your employees will no longer have to dedicate time to this task and can instead concentrate their attention on tasks that are more essential to the organization.

2.8.5 Mobile Platforms

It's been a long time since portable devices such as smartphones and laptops have become easily accessible to anyone. That has led many ERP vendors to create their applications for these platforms which serve as a distinctive feature. Online and instant access all around the world is an exciting feature for users to handle their duties anytime they want. For example, after working hours, an employee from the financial department can make online transactions in an urgent situation. The data can also be easily registered, processed, and transferred to the database. As a result, the organization can provide on-time access to the processes and data, allowing it to respond immediately to the latest requests. In this situation, mobile ERP apps make it easier to make quicker decisions and create a seamless workflow that can have a hugely positive effect on the overall productivity of the company (Al Bar et al., 2011).

2.9 ERP Companies in the Target Region

With the expansion of computer utilization, the use of information systems in Iran became increasingly popular in small-, medium-, and large-sized enterprises. From 1990 to 2000, companies were looking forward to implementing the management information system (MIS) and gradually switched to ERP. Initially, unsuccessful experiences in ERP implementation in some large-scale companies caused SMEs to cast doubt on using ERP solutions. As a matter of fact, it was implied that world-class ERPs such as SAP and Oracle were not suitable for that companies. Traditional structures, change resistance, short-sighted expectation of managers, and insufficient assessment of the real requirements were the most prominent factors shaping the pessimistic sight of ERP performance (Nikookar et al., 2010). After 2010, however, the process of using and deploying ERP systems and replacing them with MIS systems has increased considerably. In the coming chapters, the challenges, and complexities of designing a customized ERP are addressed (Aarabi & Mohammadkazem, 2014).

Basically, the implementation of ERP systems is faced with numerous challenges and obstacles. According to the statistics, the target region is one of the cases in which many ERP projects have failed or have not achieved the desired results (Babaei et al., 2015). It is important to pay close attention to issues and obstacles in the region in order to effectively implement the ERP system. It is a known fact that organizations in different areas confront technical challenges due to the incompatibility of ERP with their existing cultures. For instance, many ERPs which are technically manufactured in developed countries, may not fully satisfy the requirements of developing countries. As a result of these incompatibilities, failures to implement off-the-shelf ERP systems are very likely in such regions that are subject to certain government laws or a specific culture. Many experts believe that the unawareness of corporate executives, lack of experienced consultants, unwillingness to invest heavily, lack of technical knowledge, and so on are other challenges for the high rate of failure in the companies of the target region.

As discussed earlier, the scale of MIDHCO's requirements and the desired ERP solution, namely, MIDRP can be regarded as a unique information technology project in the relevant geographical region. By conducting the basic review of the ERP systems, the lack of practical experiences could be scientifically compensated for the project's key influencers to a certain extent. Accordingly, the basic facts of this chapter provide a significant insight for FANAP's managers to deal with MIDHCO requirements in a more realistic manner. The next activity is to build the skeleton of MIDRP to take the preliminary steps toward accomplishing the pre-defined mission which will be the concern of Chapter 3.

Note

1. American association for supply chain management.

References

Aarabi, M., & Mohammadkazem, M. (2014). A review of readiness assessment of ERP implementation in Iranian small and medium enterprises. *International Journal of Information System and Engineering*, *2*(1), 17–22.

Ahn, B., & Ahn, H. (2020). Factors affecting intention to adopt cloud-based ERP from a comprehensive approach. *Sustainability*, *12*(16), 6426.

Al Bar, A., Mohamed, E., Akhtar, M. K., & Abuhashish, F. (2011). A preliminary review of implementing enterprise mobile application in ERP environment. *International Journal of Engineering & Technology*, *11*(4), 77–82.

Allied Market Research. (2019). Available at https://www.alliedmarketresearch.com/ERP-market

Al-Mashari, M., Al-Mudimigh, A., & Zairi, M. (2003). Enterprise resource planning: A taxonomy of critical factors. *European Journal of Operational Research*, *146*(2), 352–364.

Anderson, L., Ernst, C. G., & Young, U. S. (2006). *Understanding PeopleSoft 8*. John Wiley & Sons.

Babaei, M., Gholami, Z., & Altafi, S. (2015). Challenges of enterprise resource planning implementation in Iran large organizations. *Information Systems*, *54*, 15–27.

Bahssas, D. M., AlBar, A. M., & Hoque, M. R. (2015). Enterprise resource planning (ERP) systems: Design, trends and deployment. *The International Technology Management Review*, *5*(2), 72–81.

Bradford, M. (2015). Select, implement, and use today's advanced business systems. North Carolina State University. https://books.google.com/books?id=KZRqCAAAQBAJ.

Cox J. F., Blackstone J. H., & Spencer M. S., (2002). APICS dictionary. American Production and Inventory Control Society. https://books.google.com/books?id=41ZaAAAAYAAJ

Elbahri, F. M., Al-Sanjary, O. I., Ali, M. A., Naif, Z. A., Ibrahim, O. A., & Mohammed, M. N. (2019). Difference comparison of SAP, Oracle, and Microsoft solutions based on cloud ERP systems: A review. In *2019 IEEE 15th international colloquium on signal processing & its applications (CSPA)* (pp. 65–70). IEEE.

Ganesh, K., Mohapatra, S., Anbuudayasankar, S. P., & Sivakumar, P. (2014). *Enterprise resource planning: Fundamentals of design and implementation*. Springer. Top of Form.

Gartner Glossary. (2016). Available at https://www.gartner.com/en/information-technology/glossary/postmodern-erp.

Grossman, T., & Walsh, J. (2004). Avoiding the pitfalls of ERP system implementation. *Information Systems Management, 21*(2), 38–42.

Intelligence, S. E. (2014). Avon Rubber finds maximum flexibility in Sage ERP X3 Sage Enterprise Intelligence delivers profitability, insight, and control. *Sage, 866*, 530–7243.

Jacobs, F. R. (2007). Enterprise resource planning (ERP)—A brief history. *Journal of Operations Management, 25*(2), 357–363.

Jagoda, K., & Samaranayake, P. (2017). An integrated framework for ERP system implementation. *International Journal of Accounting & Information Management, 25*(1), 91–109.

Katuu, S. (2020). Enterprise resource planning: Past, present, and future. *New Review of Information Networking, 25*(1), 37–46.

Koh, S. C. L., Gunasekaran, A., & Rajkumar, D. (2008). ERP II: The involvement, benefits and impediments of collaborative information sharing. *International Journal of Production Economics, 113*(1), 245–268.

Kumar, B. A., & Paikray, S. K. (2022). Cost optimization inventory model for deteriorating items with trapezoidal demand rate under completely backlogged shortages in crisp and fuzzy environment. *RAIRO-Operations Research, 56*(3), 1969–1994.

Lenart, A. (2011). ERP in the cloud–benefits and challenges. In *Euro symposium on systems analysis and design* (pp. 39–50). Springer, Berlin, Heidelberg.

Lindley, J. T., Topping, S., & Lindley, L. T. (2008). The hidden financial costs of ERP software. *Managerial Finance, 34*(2), 78–90.

Magal, S. R., & Word, J. (2011). *Integrated business processes with ERP systems*. Wiley Publishing.

Nikookar, G., Safavi, S. Y., Hakim, A., & Homayoun, A. (2010). Competitive advantage of enterprise resource planning vendors in Iran. *Information Systems, 35*(3), 271–277.

O'Leary, D. E. (2000). *Enterprise resource planning systems: Systems, life cycle, electronic commerce, and risk*. Cambridge University Press.

Parthasarathy, S., & Sharma, S. (2016). Efficiency analysis of ERP packages-A customization perspective. *Computers in Industry, 82*, 19–27.

Peng, G. C. A., & Gala, C. (2014). Cloud ERP: A new dilemma to modern organizations. *Journal of Computer Information Systems, 54*(4), 22–30.

Sahoo, S., & Lo, C. Y. (2022). Smart manufacturing powered by recent technological advancements: A review. *Journal of Manufacturing Systems, 64*, 236–250.

Sancar Gozukara, S., Tekinerdogan, B., & Catal, C. (2022). Obstacles of on-premise enterprise resource planning systems and solution directions. *Journal of Computer Information Systems, 62*(1), 141–152.

Software Advice. (2018). Available at https://www.softwareadvice.com/resources/ai-erp/.

Xu, H., Rondeau, P. J., & Mahenthiran, S. (2011). Teaching case: The challenge of implementing an ERP system in a small and medium Enterprise–A teaching case of ERP project management. *Journal of Information Systems Education, 22*(4), 291.

Chapter 3

MIDRP

"Organizations that avoid embracing changes are subjected to failure. The MIDRP journey was set off owing to the MIDHCO's voluntary will towards changing the way of using resources."

—**Aliasghar Pourmand**, *CEO of MIDHCO Co.*

As the main executive character of the story gains worthy knowledge over the detailed aspects of the ERP systems, it is time for configuring the MIDRP solution. Recalling the genesis of the story from Chapter 1, it has been repeatedly emphasized that MIDRP is a large-scale project. However, the supporting evidence associated with the term, large-scale has to be pinpointed. To delve deeply into the backbone of such a solution, the business scale of MIDHCO needs to be demonstrated first. The relevant introduction should go through MIDHCO's hierarchy, differentiation of products as well as the way of meeting the value chain. Second, to complete the story thread, the feasibility of possessing a total solution for MIDHCO should be exactly justified. This includes underlining the main problems, requirements, and fitness level of off-the-shelf products in the context of MIDHCO's business. Once the requirements are set, the arising question is how to map them into the precise deliverables being compatible with the ERP domain. Another prime concern is related to execution. What are the main steps toward reaching MIDRP? How the responsibilities among the engaging parties are going to be distributed? The last main issue is to highlight the promising features of MIDRP that fulfill the proposed world-class mission. In the rest of this chapter, the MIDRP is elucidated by responding to the proposed questions.

DOI: 10.1201/9781003369806-3

3.1 MIDHCO Company

Bankrolled by Pasargad Financial Group (PFG), Middle East Mines and Mineral Industries Development Company called MIDHCO has been founded in late 2007. As the organization's name suggests, its main activity is to play role in the entire supply chain of mineral industries by possessing multiple subsidiaries in a wide-geographical region. Nowadays, MIDHCO is to promote entrepreneurship in the steel-making sector using the highest technology coupled with the bioleaching industrial method. In order to capture the magnitude of the working environment of MIDHCO, two facets are required to be jointly discussed here, i.e., the differentiation of the products besides the multiplicity of the subsidiaries. The degree of differentiation would imply different volumes of products with different manufacturing processes each of which possesses specific conditions, e.g., transportation and maintenance issues. Further, as the subsidiaries are at the heart of the organization, their quantity would indicate the level of complexity in directing the MIDHCO's goals into the operational layers.

The organizational structure of MIDHCO involves a specific hierarchy, which is shown in Fig. 3.1. Herein, the subsidiary company is defined as "an entity with distinct financial procedures which may have one or several Business Units (BUs)." While the BU is defined as "an entity whose financial transactions are dependent on the company and can have one or several plants."

According to Fig. 3.2, MIDHCO has multiple subsidiaries dispersed in a wide-geographical region. For instance, ZISCO which is the organization's largest subsidiary company with more than 6,000 employees and is located in Kerman is a company below MIDHCO Holding. It has three BUs and each BU has one or more plant(s) each of which falls below its related BU in the hierarchy. Generally, this structure applies to all of the subsidiaries.

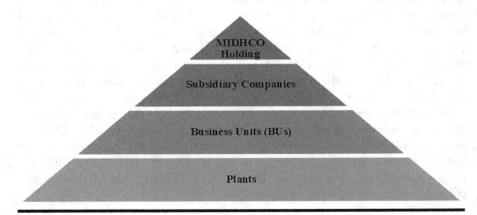

Figure 3.1   Hierarchy of MIDHCO's subsidiaries.

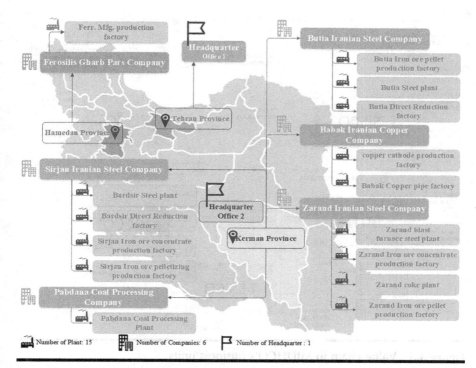

Figure 3.2   Geographical distribution of MIDHCO's subsidiaries.

These subsidiaries are interactively working together to accomplish the supply chain structure of MIDHCO's steel-making industry. Fig. 3.3 considers such a chain in a detailed manner by specifying the way of converting the input materials into the intermediate as well as final products. Considering water, natural gas, iron stone, coal, and copper ore, several types of products such as billet, iron concentrate, Ferro Silicate, and coke are manufactured throughput this chain. Precisely, Table 3.1 enumerates all MIDHCO's subsidiaries included in the MIDRP project scope in terms of the geographical location, the raw material each plant deploys as well as the products manufactured in each one of them.

It is noteworthy that in addition to Kerman and Hamadan, the headquarter office in Tehran is also involved in the MIDRP project. Totally, there are 9 BUs and 20 plants with different raw materials and products located in dispersed cities of the country. Evidently, the great number of offices, operations, and procedures inside each subsidiary company or each BU or plant as well as the relationship between these entities is expected to pose different kinds of technical and non-technical challenges to MIDHCO.

The complication of MIDHCO's internal procedures or maybe bureaucracy is intensified when it comes to the relationships among the subsidiary companies.

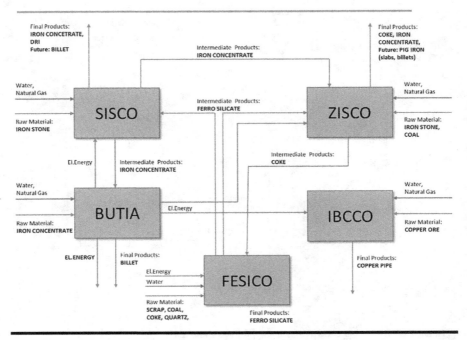

Figure 3.3 Value chain in MIDHCO's business units.

These subsidiaries have lots of communications with each other at both company and plant levels as depicted in Fig. 3.4.

Meanwhile, the geographical region of MIDHCO possesses an abundant supply of natural resources implying the urgent necessity for improving productivity to remain solvent under high elasticity. Precisely, according to the existing statistics, there have been just 420 exploited the mines in Kerman province. The share of industry and mining in the non-oil exports of the target region has reached 25%, in the past year indicating the flourishing nature of such a market. Approximately, 4,000 mines are still inactive in the geographical region of MIDHCO indicating the significant potentiality for prosperity and growth. Minerals such as Iron Ore, Copper, Steel, etc. are now being exploited in that region and companies like MIDHCO are contributing to the exploitation at the highest possible rate.

To enhance productivity and advance toward a world-class industry, MIDHCO needs to come up with the complicated nature of its hierarchy. While looking for an applied remedy, MIDHCO is determined to play a significant role in the market by setting its ambitious five-year horizon based on Table 3.2.

The sheer determination steps MIDHCO in utilizing appropriate enterprise solutions which contribute to a better decision-making policy for the entire holding.

Table 3.1 Specification of MIDHCO's Subsidiaries

Company Name	Location	No. Bus	No. Plants	Raw Material(s)	Product(s)
Zarand Iranian Steel Company (ZISCO)	Kerman	3	8	Iron Ore Lumps, Raw Coal, Iron Ore Pellet, Iron Ore Fines, Iron Scrape, Coke, Iron Ore, Coal Concentrate	Iron Ore Concentrate, Coal, Coke, Iron Ore Pellet, Steel (in future), Mine Extraction (in future)
Sirjan Iranian Steel Company (SISCO)	Kerman	2	5	Sponge Iron, Iron Scrape, Iron Ore Concentrate, and Pellet	Iron Ore Concentrate, Iron Ore Pellet, Sponge Iron, Steel Bar
Butia Iranian Steel Company (BISCO)	Kerman	2	2	Sponge Iron, Iron Scrape, Iron Ore Concentrate	Iron Ore Pellet, Billet and Bloom
Babak Iranian Copper Company (IBCCO)	Kerman	1	2	Copper Concentrate, Copper Cathode	Copper Cathode, Copper Pipe
Pabdana Coal Preparation	Kerman	0	1	Raw Coal	Coal Concentrate
Ferosilis Gharb Pars Company (FESICO)	Hamadan	1	2	Quartz	Ferrosilicon with different grades

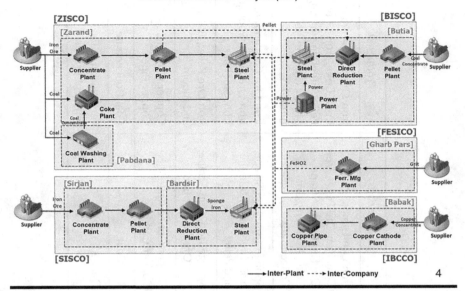

Figure 3.4   Relationship between MIDHCO's subsidiaries.

Table 3.2   Target Setting for Products of MIDHCO

Product Name	Tonnage Per Year
Raw Steel	4.2 million tons
Iron Ore Pellets	7.5 million tons
Iron Ore Concentrate	8 million tons
Coke Metallurgy	1.2 million tons
Processed Coal	1.1 million tons
Ferro Silicon	24 thousand tons
Lime and Dolomite	400 thousand tons
Copper Cathode	50 thousand tons
Copper Pipe	12 thousand tons
Electricity	500 megawatts

3.2 An Introduction to MIDRP

MIDHCO total integrated information solution or MIDRP[1] is a system for planning the organization's resources and offering an integrated connection between all its components. This solution, by its comprehensiveness, fully automates all the processes of MIDHCO Holding as well as its subsidiaries. By providing the appropriate infrastructure and accurate information, it will enable the implementation of the smart business. In Chapter 1, the concerns of MIDHCO's managers have been reviewed at a glance. However, being involved in such a risky and adventurous project needs a much more concrete reasoning that is going to be discussed here.

Concerning the aforementioned hierarchy and grand target, the presence of a smooth information flow from the top layer to the shop floor of MIDHCO is of paramount importance. There should be a total solution for all sectors and their systems, from the headquarters to the companies, business units, and plants. In fact, the lack of proper communications between different organizational units would interrupt such flow. In different sectors of MIDHCO Holding and its subsidiaries, there are various financial, administrative, and automation solutions, which leads to scattered isolated systems. Actually, the software applications lead to isolated systems when each of which generates and analyzes the data based on their own information.

In such a situation, the system components do not have a direct and integrated connection with each other and thereby it is difficult to aggregate data for obtaining the necessary information. The problem of poor communication in isolated systems resulted in resorting to interconnected systems, which is called an integrated system. Integrated systems have been created with the approach of sharing information and direct communication between all their components in the organization. According to Fig. 3.5, MIDHCO needs to replace its current isolated data collection framework with the integrated one. Under a shared database, this facilitates comprehensive access to information with a high level of accuracy in all parts of the MIDHCO as fast as possible.

Meanwhile, what features are required to realize such an integrated solution for MIDHCO? In response, the storyline in Chapter 1 should be followed. Subsequent to the occurrence of the major event, i.e., the entrance of FANAP as the key executive supervisor of the project, the Canadian TEC Company has been selected to examine MIDHCO's requirements. TEC survey has identified more than 5,000 features in MIDHCO Holding and its subsidiaries that are needed to cover the current and future scope of activities. This knowledge is obtained through accurate and precise information during various visits to all sections of MIDHCO Holding and its subsidiaries. Accordingly, it is safe to say that a system covering all of these features can be considered a fulfilling system responding satisfactorily to almost all of the current and future needs in MIDHCO. But, what about the existing best practices in passing the corresponding features? In terms of

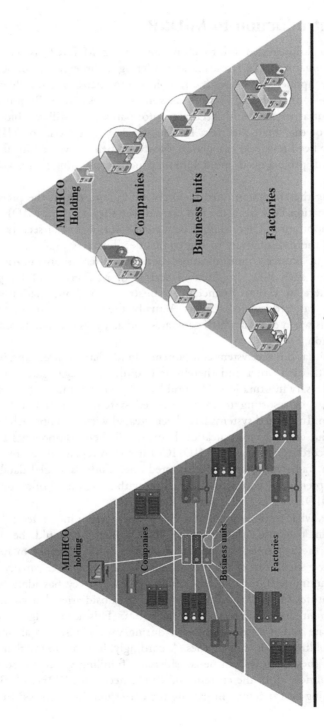

Figure 3.5 Integrated system approach versus isolated system approach.

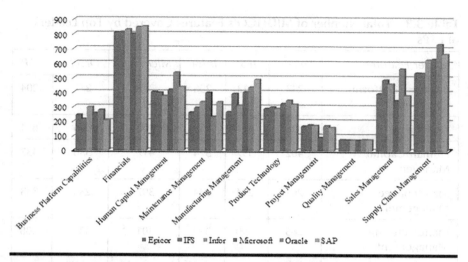

Figure 3.6 MIDHCO's requirements covered by top leaders of ERPs.

different categories, Fig. 3.6 reveals that among six well-known ERP provider companies, Oracle solution has the highest level of fitness.

However, according to the detailed result in Table 3.3, this choice could only cover around 80% of the requirements being equivalent to 4,218 features. Considering the lack of full coverage besides the prohibitive cost of buying an off-the-shelf product, the storyline is surged through building the product from the scratch (Amouzegar et al., 2020). Thus, FANAP, which has already been supposed to only contribute to the deployment of an off-the-shelf product, is now authorized as the main executive character. Complementary, a supportive character is also required to play a role as the MIDRP consultant. In this regard, the delegated consultant is POSCO ICT which is a reputable company with more than 2,500 IT specialists. Having the required knowledge and technical experience in the steel industry, POSCO ICT has conducted several international projects in the context of enterprise solutions. Originally, POSCO ICT is a subsidiary of a steel-making company called POSCO, which is headquartered in Pohang, South Korea. It had an output of 42 million tons of crude steel in 2015, making it the world's fourth largest steel-making Company. In 2010, it was the world's largest steel manufacturing company based on market value. In this way, MIDHCO, FANAP, and POSCO ICT constitute the main parties of MIDRP while working as the project's employer, executor, and consultant, respectively.

> *"Actually, POSCO ICT, MIDHCO, and FANAP are collaborating on a very meaningful project looking for promoting the knowledge of MIDHCO's business processes. To do so, POSCO ICT's relationships with MIDHCO and then with FANAP are of paramount importance."*
>
> **—Jaewoo Lim**, *Project Manager of POSCO ICT*

Table 3.3 Total Number of MIDHCO's Features Covered by Top Leaders of ERPs

Master Features	Epicor	IFS	Infor	Microsoft	Oracle	SAP
Business Platform Capabilities	243	213	296	255	277	204
Financials	808	811	829	800	846	851
Human Capital Management	402	397	374	417	536	437
Maintenance Management	261	294	334	397	233	333
Manufacturing Management	265	390	310	401	435	488
Product Technology	288	298	289	323	345	318
Project Management	167	176	173	90	171	159
Quality Management	77	76	76	74	78	77
Sales Management	394	488	461	347	564	381
Supply Chain Management	538	536	626	633	733	666
Total	**3443**	**3679**	**3768**	**3737**	**4218**	**3914**

It is necessary to form a joint operational collaboration among the main parties of MIDRP to execute such a huge project. The corresponding collaboration is realized by considering some committees illustrated in Fig. 3.7.

Accordingly, with the formation of executive and specialized committees, strategies and executive methods of the project are determined and communicated. Representatives of MIDHCO, POSCO, and FANAP are present in all executive groups and committees. These committees include the following:

- *Steering Committee:* Determining the macro and strategic policies of the project.
- *Coordinating Committee:* Coordinating and supervising the implementation of all steps of the project.
- *Expertise Committee:* Forming the professional teams for all product groups.
- *Training Committee:* Policymaking and holding of training courses.
- *Public Relations Committee:* Conducting acculturation process and public relations affairs.

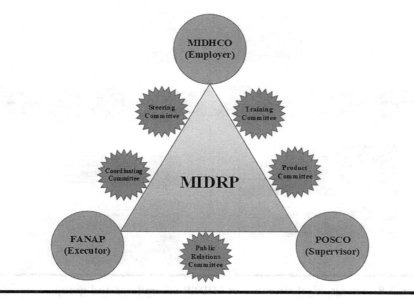

Figure 3.7   Collaborative basis of MIDRP project.

The purpose of these committees is to engage the related experts of MIDHCO, POSCO, and FANAP in the main required activities of the project, simultaneously. These activities embrace recognizing, implementing, and validating organizational processes besides performing user acceptance tests and providing data structures throughout the entire hierarchical structure of MIDHCO.

Primarily, Fig. 3.8 depicts how different teams are acting under the umbrella of the steering committee. Precisely, under the surveillance of the steering committee, any change to the project process must be approved by the Change Control Board (CCB). Further, the risk committee is supposed to identify, analyze, and evaluate the terms making the project vulnerable. The issues of CCB alongside with the risk committee are registered by the Project Management Office (PMO) and reported to the steering committee as well. Additionally, the task of deploying MIDRP products, being gradually delivered from the implementation group, is delegated to the deployment team. After producing the different products, in order to run the processes without any problem in real conditions, different tests must be performed by the test team. The adjustment group evaluates and assures that the delivered products comply with what is required on the employer's sites. There is also a data management and infrastructure group which is in charge of facilitating the product deployment in different hierarchical layers of MIDHCO.

Meanwhile, concerning the aforementioned multilateral structure of cooperation, what are the pillar concepts that are going to be dealt with by the involved parties? The relevant response to this concern would definitely make up the skeleton and body of the MIDRP project. In fact, the deliverables, accomplishments,

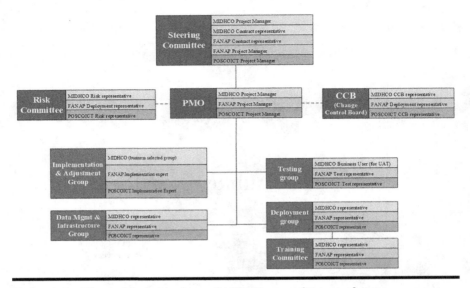

Figure 3.8   Hierarchical structure of MIDRP committees and groups.

and highlights of the project are among the critical entities that need to be specified for the involved parties in advance. First, the deliverables illuminate the MIDRP trajectory by converting the MIDHCO's requirements or equivalently the corresponding multiple prescribed features into tangible outputs in terms of the ERP context. Second, the way of accomplishing the project is another key concept that could shape the project body by specifying the execution method and the sequence of handling the deliverables. Finally, the involved parties deal with the clarification of the key features, realizing the main mission of MIDRP, namely, delivering a world-class product. These triple sets of pillar concepts are the subject of the next sections.

3.3 MIDRP Skeleton

To map the MIDHCO's requirements, known as TEC features in the storyline, into the tangible ERP deliverables, a special approach has been adopted under the cooperation of FANAP and POSCO ICT. In this approach, the prescribed features have been broken into a number of prime product groups and are subsequently drilled down to products and business processes, respectively. The product groups, indeed, meet all the needs of MIDHCO Holding and its subsidiaries. Totally, MIDRP possesses 13, 38, and 202 product groups, product, and business processes, respectively. As can be observed in Fig. 3.9, the product groups are divided into two general categories. The main category concentrates on the core processes being inclusive of quality management, supply chain management (SCM), manufacturing, commercial management, and maintenance management modules.

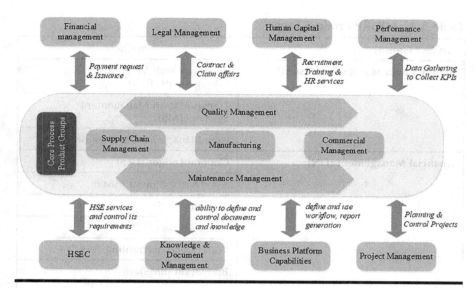

Figure 3.9 Big map of MIDRP.

The other product groups are closely connected to the core ones and play a role as the supportive modules. Moreover, the products are listed in Table 3.4, whereas the associated business processes are shown in Fig. 3.10. In what follows, the product groups and the enclosed products are elaborated.

3.3.1 The SCM

The SCM solution provides an integrated approach for the planning and control of materials and information while being transferred from the suppliers to customers in an organization. In this solution, organizations can easily coordinate the material flow between several departments or organizations. Using the latest technology and tools in the world, the solution is able to trace the materials along the route from origin to destination and record their information at each stage. This product group includes the following products.

3.3.1.1 Inventory and Warehouse Management (IWS)

This product includes important activities such as configuring the organization's warehouses and their items, locating the goods, registering the entry and exit of goods, managing requests, ordering, and warehousing. The features of this product are as follows:

- Adjusting the characteristics of the company's items such as determining the order point and safety stock, supply method, methods of leaving goods, and

Table 3.4 MIDRP Product Layer

Product Groups	Products
Supply Chain Management (SCM)	Inventory and Warehouse Management (IWS)
	Transportation Management System (TMS)
	Item Management System (IM)
Financial Management (FIN)	General Ledger (GLS)
	Asset Management (AMS)
	Treasury (FCS)
	Stock Affairs (SAS)
	Warehouse Accounting (WAC)
	Budgeting (BMS)
	Cost Accounting (COA)
	Cash Management (CSM)
	Loan and Credit Management (LCM)
Human Capital Management (HCM)	Recruitment Management (RCS)
	Human Capital Deployment (EMS)
	Payroll and Compensation (PCN)
	Training and Development (TRS)
Commercial Management (CMG)	Purchasing Management (PUR)
	Sales and Pricing Management (SMS)
	Relationship Management (XRM)
Manufacturing Management (MFG)	Manufacturing Engineering (MET)
	Production Planning (PMP)
	Manufacturing Execution (MES)
Quality Management (QMS)	Quality Assurance (QAS)
	Quality Control (QCS)
Maintenance Management (MTC)	Maintenance Management (MTC)
Health, Safety, Environment, Community (HSEC)	Health, Safety, Environment, Community (HSEC)
Project Management (PJS)	Project Management (PJS)

(Continued)

Table 3.4 (Continued) MIDRP Product Layer

Product Groups	Products
Legal Management (LMS)	Contract Management System (CMS)
	Claim Management System (CLM)
Business Platform Capabilities (BPC)	Platform (PFS)
	Portal and Office Automation (PAT)
	Workflow Management (WFM)
	Reporting (RPT)
Knowledge and Document Management (KDM)	Document Management (DMS)
	Knowledge Management (KMS)
Performance Management (PMS)	Business Intelligence Service (BIS)
	Data Analysis and Evaluation (DAE)

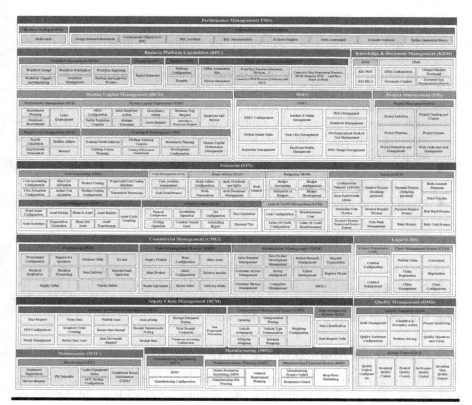

Figure 3.10 Business process layer of MIDRP.

specifying the requirements for quality control, serial number registration, and expiration date when items enter and exit the warehouses.

- Automating ordering of the organization's goods for optimal warehouse replenishment.
- Providing various types of reports related to warehouse transactions (such as receipts, remittances, orders, product requests, etc.) for each document in detail.
- Restricting access to items of different organizational units to register the request for goods.
- Specifying multiple units of measurement per product with the ability to convert to each other and perform warehouse transactions.

3.3.1.2 Transportation Management System (TMS)

This product was created to facilitate communication between order and warehouse management, allocate vehicles, and perform weighing tasks. The features of this product are as follows:

- Transferring the exact weight of the load from the scales to the weighing bill and recording and confirming the weighing remittance and receipts automatically.
- Calculating the remaining load of each shipping permit (trade and sales) based on the received information from the scales.
- Getting access to various types of reports related to transportation processes such as weighing times, the tonnage of each bill, the amount of load remaining from each shipment, and viewing receipts and remittances issued separately.
- Specifying a special vehicle and its license plate number and other features (such as refrigerated and containerized, etc.) to carry cargos.
- Loading and unloading the vehicles waiting in line.

3.3.1.3 Item Management System (IMS)

In this product, all items of the organization including services (such as welding or casting) and goods (such as raw materials to final products) are defined and classified. Each of them is also given an ID. An item may look exactly like another item, but one of its specifications is different.

3.3.2 Financial Management (FIN)

This product group covers all financial processes, including accounting, budgeting, costing, etc. This product group integrates accounting of all levels of the organization; thus, making it possible to handle macroeconomic and financial decisions using integrated and aggregate reports at the level of holding and subsidiaries. The following are the products of this group.

3.3.2.1 Asset Management (AMS)

This product manages and monitors all processes related to the organization's financial assets from the moment of possession to abandonment and elimination from the system. Features of this product are as follows:

- Recording public information, value, deliverable, and asset position from the moment of identification and in connection with the purchase and inventory control system.
- Recording price changes of assets, including corrections, repairs, and accounting documents.
- Calculating the depreciation of assets in financial periods and the possibility of predicting the future depreciation of assets.
- Determining the outflow of assets and the responsibility for the outflow cost.

3.3.2.2 Warehouse Accounting (WAC)

This product includes a set of operations to determine the price of warehouse inventory. The operation includes determining the price of the items entering the warehouse and the financial documents issued by the warehouse. The features of this product are as follows:

- Automatic pricing of purchasing receipts based on invoices and ancillary costs.
- Automatic pricing of production receipt documents based on cost.
- Estimated pricing in different ways.
- Remittance documents pricing by average method, special identification, and FIFO.
- Adjustment of the receipt rate and remittance.
- Automatic issuance of all the related accounting documents and receipts.

3.3.2.3 Cost Accounting (COA)

Using this product makes it possible to measure, record, report, and analyze cost-related information to plan and control operations, improve quality and efficiency, and make decisions. The features of this product are as follows:

- Calculating the cost of goods and services in a standard and realistic way.
- Calling the information needed to calculate the cost of processes.
- Allocating costs, based on activities and traditional methods such as cost sharing and distribution.

- Calculating and presenting deviation reports.
- Calculating the price of products and services separately for cost components (such as wage, energy, depreciation, maintenance, and other costs).

3.3.2.4 Treasury (FCS)

This product includes liquidity management, financing, recording, storing, and reporting in the field of all received and paid transactions in cash in the organization. The features of this product are as follows:

- Capability to plan cash reserving using liquidity report.
- Ability to view and identify contradictions of cash using bank cards, capital, and fund.
- Ability to receive and pay in foreign currency and view the current balance of the bank accounts and the fund.
- Capability to barter various suppliers and customers and register an automatic document using the bartering process.
- General Ledger (GLS).
- This product has a set of operations, including recording, storage, and reporting of all financial transactions in the organization. Product features include the following.
- Automatically recording documents of purchasing, sale, warehouse, treasury, salary, etc. without the possibility of change by the accountant (using prespecified approvals).
- Issuing a manual document using the template.
- Registering foreign currency, documents and currency reporting.
- Entering basic information about items and accounting documents, etc. via Excel.
- Defining account tree and standard document templates at the holding level.
- Tagging and categorizing entities in financial documents in order to issue an automatic document.

3.3.2.5 Budgeting (BMS)

In addition to evaluating the performance and control of resources and expenditures in the organization, the budgeting solution can also serve to measure the realization rate of the organization's strategies and goals. This solution leads the organization to calculate the prime cost of goods and services and provides the user with the tools needed to perform operations related to budgeting. The most important features of this product are as follows:

- Creating budget division based on the budget ratios and expenditures of organizational units.
- Predicting budget based on records of the organization.

- Defining proposed, approved, and actual budgets.
- Controlling the allocated budget directly with the financial system.
- Controlling the realization of planning using comparison reports.
- Providing advanced reporting tools to create all custom reports indefinitely.

3.3.2.6 Cash Management (CSM)

This solution helps the organization plan and control the liquidity situation by providing various reports on the liquidity situation and related resources and expenses. Two of the most important features of this master product are as follows:

- Liquidity Report for Future Forecasts.
- Preparation of cash flow report.

3.3.2.7 Loan and Credit Management (LCM)

This solution allows the organization to record, receive and settle the financial loan and maintain all the related information, and due to integration with the financial system, accounting, and treasury, covers all the related financial processes. Features of this product include the following:

- Announcing the due date of installments to stakeholders.
- Receiving financial loan reports and financial calculations such as interest rate calculations.
- Receiving loans in different currencies and settling them in the desired currency.
- Defining interest forgiveness and late payment penalty.

3.3.2.8 Stock Affairs (SAS)

In this solution, all general information about stocks and stockholders along with their financial and trading details are recorded so that it can be used in various forms. Features of this product are as follows:

- Ability to transfer stocks, increase or decrease capital.
- Receipt and payment generation to stockholders.
- Capability to calculate earnings per share, according to accounting standards.
- Capability to print stock shares and issue stock certificate.
- Comprehensive and analytical report.

3.3.3 Human Capital Management (HCM)

The most important point of this solution is the capital-oriented approach to the organization's human resources. The processes of this solution are empowering drivers to improve the management system of the organization in the field of human capital and maintain it at the appropriate level. With the Human Capital Management solution, it is possible to recruit, employ, train, motivate, and promote human capital in a simple way.

3.3.3.1 Recruitment Management (RCS)

In this solution, all services related to recruitment planning, interviews, and employment of manpower are performed. Features of this product are as follows:

- Providing the required job items and types of job application status.
- Receiving information about the job applicants and their resumes through the web and controlling the registration of their information.

3.3.3.2 Human Capital Deployment (EMS)

This product includes all the processes of the human resources department that relate to the employees of the organization. Features of this product include the following:

- Defining employee contract.
- Issuing employee action.
- Managing timesheet of employees.
- Defiling disciplinary action.
- Sending leave requests and business trip requests.
- Defining attendance permission request.
- Providing employee self-service facilities.

3.3.3.3 Payroll and Compensation (PCN)

Accurate calculation of staff salaries with high flexibility in the face of changing laws is one of the most important tasks of the PCN solution. Features of this product include the following:

- Creating fiscal years without restrictions and keeping the records for each year separately.
- Calculating the cost of salaries at the standard rate to calculate the prime cost of projects or products.
- Sharing salary costs of the project, cost center, and activity (or product) and issuing their accounting document.
- Calculating the retirement bonus, severance package, and the new year bonus according to the rate announced by the Ministry of Labor automatically.

- Calculating personnel settlement, redemption service, and employment termination.
- Providing welfare affairs and reward for personnel.

3.3.3.4 Training and Development (TRS)

Education and training of human resources are two key roles of a progressive organization. New recruits need to receive enough training to become skilled employees who can do their tasks independently. Organizations, on the other hand, need to plan so that whenever one person leaves the organization, they can immediately replace it with a suitable successor. Therefore, the TRS solution allows organizations to conduct a training needs assessment at first, then plan and execute a fixed training program for employees according to their training needs. Actually, this solution helps to examine the effectiveness of training courses. Another feature of this product is planning for training successive forces as well as managing the performance evaluation of the organization's employees.

3.3.4 Commercial Management (CMG)

This solution comprehensively provides the organization with a complete chain of marketing, sales, and customer relationship processes. In this solution, different modules of the sales management system become available. Undoubtedly, Extreme Relationship Management (XRM) is one of the features of this solution that facilitates effective communication with customers.

3.3.4.1 Purchasing Management (PUR)

This product was created to facilitate communication between order and warehouse management, item purchasing, as well as the connection between the financial system and the treasury. The features of this product are as follows:

- Sending purchase orders from inventory control and warehouse management in an integrated manner.
- Registering the purchase of the requested services from organizational units.
- Registering ancillary services including transportation of raw materials.
- Registering independent ancillary services in foreign trade and connecting to the purchase order.
- Planning and partitioning based on the variety of purchases.

3.3.4.2 Sales and Pricing Management (SMS)

This solution is a tool for handling the optimal sales of an organization's products efficiently in a way that reduces the organization's costs while increasing customer satisfaction. Product features include the following:

- Performing all sales steps from order booking to systematic delivery through online platforms.
- Creating a systematic connection between sales and warehouse.
- Controlling the sales unit based on the amount of load delivered to customers daily.
- Announcing daily quotas for delivery to the warehouse.
- Eliminating non-systemic and time-consuming communication.
- Establishing a systematic relationship between sales and treasury.
- Announcing and sending a system request (pre-receipt and receipt) from the sales to the treasury.
- Notifying and systematically monitoring the sales unit based on the amount of money received from the customer.
- Controlling systematically to prevent unloading more than the amount received.
- Providing systematic permit management in case of unloading more than the amount received.
- Monitoring directly the accuracy of the registered invoices of the sales and accounting unit.
- Generating sales invoices.
- Revising invoices.

3.3.4.3 Relationship Management (XRM)

Customer Relationship Management is one of the most important parts of an organization. However, organizations need relationships with other stakeholders to pursue their goals, for example, communication with employees, partners, suppliers, distributors, sellers, and many other stakeholders. In fact, as the name implies, XRM can be used to define communication with anything (Britsch et al., 2012). This product helps to enhance the value of all relationships, improve business relationships and lead to operational excellence.

3.3.5 Manufacturing Management (MFG)

This solution, using comprehensive production system configuration, product production planning, optimal machine scheduling, and production control, provides effective management of the organization's production processes. Also, at the integrated *Manufacturing Execution System (MES)* layer with the process control system, real-time data from the programmable logic controller (PLC) equipment of the production lines are always exchanged. Moreover, the possibility of making decisions and issuing orders to the production lines will be available to the managers. The products of this group are as follows:

3.3.5.1 Manufacturing Engineering (MET)

This solution encompasses the following features:

- Providing the necessary facilities to configure the structure of the production system according to the actual production conditions.
- Creating routing and Bill of Material (BOM) of products.

3.3.5.2 Production Planning (PMP)

The following features are enabled by means of PMP:

- Defining the master production plan periodically and controlling the realization of each period separately by product.
- Calculating the raw materials required separately by planning horizons.
- Increasing the predictive power of the production situation.

3.3.5.3 Manufacturing Execution System (MES)

There are critical features that are activated using MES:

- Issuing production schedule for each product and scheduling it separately for each operation per shift.
- Reserving inventory automatically to order production based on the initial quantity required.
- Recording production performance and reporting various work centers, including information on production values, raw material consumption values, and energy carriers.
- Providing diverse and multidimensional reports of all information available in production.

3.3.6 Quality Management (QMS)

This solution meets the customers' satisfaction with the comprehensive implementation of quality control of final products, raw materials, inventory, and work-in-process, besides analyzing the results and reviewing the feedback. Also, an appropriate methodology to implement the requirements of ISO 9000 series standards in the organization is provided. The products of this group are as follows:

3.3.6.1 Quality Assurance (QAS)

Quality assurance is a process to ensure that the system is designed to meet its objectives. This product strives to provide the design of processes that deliver consistent results each time. QAS product focuses on system and process compliance with system requirements such as ISO 9001 standard series. The features of this product are as follows:

- Managing and conducting internal audits in the organization.
- Managing and defining corrective and preventive measures and determining implementation methods.
- Offering different problem-solving approaches.
- Performing monitoring and controlling the production process.
- Defining quality objectives and vision.

3.3.6.2 Quality Control (QCS)

Focusing on planning and controlling the quality of the organization's items, the QCS solution is trying to increase the quality and customer-friendliness of all manufactured and non-manufactured goods. Hajipour et al. (2021) provided an overview of the MIDRP's QC module and highlights the most important features of the product as follows:

- Planning the activities of the quality control unit in the system.
- Communicating with the processes of purchasing and production and controlling them.
- Instantaneously reporting the quality status of input items and products.
- Categorizing all the items of the organization in the system and determining their quality status.
- Performing qualitative analysis of suppliers using valid recorded data.
- Detecting quality issued using data recorded in the system.

3.3.7 Maintenance Management (MTC)

This product has an integrated and coordinated process structure of all technical, executive, and managerial measures related to the organization's equipment during its life cycle. The MTC approach is based on achieving the desired level of performance and reliability of the equipment. This product group does not have a specific product and includes the following features:

- Managing and developing the equipment structure and ID as well as keeping the history of changes and actions taken.
- Providing the capabilities of planning, scheduling, allocating resources, controlling the effect of stops, issuing action permits, and registering agendas.
- Performing the analysis of the events' root causes based on standard data in corrective actions.

- Defining scheduling and planning for preventive measures based on time-based and functional patterns.
- Offering condition-based maintenance by monitoring the condition of the equipment at level 2 and determining corrective or preventive measures at level 4.
- Calculating key management and performance indicators.

3.3.8 Health, Safety, Environment, Community (HSEC)

With the slogan of sustainability in the structure, this system has managed the health, environment, and safety issues in the whole organization in order to progress toward a green business. Borrowing from Hajipour et al. (2021), product features include the following:

- Systematic recording and evaluating incidents and near-misses.
- Instantaneous observation of incident and near-miss statistics and key organizational indicators in the system.
- Capability to record incidents and near-misses as soon as it occurs through the mobile application.
- Systematic review and issuance of work permits through the mobile system and application and the current status of permits.
- Systematic record and evaluation of risk types, risk areas, and high-risk activities.
- Systematic reminder of the due dates of periodic risk reassessment.
- Automatic recording of identified risks arising from incidents and near-misses.
- Capability to plan and execute HSE visits with periodic or intermittent evaluation dates.
- Systematic reminder of the date to conduct the inspection.
- Periodic planning of tests and examinations in the system and control of health indicators.

3.3.9 Project Management (PJS)

This solution allows organizations to advance the management of projects, resources, time, and costs. Through this solution, it is possible to perform all activities related to project management, including scheduling, allocating and leveling resources, managing staff tasks and time sheets, managing approvals, management reports, and risk management on a secure platform using an integrated database. Among the most significant capabilities of this solution is the possibility of defining multiple users with different levels of access to project information. Using this information system, managers will be able to carefully monitor the status of projects and monitor the activities of executive teams. This solution allows project managers to make various reports based on the project's progress.

3.3.10 Legal Management (LMS)

For all legal and contractual matters in the organization, the product group of legal affairs management is activated. The products of this section are as follows.

3.3.10.1 Contract Management System (CMS)

Recording, observing, and tracking the history of contract changes from the stage of preparing the draft until its completion, controlling the number and the budgets of the concluded contracts, as well as monitoring the progress of the implementation of the provisions of the contracts is the most important achievements of the CMS solution. The most important features of this solution are as follows:

- Defining different contract types and determining access levels and parameters related to each contract type.
- Defining how to select a contractor through tender, ordinary contract, etc.
- Managing the contract process based on the financial transaction regulations appropriate for the organization.
- Conducting tenders and bids in accordance with the organization's regulations and simple management, reporting and archiving all relevant documents.

3.3.10.2 Claim Management System (CLM)

Claim management is crucial in managing, planning, and controlling a project or organization. All processes related to registration, management, and publication of claims are available in the CLM solution. The features of this product are as follows:

- Registering contracts, amendments, and minutes of meetings to provide the basis for the prospective justification of delays and overtime.
- Providing the financial claims.
- Issuing a claim document in case of any conflict between actual and planned work.

3.3.11 Business Platform Capabilities (BPC)

These products are a set of supportive capabilities of the MIDRP solution. Document management, knowledge management, balanced scorecard (BSC), portals, office automation, reporting, etc. are provided in the form of a BPC solution. Here, full integration with other solutions is provided in such a way that it is easy to use the corresponding processes in other products. The products of this group are:

3.3.11.1 Platform (PFS)

The platform configuration is handled in this product. It, in fact, can be regarded as a must for MIDRP to ensure that the BPC solution works well and generates the required outputs.

3.3.11.2 Portal and Office Automation (PAT)

With the help of the PAT solution, one can manage meetings, portals, office affairs, and other tasks related to office automation connected to other processes. The main features of this product are as follows:

- Office Automation BPs.
- Meeting management.
- Portal basic function (attachment, revision, ...).
- Connection to CRM processes (Marketing and sales).
- Connection to other processes (HCM, FIN, SCM, ...) and the display of the result of the portal.

3.3.11.3 Workflow Management (WFM)

Process and workflow management is able to define smooth workflow by identifying the needs and processes and considering the appropriate scheduling for the implementation of the task. By creating a workflow, the organization's processes are simply performed automatically step by step, and the responsibilities and thus the duties of individuals in the organization are clear and controllable. Management, design, enabled notification, report generation, and scheduling of workflows are included in this product.

3.3.11.4 Reporting (RPT)

One of the most important parts of information systems is their capability to build the required and special reports by the organization or the project, which is one of the important criteria for managers to choose the right solution. The generation of various reports from multiple data in a system based on the operational needs of the organization is one of the features that any solution or software should have. In fact, in this way, managers and other users can prepare comprehensive reports based on their needs, without the need for additional efforts. This valuable feature of the web reporting tool allows managers and users to prepare a variety of comprehensive reports.

3.3.12 Knowledge and Document Management (KDM)

With the presence of this solution at the level of MIDHCO Holding and its subsidiaries, many documents can be produced. There is also a need for preserving the knowledge produced in the MIDRP project to empower FANAP and MIDHCO employees with previous experiences. The products of this group are as follows:

3.3.12.1 Document Management (DMS)

A document management system can be defined as a product that controls and organizes documents in an organization. It should be noted that this product is used to define, track, view, store, and control documents. In general, how to store, manage, and track electronic documents in the organization can be defined as document management. Versioning documents and obsolete versions, as well as managing document data, are important features of this product.

3.3.12.2 Knowledge Management (KMS)

The knowledge management solution provides a secure and reliable resource for logging, observing, and disseminating organizational knowledge and can facilitate interactions within defined groups and individuals. The most important features of this solution are as follows:

- Defining access level to classified information for defined groups.
- Providing the capability to log, publish, and manage the lessons learned along with assessment capabilities.
- Communicating with other organizational systems with the aim of searching, receiving, and sending content.
- Submitting the lessons learned via text, video, outlook, or email.
- Creating people profiles.
- Defining expertise and evaluator.

3.3.13 Performance Management (PMS)

One of the goals of this solution is to make the organization smarter. Therefore, by providing completely analytical reports at different levels of the organization and offering business intelligence (BI), it is possible to make more accurate decisions in the organization. The products of this group are as follows:

3.3.13.1 BI Service (BIS)

This product plays a key role in deciding and showing the right way for the current and future situations of the organization. To make the right decision, the organizations need to prepare the right reports in explicit form. This product allows the organization to use analytic tools in BI and display them on the dashboard.

3.3.13.2 Data Analysis and Evaluation (DAE)

DAE supports organizations in achieving their strategic goals by enhancing internal and external communications and by monitoring the performance of the organization. This tool provides the managers with a performance measurement framework that measures non-financial, strategic performance against traditional financial criteria to give them a more balanced view of the organizational performance. The most important features of this product are as follows:

- Designing and managing balanced scorecards (BSC).
- Linking objectives to BSC.
- Providing BSC feedback.
- Evaluating supplier, customer, and sale.
- Defining assessment basics.

The aforementioned body of MIDRP provides a crystal-clear perspective on the extent of such a large-scale project. Now, the next upcoming challenge is associated with the way of accomplishing the corresponding number of product groups being inclusive of several products as well as business processes. This concern is taken as a hint of the next subsection.

3.4 Accomplishment

Eliciting from the gist of the story, FANAP could not presumably deliver the entire body of MIDRP at once. It stems from the completely new nature of the project which demands a gradual development procedure. Against the backdrop of such logic and prescribing an efficient roadmap for accomplishing the project, there is a long history that will be discussed in the next chapter. In the meantime, some aspects of the proposed methodology are implied herein. Generally, to realize the body of MIDRP, the product groups and enclosed details should pass the general procedure specified in Fig. 3.11. Adopting an incremental development process, the pre-specified segment of the body is going through the scope review, which maps the TEC features into the product groups and enclosed details. Subsequent to conducting the system analysis, the related committee provides the necessary feedback to align the new processes with the MIDHCO's requirements in practice. When the requirements of each process are met, the software design and development are carried out. Consequently, the integration test ensures that the connectivity among different business processes is

Figure 3.11   General MIDRP accomplishment procedure.

preserved. Now, the developed product can be gradually deployed across the entire hierarchical structure of MIDHCO in a step-by-step manner.

However, how could the whole bunch of business processes be injected into the above briefly described accomplishment procedure? Entailing a detailed story that would be explained later, FANAP has come across three phases of preparing the deliverables. Thus, the corresponding procedure is fed up based on the content of each phase. Fig. 3.12 shows the sequence of delivering the products within the three

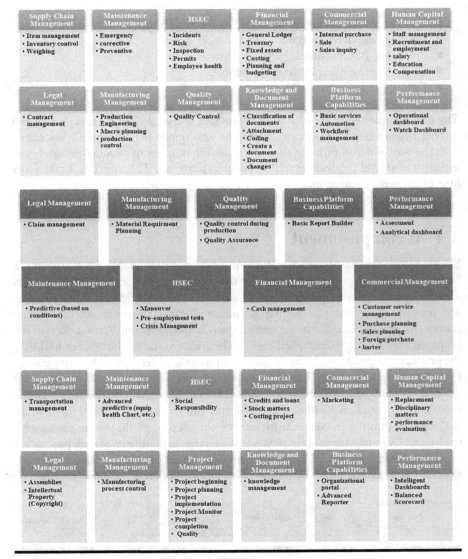

Figure 3.12   Phasing deliverables of MIDRP.

parts, namely, MIDRP I, II, and III. MIDRP I is a group of products that lead to omit the overall isolated software across the hierarchical structure of MIDHCO. MIDRP II works as a complementary package that fulfills the MIDHCO's requirements by going beyond the provided features in MIDRPI. Finally, MIDRP III enhances the quality of decision-making and performance of data entry by involving artificial intelligent techniques in the MIDRP framework. In the meantime, do the involved parties merely look for delivering MIDRP I, II, and III? The response is related to the pre-defined mission issue of Chapter 1 that is going to be discussed in the next subsection, in depth.

3.5 Highlights of MIDRP Solution

Sticking to the storyline, it has been implied that FANAP sets out to promote the MIDRP capabilities on the scale of world-class products. In fact, the involved parties are supposed to cover the aforementioned numerous features issued by TEC Company to correctly satisfy MIDHCO's requirements on the one hand. On the other hand, the quality of attaining the proposed solution constitutes the main mission of MIDRP. Under the reasonable time and cost trade-off, a framework needs to be developed that could smoothly provide a variety of advantages among the entire hierarchical structure of MIDHCO. These include integration, comprehensiveness, accessibility, flexibility, customization, real-time monitoring, supportability, and smart decision-making. Among the others, an integrated framework prevents the storage of duplicated data and facilitates the efficient data flow throughput MIDHCO. The comprehensive MIDRP should also guarantee that there is no necessity to purchase any external software package for meeting the whole MIDHCO requirements. Instant access to the MIDRP system in order to enhance the mobility of the users has to be deemed as another key advantage of the framework. To reach the required level of flexibility, the proposed system should avoid a task-oriented structure bringing about a major barrier to responding to the changes (Khosrowpour, 2000).

In response, a holistic and macro view of the organization instead of a partial view needs to be intensified by means of a process-oriented development (McCormack & Johnson, 2001). Customizing the product besides preserving the local compliance with the MIDHCO's business environment is the constant part of the MIDRP development stage. When designing MIDRP, the capability of ongoing support should be taken into account as the other prime merit of MIDRP. The supportability would be enhanced in case of effectively handling the new operation of MIDHCO at an affordable cost as time goes on. Providing a basis for embedding the decision-making with intelligent choices is also regarded as a complementary action for carrying out the pre-defined mission. In fact, the huge amount of data stored and transmitted in these solutions increases the complexity of analysis and decision-making. Therefore, the system must quickly provide the

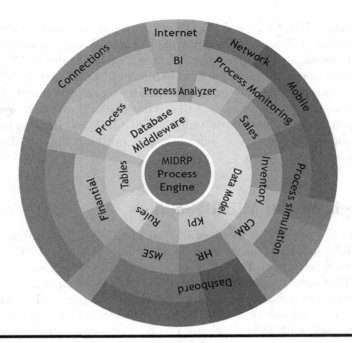

Figure 3.13 Enhanced highlights of MIDRP mission.

users with accurate analyzes using artificial intelligence tools. Such a tool helps managers to make the right decisions and predict the future, which is the goal of MIDRP III.

To fulfill the above advantages, Fig. 3.13 illustrates how a groundbreaking infrastructure with a variety of advantages has been projected by the MIDRP engine.

In this regard, the core engine of MIDRP is built based on the business process management system (BPMS) terminology. BPMS considers the processes as the key resources of the system and allows for modeling the business environment at detail levels through a special notation called BPMN. Indeed, BPMN is a standard, including symbols and rules that are easily understood by all business process users (Pajk et al., 2011). By simply converting the BPMN to the development codes, BPMS injects flexibility into the body of MIDRP in practice. The engine provides different connection methods for improving the accessibility of users such as internet, mobile as well as a hybrid cloud framework. Under such a framework, MIDRP is endowed with a technology-driven process of BI which underpins decision-making by analyzing the advanced data. To further optimize the ongoing processes of MIDHCO, the engine is also accompanied by a process simulation tool. This tool plays a core role in shortening the main engineering cycle of design, research & development, and operation.

Furthermore, the customized process engine proposes a systematic approach by enhancing the shop-floor monitoring through integrating the manufacturing execution system into the body of MIDRP. The presence of an applied dashboard coupled with key performance indicators (KPIs) also completes the BI cycle by collecting information on the performance of the different MIDRP entities. Moreover, by defining the business rules engine, the condition related to running and stopping specific applications could be handled in an interactive platform. The platform enables the users to adjust their desired conditions without the necessity of changing technical codes. Additionally, the database middleware has been laid out to enhance the interoperability between software entities and capture the scaling concern in the MIDRP engine. In the light of automating the workflow, data models are another key component of the engine toward consolidating the cohesiveness between various product groups of MIDRP. Finally, the motif of the proposed engine is to streamline the communication of the corresponding product groups and bring about a fully integrated basis for meeting the requirements of MIDHCO.

3.6 Conclusion

Herein, the general discussion about the MIDRP product has been opened up including facets regarding the context, execution, and blueprints. Nevertheless, the aforementioned aspects still demand a much more detailed exploration to puzzle such a venturesome journey out. In this regard, there are a significant number of derivatives that are out of the current chapter. Chapter 4 aims at devising the exact roadmap of the MIDRP accomplishment procedure. The chapter would narrate the way of achieving the ideal MIDRP methodology and the related technical issues in realizing a great number of deliverables.

Delivering the explained blueprints strictly engages with the approach to designing the fundamental structure of the system known as system architecture. Chapter 5 elucidates the multi-layer architecture that has been devised to surmount the restriction of the classical two-layer scheme. A poor architecture would interrupt the development process of MIDRP and hedge against fulfilling the predefined goals of the mission. Chapter 6 concerns the most important step in terms of identifying the existing condition, drawing the ideal working procedure, and specifying the special business requirements of MIDHCO. The reasons behind the composition of product groups and the enclosed items are clarified in the context of system analysis. Enlarging the technical side of developing MIDRP is the other key concept that needs to be considered as a distinctive part of Chapter 7. Moreover, MIDRP would be absolutely meaningless in the lack of interconnection among the several developed entities related to product groups. Chapter 8 is the matter of infusing the usefulness into the functionality of MIDRP by integrating different targeted processes.

The deployment of such a large-scale product would not definitely be a straightforward process. The involved parties have experienced partial failures in settling MIDRP within the hierarchical structure of MIDHCO Holding. The remedies to surmount the underlying challenges of deployment has their own long story that is going to be demonstrated in Chapter 9. Eventually, Chapter 10 is the end of the story that goes around the remarkable segment of MIDRP, i.e., the use of intelligent maneuvers in response to the pre-defined world-class mission of the project. Fig. 3.14 outlines the inquiries that lead to extending the content of the current book over the practical issues surrounding the MIDRP story. This story is named adventurous journey since there are no quick-fix solutions for the corresponding inquiries. In order to come up with a workable solution, the involved characters have been supposed to take the rocky path of the project accomplishment.

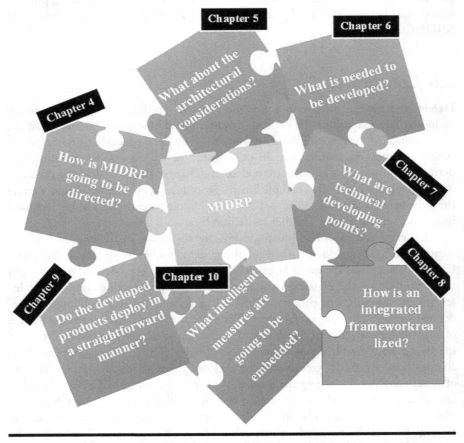

Figure 3.14   An overview of pieces of the MIDRP's puzzle throughout the next chapter.

Note

1. This acronym is a combination of the two words: MIDHCO and ERP.

References

Amouzegar, H. R., Hajipour, V., & Jalali, S. (2020). An enterprise solution in practice: Issues and challenges. *Journal of Applied Intelligent Systems and Information Sciences*, *1*(1), 44–49.

Britsch, J., Schacht, S., & Mädche, A. (2012). Anything relationship management. *Business & Information Systems Engineering*, *4*(2), 85–87.

Hajipour, V., Amouzegar, H., & Jalali, S. (2021). A practical integrated solution into enterprise application: A large-scale quality control system development case study. *International Journal of Quality & Reliability Management*, *38*(7), 1487–1519.

Hajipour, V., Amouzegar, H., Gharaei, A., Abarghoei, M. S. G., & Ghajari, S. (2021). An integrated process-based HSE management system: A case study. *Safety Science*, *133*, 104993.

Khosrowpour, M. (2000). *Challenges of information technology management in the 21st century*. Idea Group Publishing.

McCormack, K. P., & Johnson, W. C. (2001). *Business process orientation: Gaining the e-business competitive advantage*. CRC Press.

Pajk, D., Indihar-Štemberger, M., & Kovačič, A. (2011). Enterprise resource planning (ERP) systems: Use of reference models. In J. Grabis & M. Kirikova (Eds.), *Perspectives in Business Informatics Research. BIR 2011. Lecture notes in business information processing* (Vol. 90). Berlin, Heidelberg: Springer. doi:10.1007/978-3-642-24511-4_14

Chapter 4

Project Management Methodology

"Amidst pages of the current book, curious audiences endeavor to trace the critical factors that build the basic success origins of MIDRP. It's not an overstatement that half of the factors stem from the methodology of laying the project's foundation guaranteeing MIDRP survival in the tortuous accomplishment path."

—Project Management Office of MIDRP

Borrowing from the previous chapter, one of the key pieces of the story's puzzle has been associated with the way of directing the project. In terms of scale, MIDRP can be even regarded as a unique practice throughout the Middle East. Hence, advancing a project at this scale entails a delicate, transparent, and efficient roadmap to illuminate the holistic way of achieving the desired goals. This roadmap is analogous to project management methodology. Devising the methodology of MIDRP is probably the potential challenging decision faced by the involved parties throughout the project lifecycle. For the executive character of the story who is practicing a completely new experience, the recipe of the appropriate project methodology is not going to be figured out at once. In fact, the customized methodology would be realized through a progressive procedure by studying the best practices and grilling the supporting character on many facets of the project. This chapter draws the key notifications and highlights on the way of approaching the best fit for organizing MIDRP methodology. In this regard, to provide a preparation basis for narrating the showcase of MIDRP methodology, the related best practices are reviewed in Section 4.1. Then, Section 4.2 steps into describing how MIDRP methodology has evolved during an adventurous journey. The

DOI: 10.1201/9781003369806-4

section focuses on the methodology that has been adopted initially leading to several ramifications and thereby improved regarding certain measures. Section 4.3 deals with the project collaboration by enumerating the opportunities for co-operation and participation of individuals in the MIDRP. Finally, Section 4.4 concludes the maturing trend of MIDRP methodology and responds to possible inquiries that may come to readers' mind.

4.1 An Introduction to Project Management Methodology

Concerning software-based cases, the project management methodology is to provide a systematic framework for structuring, planning, and process monitoring of an information system. It should equip the project team with swift process development and sifting through the project accomplishment phases in order to remove the obstacles in advance. The functionality of such a methodology is highlighted when dealing with the integration of the software projects and the fulfillment of the special requirements. It also works as a preceding notification for the project teams to be aware of their upcoming tasks. Under the project management methodology, the work is broken down into different tasks and phases in order to facilitate better planning and management of the project.

Herein, the studies related to the background of the software development project methodology are reviewed in an organized manner. First, the existing traditional versus recent emerging methodologies in the literature are compared and the controversial ideas on their application to large-scale projects are studied in Section 4.1.1. Second, Section 4.1.2 briefly introduces some of the best practices recommended by consultants and popular software development companies. The final part of the literature review in Section 4.1.3 considers the practical experiences of previous research on employing the recent methodologies in case of large-scale software projects.

4.1.1 Prevailing Methodologies for Software Project

Studying appropriate methodologies of accomplishing software projects, most of the previous works unanimously have put the performance of heavyweight methods versus lightweight ones into consideration. Heavyweight methods are sequentially laid out based on a series of stages whose fixed durations should be set in advance while predicting the prospective arising problems (Bianchi et al., 2020). The predictive approach is the embodiment of the heavyweight methods which strictly rely on detailed upfront setting and heavy documentation. However, lightweight methods are attributed to the agile terminology which is devised based on incremental and iterative development rather than a fixed pre-specified manifesto (Islam & Storer, 2020). According to Leau et al. (2012), agile versus traditional approaches are comparable in terms of user requirement, rework cost, testing, customer involvement, and required personal traits and skills of the participants. The user requirement should be fully and iteratively determined in terms of traditional and agile approaches. The rework cost and customer involvement of the agile approach are lower and higher than the traditional ones, respectively, due to several double-checking the details within short time intervals. In addition to programming skills, the agile method demands developers to have interpersonal skills as well as basic business knowledge since there exists close interconnection between developers and customer. Besides, despite conducting a single test at the end of the coding stage of the traditional methods, the testing practice would be repetitively conducted per iteration in the context of the agile approach.

The most popular branches of the agile approach are Scrum and Extreme programming (Ellis, 2016). Scrum concentrated on the project management facet of agile development concerning pervasive monitoring of project progress. It also gives prominence to customer satisfaction, and breaks down tasks' duration into smaller periods, known as the sprint. However, extreme programming deals with a set of measures for propelling incremental production through agile development. Meanwhile, there exist very close similarities between the proposed mechanisms of both approaches pertaining to continuous development cyclically. Their similarities involve setting release planning based on the project vision and further conducting sprint planning for the sake of implementation. During the implementation stage, daily Scrum is regularly carried out while sprint review and retrospective meetings are subsequently convened. The most salient problem of embedding agile methods into large-scale projects is its holistic way of thinking which inhibits minor changes to cope with the corresponding challenges. Rather, this approach entails entire organizational changes and hedging against the inertia and bureaucracy of large companies.

However, there is a hypothesis that agile approaches generally fit well small-scale projects and do not apt for larger ones (Jalali & Wohlin, 2012; Saeeda et al., 2015). In contrast, several relevant studies have advocated the promising performance of the agile approaches in such projects (Ebert & Paasivaara, 2017; Lagerberg et al., 2013). To find out more about such a concern, Jørgensen (2018) designed a questionnaire-based survey with respect to a hundred Norwegian software projects. Using statistical analysis, the superiority of the agile approaches was concluded in the case of large-scale projects. It was discussed that the controversial feedbacks over the performance of the agile approaches stem from different factors. There was a lack of a good definition of agile principles and practices while the existence of the other influential factors on the software project success might intervene in the results. Furthermore, the indefinite perception over the extent of a large-scale software project besides the personalized interpretation of the effectiveness of the agile approaches were crippling items causing misunderstanding.

4.1.2 Best Practices Associated with Software Project Methodologies

The best practices of scaling agile approaches are mainly proposed by professional consultants and global technology leaders. Owing to the significant role of the top software-based methodological experiences, four prime approaches are briefly reviewed in what follows.

4.1.2.1 Accelerated SAP

Accelerated SAP methodology (known as ASAP) is an agile-based implementation strategy being employed by popular ERP vendors, in order to facilitate the rapid building pattern of the customized coding (Kalaimani, 2015). Coupling with Scrum standards, the most salient achievement for SAP was to make sure that has ensured that almost no segment of the developed software would deviate from the customer expectations. The magnitude related to the involved teams and the complexity of the project landscape and scheduling was the overriding pitfall in the agile implementation of SAP. To remedy this, SAP has considered a step-by-step procedure for mapping its proposed agile strategy with the basic project management processes of initiation, planning, execution, monitoring, and closure. Hence, the two former processes are aggregated as the preparation step of the agile methodology while execution is decoupled into the blueprint, realization, and final preparation steps.

The Go-live and support besides operating steps are representatives for the monitoring and closure processes. Next, the deliverables of each step have been specified. For instance, the project preparation entails adopting best practices, setting work broken structure, determining infrastructure requirements, managing data, and defining training strategy. Moreover, the business blueprint, realization, final preparation, and Go-live steps are typically expected to finalize gap analysis, user acceptance testing, cutover planning, and transition framework, respectively. Certainly, these steps are not isolated from each other and 70% of the deliverables of each step depend on the completion of the previous ones. SAP experts stated that one of the most helpful tools to get familiar with the new methodology was related to the utilization of the product canvas after the completion of each release. The product canvas collaboratively involves user-stories, scenarios, and design sketches to reach a validated blueprint for developing the next release.

4.1.2.2 Large-Scale Scrum

Being released in 2005, the Large-Scale Scrum (LeSS) approach endeavors to extend Scrum's guidelines to the structure of the enterprise scale (Larman & Vodde, 2016). This approach provides a bridge between two consecutive sprints through a systematic framework that involves an organizational system/design related to groups, roles, hierarchy, and policies. The initial input of a new sprint is the updated list of all works that need to be done for a product, known as the product backlog, being prepared by the product owner. To possibly manage several interconnections among multiple teams, LeSS focuses on organizational changes and recommends considering different product owners to do necessary coordination about product backlog. Similar to the prevailing procedure of the Scrum method, sprint planning, and review sessions are regularly carried out.

Based on the product backlog, sprint planning is convened in two sessions to clarify what the goal of the current sprint is and how it should be realized. The former session is a meeting among all engaged teams to select items from the product backlog and specify which items will be accomplished by which team. The latter meeting is inner-team planning to design and plan for getting items to be done during the sprint. The results of both meetings comprise the sprint backlog, including a set of plan actions and tasks. Similar to the team definition in a one-team Scrum, the engaged teams in LeSS attempt to fulfill a couple of product backlogs during the per sprint. The Scrum master is the key individual in monitoring a team's performance toward not being derailed from the sprint goal while reminding the whole product's focus.

In contrast to the one-team Scrum, the daily short meeting of LeSS can be managed in the presence of people from other teams for the sake of significant coordination. In the middle per sprint, the ongoing product backlog entails refining as the preparation step for the next sprint planning. It is first refined under the supervision of the product owner and representatives of each team. Then, the refinement is detailed in attendance of the users and stakeholders and a mixed group of teams. The output of the current sprint is entitled potentially shippable product increment and is associated with entire works that have been done for currently implemented features. In fact, all teams are supposed to integrate their done work in order to shape the incremental product at the end per sprint.

4.1.2.3 Scaled Agile Framework

Introduced by Leffingwell (2007), the Scaled Agile Framework (SAFe) has also been developed to respond to empowering software projects at scale. Concerning the combination of agile and lean practices, SAFe is a layer-based method that considers four categories in its big picture including team, program, portfolio, and value stream levels. Pertaining to the team level, SAFe combines the Scrum method with extreme programming or even lean measures such Kanban tool. The backdrop of such a combination is the fact that agile methods may be unable to manage the interdependencies of multiple teams efficiently and lean measures can capture the underlying dilemmas. The program level is related to realizing the facts that enhance business capability or value. This realization would be accomplished by assigning teams to the program level. Further, the value stream level is to ensure the existing multiple teams' functionalities and goals are continually working in the same direction and converged.

The portfolio level provides a basis for the involved teams to seek innovative ideas for resolving ongoing challenges and increasing productivity. Agile Release Train (ART) is another critical concept of SAFe that needs to be set. It signals the purpose of multiple teams to reach a common value stream of the business. Subsequent to the creation of the implementation plan, the condition for launching ART is prepared. Training teams and coaching ART execution are indispensable parts of its realization. Actually, the continuous practice of SAFe, requiring sustainability and improvement, is to launch and adhere more and more ARTs to the portfolio level.

4.1.2.4 Disciplined Agile Delivery

Disciplined Agile Delivery (DAD) is a hybrid agile approach by extending Scrum with promising methods such as agile modeling, extreme programming, LeSS, and SAFe (Ambler & Lines, 2012). One of the main characteristics of DAD is to support several delivery lifecycle addressing all the ways of delivering the products to the customers rather than the mere development-led viewpoint of Scrum. This characteristic is achievable through the key component-based principle of DAD, namely, context counts. Simply, it means that DAD could adjust its methodology to any specific working framework of the organization. In other words, the unique, engaging set of employees, teams, targeted customers, and stakeholders necessitate the fact that the organizational structure has to be tailored to its specific context. To recognize the context of an organization and further construct teams, the potential criteria are categorized into the selection and scaling factors. Selection factors are the main initial drivers of adopting the new structure being affected by the participants' skills of a team, organizational culture, the nature of the problem, and underlying constraints. Additionally, the scaling factors are motivators of tailoring the new structure under consideration of team size, the geographical distribution of customers, different branches of the organization, and inherent technical complexity.

Another key characteristic of the DAD approach corresponds to the robust design of roles that are involved in delivering agile solutions. Primary and supporting roles imply the responsibilities that permanently and temporarily existed in DAD projects concerning scaling issues, respectively. The primary roles consist of the associated team and stakeholders' participants. Here, team roles are product owner, team leader, architecture owner, and team member. Additionally, the supporting roles will be added to DAD's structure, including specialist, independent tester, domain expert, technical expert, and integrator. Contrarily, any other agile method such as Scrum considers a significantly lower number of roles such as Scrum master and product owner. The presence of multiple influential roles in DAD indicates the high level of DAD's emphasis on all aspects of the deliverable solution. Accordingly, not only the issues related to leadership and change management are satisfied but also a considerable concentration is made on the technical-oriented part of the output delivery.

4.1.3 Related Experiences in Adopting the Recent Methodologies

To preserve the thread of the aforementioned best practices, some of the studies related to their functionalities in real cases have been investigated as follows. Brenner and Wunder (2015) investigated the applicability of the SAFe method in a large-scale integration software products company with 40 teams and four ARTs. It was implied that the key feature of SAFe is related to its capability in improving the collaboration among multiple teams when it comes to incremental planning. Alqudah and Razali (2016) reviewed agile methods in large-scale software developments and highlighted the discrepancies among them in terms of different criteria, e.g., team size, training, adopted practices, and organizational type. For instance, comparing DAD, SAFe, and LeSS in terms of required technical practices, it was mentioned that DAD entails adopting the highest level of technical skill. Meanwhile, SAFe and LeSS almost require a medium/low level of skills to get familiar with portfolio and Scrum concepts, respectively. Concerning a large-scale software project at Nokia Company, Paasivaara and Lassenius (2016) justified that the pain point in running the LeSS method stemmed from the lack of cohesiveness coaching the elements associated with the organization, team, and technical levels. Additionally, the high workload to deliver the products to the existing customers along with market pressure, leading to the new contracts forced the team members to skip unnecessary meetings. Unfortunately, this instigated miscommunication and brought about major bugs and rework costs at times of integration. Paasivaara (2017) explored the critical success factors on the implementation of SAFe in a globally distributed software development company. The research revealed that investing in coaching and training to engage people besides well preparing for the first planned event led to utilize the agility's benefits as much as possible.

Despite proposing different new generations of doing work in an agile manner, Conboy and Carroll (2019) stipulated that the literature lacked empirical studies on original framework papers in the wild. Conducting an extensive survey, they figured out that one of the most problematic issues stemmed from the absence of any assessment model for choosing between LeSS, SAFe, DAD, and so on. Concerning the interactive role of clients-vendors in agile software development, Shameem et al. (2017) identified three success factors embracing rich technological infrastructures, managerial commitment, and in-depth requirement analysis. Uludağ et al. (2019) have enumerated the prime challenges of an automobile company in employing the LeSS method of interviewing corresponding experts. One of the typical complaints was about the efficient reduction in teams' members due to take part in so many meetings and consequently losing energy and concentration to undertake their responsibilities. The existence of dual leadership for each product causing managerial divergences was also reported since each product had two owners: one to cover information technology facet and another one to monitor the business. It was believed that the organizational position of middle-level managers was prone to be degraded due to continual retraining by the product owner. Furthermore, a lack of an agile mindset was among the main reasons leading to considerable dilemmas in adaptation to the LeSS methodology in that company.

Therefore, previous studies emphasize the prominent position of studying the methodological aspects of a real case study such as MIDRP project. In fact, it is worthy to investigate the process of transforming the classical methodologies into agile ones which is going to be the main concern of the next section.

4.2 Toward Maturing MIDRP Project Management Methodology

After declaring the necessitous background, it is now prudent to review the evolving procedure of the MIDRP methodology from beginning to end. In this regard, Section 4.2.1 discusses the foundation of this methodology that definitely originated from the content of the contract between MIDHCO and FANAP. Section 4.2.2 focuses on the performance of the initial methodology in practice and highlights its restrictions on achieving project success. Section 4.2.3 proposes the new methodology and enumerates the measures to align with it, while Section 4.2.4 keeps the involving processes in perspective.

4.2.1 Methodology Origin

There is a long story corresponding with MIDRP methodology needing to review key events of the project history. The negotiation surrounding signing the contract between MIDHCO and FANAP broke in 2014. It took almost a year and a half for the involved parties to conclude the negotiations and reach an agreement on the detailed content of the contract as summarized in Fig. 4.1. Quoting from the head of the FANAP PMO, this apparently long interval sounds reasonable since a software-based practice at such scale was a relatively new experience even in the region of the Middle East.

> "Negotiation surrounding an ERP contract is certainly burdened by forming the mindset of the customer over what terms are going to be realized throughout such a project. Clearing the scope and deliverables of the project, its conveyance to the customer, and subsequently, its conversion to the monetary terms were real challenges towards initiating MIDRP."
>
> –PMO

Based on what was mentioned in Chapter 1, MIDHCO looks for a significant spike in its annual steel production equal to 4.2 million tonnes. To reach this, an

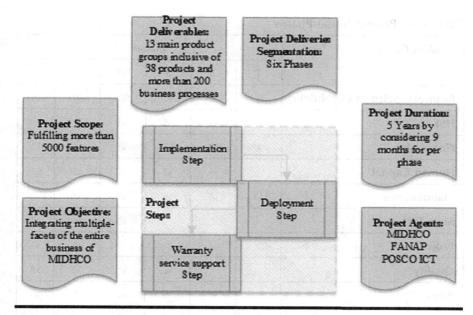

Figure 4.1 Contract-based methodological setting.

enterprise solution to increase the productivity of its entire business was a crucial must. Accordingly, the main objective of the MIDRP project was to provide a systematic platform for integrating the whole processes of MIDHCO holding and its business units. Further, the project scope has matched the TEC features.

Then, the largest chunk of the pre-contract assessment originated from attempting to map the TEC features (or synonymously project scope) to the project deliverables based on the logic behind the process-oriented development of FANAP. As discussed in Chapter 3, the features were converted to the 202 business processes, 37 products, and later formed the 13 main product groups which constituted the main deliverables of the project. To frame the progress plan, each process was further weighted in terms of the percent of satisfying the TEC features. For the sake of monitoring and progress checking, the project was also subdivided into implementation and deployment accompanied by the support service during the warranty period. The implementation aims at producing the proposed business processes one by one under the official confirmation of the customer. The deployment is to put the developed business processes into practice for the candidate customers' subsidiaries.

As implied before, the whole requirements of MIDHCO, namely the product groups, could not be developed at once, according to the contract content, the work was broken into six phases. Table 4.1 shows how the project components were initially supposed to be delivered. The completion time per phase was set equal to nine months by considering a six-month for accomplishing the deployment and

Table 4.1 Project Initial Phases

Product Group	Phase					
	1	2	3	4	4	6
Business Platform Capabilities	☑	☑	☑	☑	☑	☑
HSE		☑	☑	☑		
Financials	☑	☑	☑	☑	☑	☑
Human Capital			☑	☑	☑	☑
Maintenance	☑	☑	☑	☑		
Manufacturing				☑	☑	☑
Project					☑	☑
Quality			☑	☑	☑	☑
Sales		☑	☑	☑	☑	☑
Supply Chain	☑	☑	☑	☑	☑	☑

development steps, distinctively. Notably, the start time of the development step has three months intersecting with the development interval. Aggregately, it would take 54 months for the MIRP to be completed. A one-year warranty period was also considered in the contract entailing FANAP to support the MIDRP product free of charge. By adopting a professional consultant and starting the execution of the project, the project agents are MIDHCO (employer), FANAP (contractor), and POSCO ICT (consultant).

4.2.2 Initial Methodology in Practice: Issues and Challenges

At the inception of steering the project, the methodology used to be laid out based on the predictive approach to complete the MIDRP life cycle. In fact, the MIDRP life cycle operated in a waterfall sequential manner illustrated in Fig. 4.2 in two general and detailed levels. The initiation step can be attributed to the required activities and time that has been devoted to signing the contract. Next, the preparation step has been conducted under the collaboration of FANAP and POSCO. It is considered in defining the project management methodology to identify how the pre-determined scope is going to become ready for the final users' exploitation. Furthermore, the implementation step can be detailed in the execution and confirmation sub-steps. The execution is equivalent to whatever is needed to shape the MIDHCO's requirements into the appropriate software-based system ranging from the process analysis to the integration test. The output of the execution sub-step has to be

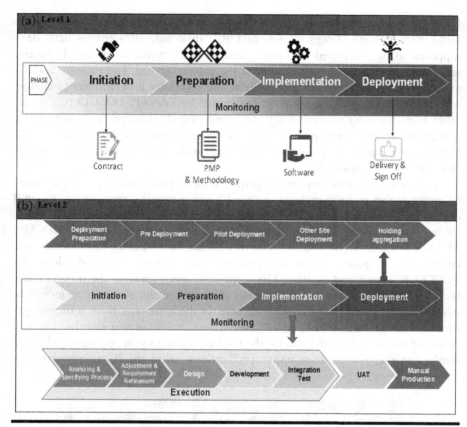

Figure 4.2 **Project management lifecycle in general (a) and detail (b) perspectives.**

confirmed by the customer, bypassing the user-acceptance test (UAT) and providing the training manual of the corresponding production. The deployment step is divided into the sub-steps to assure its pre-requisites, institutionalization of the developed products in the pilot business units, as well as the other sites and preserving the aggregation.

Under this classical approach, the accomplishment of the first phase has lengthened two times the planned duration leading to three years increase in the project duration as a result of the rescheduling plan. In addition to the scheduling intervention of the implementation step, the components that were supposed to be deployed in the first phase could not satisfy the customer's expectations in practice. Indeed, MIDHCO could not switch its isolated software with the delivered product in the first MIDRP phase and had to make wasteful attempts to manually synchronize its old software with that incomplete package. The disappointing result has forced the involved parties to detect the underlying reasons for the resulting delay and look for effective solutions.

Prior to describing their proposed solution, let's review the skeleton of the initial project methodology of the MIDRP. In detail, all activities have been supposed to be completed in a row through the contribution of the distinctive teams related to the key participants of the project agents. The primary team is made up of a number of business analysts and computer programmers to analyze and develop each product group being directed by FANAP. POSCO ICT is another team focusing on evaluating and presenting the best practices per group. The implementation group (IG) team, on the other hand, is a committee of the MIDHCO's experts that are quietly familiar with the product groups and are aware of the requirements.

The associated teams are then engaged in the development and deployment phases being scheduled to be completed during 12 and 6 months, respectively. Fig. 4.3 depicts the scheduling related to the implementation and deployment steps by specifying the involved agents in accomplishing each sub-step, i.e., F (FANAP), M (MIDHCO), P (POSCO). Meanwhile, the development distinctively encompasses scope assessment, business analysis, IG adjustment, software development, POSCO ICT test, and IG test. The scope assessment involves the mutual collaboration of FANAP and POSCO within the expected duration of one month in which FANAP plays a more critical role here. In the same vein, there is the engagement of FANAP and POSCO to fulfill the system analysis in two months. Taking a period of two months into account, the resultant business processes have to be customized to the pilot business units' specifications, called the IG adjustment step.

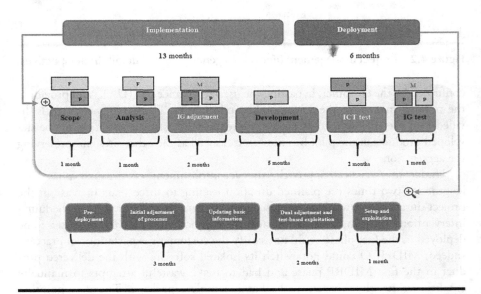

Figure 4.3 Implementation and deployment scheduling under the initial methodology.

In this step, MIDHCO is the main decision-maker while both POSCO and FANAP have participated in the necessary judgments.

Further, the software development is exclusively carried out by FANAP for five months. In the presence of FANAP, POSCO ICT should evaluate the software functionality in two months and try to provide constructive comments for its improvement. Concerning a one-month interval, MIDHCO as the core owner of the IG test also examines the software and notifies POSCO and FANAP of the required modifications. Going through the deployment step, the preparation, initial adjustment, and information tuning take three months while the dual adjustment is completed within two months. One month is also considered for exploiting the software. It was a difficult task to consider fully planning practice and predict fixed durations for such sub-steps due to the uncertain nature of the project.

> "Suppose the customer needs a business process to utilize the benefits of the material resource planning (MRP) feature. To forecast a rigid duration and define up-to-scratch planning in a predictive manner, the way of integrating MRP with other product groups such as purchase, and warehouse should be clarified in advance. To reach a significant level of clarification over the type and degree of integration, an analysis is needed to be conducted. Meantime, how long does it exactly take? The response is quite straightforward: it is an uncertain fact, since the detail aspects of such a business process are opaque to us prior to being engaged with it."
>
> –PMO Manager

Under the predictive methodology, the first trial in accomplishing the initial phase of the project was disapproved by the involved parties. Thus, the steering committee, including key participants of FANAP and MIDHCO endeavored to identify the causes of the deadline extension and provide significant solutions using brainstorming. In response, the committee highlighted the drawbacks of the initial project methodology in six general categories of scope, analysis, IG adjustment, software development, tests, and deployment. The drawbacks chiefly stemmed from a set of rework operations being highlighted with curved braces in Fig. 4.4. The scope definition was merely based on the TEC features without being customized for the customer's requirements. Hence, the developed business processes and products could not get the approval of MIDHCO in the UAT step. In terms of analysis, underestimating the importance of MIDHCO's involvement during two consecutive months caused a large chunk of underlying initial phase accomplishment delay. Such ignorance entailed reassessing MIDHCO experts in the context of the IG test during a two-month interval.

IG adjustment, per se, lacked rigorous engagement of MIDHCO's participants in facilitating a prompt yet comprehensive control over the business processes

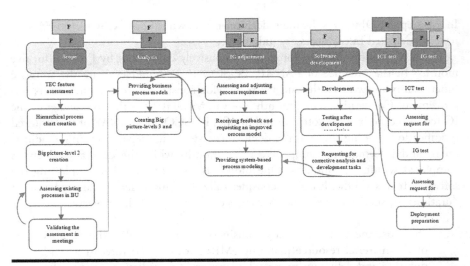

Figure 4.4 Highlighting rework actions of the implementation mechanism under the initial methodology.

derived by FANAP. In addition to the implementation unevenness, the deployment step suffered from critical problems such as the decentralized data collection and variable demands of different business units over the proposed products. Further, the inherent characteristic of such a committee demanded a delicate and technical perspective of each distinctive professional product group. Apparently, the current composition of the IG committee, including a significantly large number of top-level directors of MIDHCO with a broad level of managerial views over different organizational aspects, did not fit well such a characteristic. Various and dispersed attitudes toward any sort of issue in the committee also implied the number of participants that needed to be lessened. In the same vein, the software development had been conducted by FANAP in the absolute absence of monitoring of the other parties during the corresponding five months.

Amid this long-lasting isolated interaction, the members of the IG committee gradually missed their expectations, requirements, and prescribed comments related to the features of the software. Therefore, the resultant software package was far from the anticipation of the committee causing MIDHCO's dissatisfaction. Finally, the quality of testing had been imprecise and could not reflect the exact capabilities and drawbacks of the software. Furthermore, it was an exhaustive and time-consuming practice for FANAP to apply the specified comments and modifications stemming from the separated test results of POSCO and MIDHCO. Moreover, to experience a seamless deployment of the deliverables, the segmentation of the phases needs to be revised. Actually, the components of each phase should be selected in a way that could be linked to a coherent output. Such output must aim at meaningfully stepping into a smooth

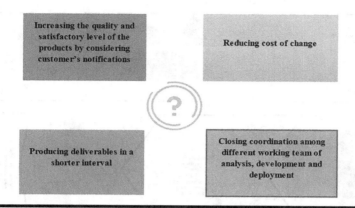

Figure 4.5 **Necessitous facets for improving the MIDRP project methodology.**

integration of MIDHCO's affairs. All in all, the PMO of FANAP enumerated the underlying exigencies and problems related to the completion of the first phase. In this manner, the foremost interrupting dilemmas were labeled as facing a lengthy delay, causing MIDHCO's dissatisfaction with the initially developed product, disharmonized interactions among the involved parties, and escalated production costs. Therefore, the upgraded methodology must center on removing such dilemmas by responding to the highlighted necessitous areas of Fig. 4.5.

4.2.3 Designing the New Methodology

Thenceforth, the PMO was appointed to be in charge of approaching a much more efficient methodology to circumvent the malfunctions of the current scheme. As the basic step, this office has begun exploring whether the experiences of the best available practices could surmount the challenges of the MIDRP project or not. Accordingly, the software development methodologies of popular ERP vendors, such as SAP, Oracle, and IBM, have been studied and compared. It was discovered that in large-scale projects the mere exposition of a specific methodology like predictive or agile approaches would not effectively work. In contrast, a hybrid methodology has been suggested in which the specific steps would be planned via the predictive method while the other ones would be controlled through the agile way. In terms of the MIDHCO case, steps like deployment and a large chunk of system analysis could not be synched to the agile method while the development process nicely fits such a method. By combing through the recent models, e.g., LeSS, DAD, and SAFe, PMO has considered the Scrum framework for large-scale cases as the appropriate methodology for the agile part of the production. Thus, the new version of the MIDRP methodology works based on the hybrid method presented in Fig. 4.6.

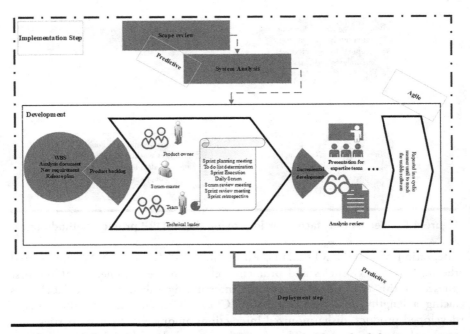

Figure 4.6 Schematic representation of the new hybrid methodology.

In this regard, the scope review and system analysis of the implementation step besides all activities of the deployment step are methodologically based on the predictive method. Meantime, the software development part of the methodology is in an agile format. Concerning the agile part and recalling from the literature review of Section 4.2, the input and output per sprint session of the standard LeSS are product backlog and increment, respectively. For the MIDRP case, the product backlog is extracted from a sequential chain of work breakdown structure (WBS), analysis documents, new issues, and a release plan. WBS is the detailed plan of the whole project being prepared based on the content of the contract and later updated with respect to the new methodology modifications. Now, the release plan is a subset of WBS activities that is going to be accomplished in the next three/six months determined by the product owners. The release plan is also affected by the result of system analysis besides the new issues that are derived from recent requests of the MIDHCO throughout the development period. At the end per sprint, the incremental product is presented to the MIDHCO's influencers, and based on their prospective comments the process analysis will be reviewed. Subsequent to sprint planning and in the middle of the sprint execution by different product group teams and under the monitoring of Scrum master, the retrospective, sprint, and daily Scrum meetings are conducted. Notably, the product owner and technical leader are the main leaders per product group.

Following, the main specifications of the proposed hybrid methodologies are briefly discussed.

4.2.3.1 PDCA Improvement Cycle

The utilization of the Plan–Do–Check–Action (PDCA) cycle has been taken into account for propelling the continuous improvement of the new agenda and procedures associated with the modified methodology. Borrowing from quality control knowledge, PDCA iteratively involves planning, doing, checking, and acting in order to consolidate a standard and effective way of conducting a specific procedure (Patel et al., 2015). In terms of modifying the initial methodology, it would be essential to establish the required objectives and processes within the planning module of the PDCA cycle. Then, it comes to putting the provided plan into practice within a short interval, probably each sprint related to the scrum approach. Data and outcomes resulting from the DO module of PDCA are evaluated and compared with the expected output. In such a comparison, it is also testified that how much the prospective changes in the plan module have contributed to the increment in the quality of the outcomes. By investigating the records from Do and Check modules of PDCA, the action is to improve the instructions, standards, and goals by removing non-conformities as much as possible. Now, the plan module of the next cycle has a further qualified and realistic baseline to proceed.

4.2.3.2 Adapted Organizational Hierarchy in a Team-Oriented Manner

Organizational hierarchy has been supposed to be settled with all details pertaining to the implementation of the agile methodology. The details can be classified in terms of aligning the top-level managers, constructing the necessitous working teams, and applying modifications in the Organigram. Primarily, top-level managers should be informed about its structural functionality and outstanding advantages. In the midst of inducing such a methodology, the most challenging facet has been associated with accustoming the managers to their new managerial roles. In detail, under the scrum charter, the cross-functional teams are working horizontally to achieve a common goal breeding an environment for better collaborations. Further, the teams are needed to have specific authorization rights in prioritizing the sequence of accomplishing the pre-defined tasks as well as adopting the appropriate development method. Indeed, while maintaining the prestigious position of the managers, the scope of their authorities and responsibilities should be clearly defined with regard to the scrum basis. The backbone of the organizational changes is updated using the DAD model.

This model fulfills the inherent practical gaps of the scrum approach and enables the formation of the team-oriented structure and re-designing of the Organigram. In the updated structure, the top-level managers are clustered together in the leadership team undertaking the responsibility of constructing cross-functional teams and monitoring the performance of the members. Especially, they concern about checking and tracing the related issues subjected to the integration among different product groups of the MIDRP. In such a large-scale project, all details associated with the integration should be bordered, clarified, and assessed. Subsequently, the most significant mission of leadership is to interactively follow up on these cases.

The modified structure has rearranged the entity of the single skilled-based analysis, development, and test groups by dividing their experts into the cross-functional teams corresponding with each product group. The experts' selection per the product scrum-based team, known as DAD sub-team in the literature, is made under the supervision of the top-level managers. Instead of being professional-oriented, the teams are now production-oriented possessing a portfolio of system analysts, developers, and testers being appointed by the managers. Empowering this new experience demands the usage of teamwork maneuvers as well as professional educational workshops.

As the pilot case toward team-making, FANAP began with the participants of two product groups, namely MTC and SCM. After a short while and by gradually getting positive pulses from their performance, in the early months of 2017, all other teams were compromised according to the agile manifesto.

4.2.3.3 Cultural and Educational Promotion

Actually, promoting consistency toward the concept of the agile culture is another critical aspect needing to be localized in the project's participants and stakeholders by the PMO of FANAP. To do so, incentive measures, e.g., designing the incentive cartoons for the participants' preparing to move from traditional approaches to the agile ones, have been devised. Further, in order to make the involved individuals familiar with the functionality of the LeSS, they have received pedagogical notifications on its basic concepts, artifacts, and events. These simple yet efficient measures could significantly work in MIDRP, as stated by the head of the PMO.

> "At the beginning, forcing the developers to take part in the simple standup meeting was a real headache. However, after settling the cultural and educational promotion, the developers argued against canceling a specific daily meeting with the Scrum-master."
>
> –PMO

Apart from the skill-based factors, the characteristic types of individuals play a critical role in increasing the efficiency and effectiveness of the constructed teams in the scrum approach. Using professional team-making models, delicate psychological terms were considered to yield self-organizing and cross-functional teams and enhance the spirit of intensive cooperation. For selecting individuals in each team, their ways of acting, thinking, sensing, working under pressure, and communicating with others, coupled with their strengths and weaknesses were taken into account. Furthermore, several educational workshops were held to promote teamwork, time management and problem-solving, stress management, anger control, and efficient communication. To accentuate the value of team working, the bonus distribution among individuals was synchronized to the performance of each team. It is also a standard practice to share any sort of applied modifications to the project's employer and consultant, respectively. PMO of FANAP has been responsible for lining both employer and consultant up with the new methodology by introducing its special mechanism and unique advantages. All elements of the MIDRP are supposed to be elaborated on the functionality and features of the underlying methodology. In particular, the project's stakeholders are justified within the steering committee.

4.2.3.4 Expertise Team Constitution

In spite of sticking to the scrum approach and enhancing the project's procedures based on its rules, there are still disrupting factors requiring to be surmounted. Clearly, the new methodology should also entail finding a specific measure to circumvent the underlying inefficiency of the IG team as well as the lack of coordination among the project's participants. To cope with it, PMO of FANAP has created a number of professional teams corresponding with each product group being entitled expertise team. Depending on the impression of the steering committee, it is possible to assign multiple expert teams to a specific product group. Each expertise team includes two, one, one, and two/three number of influencers of FANAP, POSCO, MIDHCO ICT, and MIDHCO, respectively, alongside one business expert. The expert team is a substitution for IG one. In the new methodology, the responsibilities of the IG team are delegated to two or three expert members of MIDHCO that are interactively engaged throughout the project in the agile manner.

4.2.3.5 Revising Project Phases and Scheduling

By revising the main segment of the project, the new methodology has come across three updated phases of MIDRP version 1.0, MIDRP version 2.0, and MIDRP version 3.0. MIDRP 1.0 looks for developing and deploying any sort of business processes and features that fulfill the basic requirements of MIDHCO leading to putting aside the old isolated software. MIDRP 2.0 includes complementary business processes for stabilizing the MIDRP component as a total integrated mining solution in the business units of MIDHCO. MIDRP 3.0 is a smart companion to the MIDRP product intending on providing intelligent solutions in different working scopes of MIDHCO. The underlying business process of MIDRP 3.0 substitutes the current experience-oriented decision-making with the optimal one through resorting to artificial intelligence. Under the hybrid methodology coupled with new phasing segmentation, the project schedule is subjected to change. In comparison with both

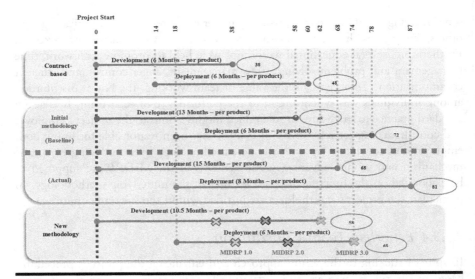

Figure 4.7 Changes in project scheduling (numbers are in terms of months).

baseline and initial actual scheduling of the previous methodology, Fig. 4.7 shows how the corresponding new combination leads to a closer completion gap to the contract-based setting. It will be finished 4 and 13 months sooner than the baseline and actual plans of the previous methodology, respectively. Fig. 4.8, specifically, concentrates on the completion time, number of involved business processes, and estimated weight factor in terms of each new phase of the hybrid approach. For an in-depth assessment and as a prime instance, it is prudent to consider the detailed scheduling of the lengthiest activity, namely software development, and testing.

As discussed earlier, the main reason forcing FANAP to employ the necessary changes in the initial project methodology was the considerable delay in accomplishing the first phase of the project. Now, it should be reviewed how the new methodology has improved the previous scheduling which is schematically represented by Fig. 4.9. In the re-scheduled plan, the scope assessment still takes one month while the analysis and IG adjustment steps are merged into a single activity demanding three months to be completed. The software development, which is coupled with the consultant and employer tests, can be accomplished within five months, whereas a new activity, called integration test, is expected to be done in half a month. Therefore, the total length of the production process is presently equal to 10.5 months being 2.5 months less than the initial methodology.

Additionally, the software development and testing demand cyclic feedback from the consultant and employer to hedge against failures of the previous methodology. Thus, there is a real necessity to consider a systematic procedure for the close and active engagement of the expertise teams as well as the scrum-based teams in the new methodology. In this regard, the completion period of the software development and

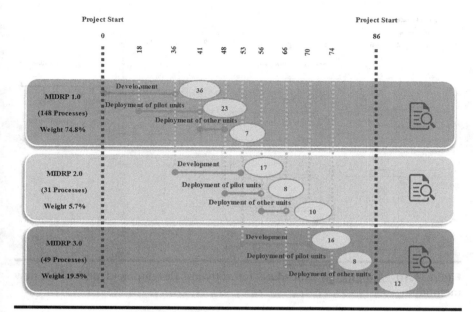

Figure 4.8 **Project scheduling under reorganized phases (numbers are in terms of months).**

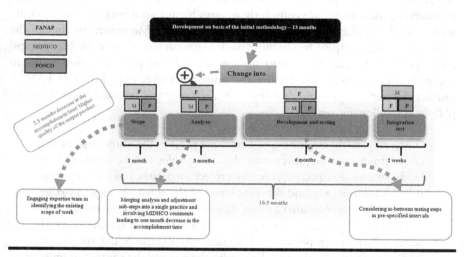

Figure 4.9 **Implementation scheduling under the new methodology.**

testing is approximately decoupled into 12 consecutive intervals each of which includes two weeks. According to the illustration of Fig. 4.10, the corresponding third, sixth, and ninth intervals are devoted to a demo presentation of the product groups, quality assessment of the software, and process analysis arguments. By convening such sessions, three teams of the product groups are evaluated by the expertise team per day.

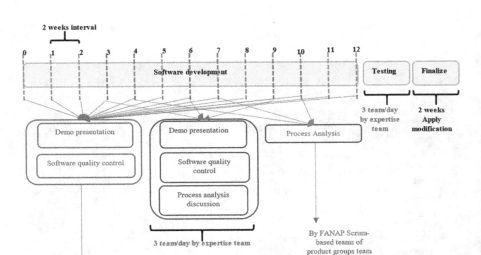

Figure 4.10 Monitoring procedure for software development under the new methodology.

In the fourth, seventh, and tenth intervals, the process analyses are subjected to be reviewed by the constructed Scrum-based teams of the product groups. Within all intervals, these teams are constantly responsible for arranging the coordinating sessions of demo planning and software quality control. Moreover, the time of the expertise team is occupied by checking the integration test of three product groups' teams per day. It takes two weeks for the scrum-based product group teams to apply the modifications and finalize the implementation step. PMO of FANAP justifies the reasoning behind devising such a rigorous and interactive development plan in the following sense.

> "Generally, at the beginning of a software project, the knowledge of the contractor versus employer over the deliverables can be attributed to levels 10 and 1, respectively. As the project progresses and the employer receives information, and different views of the software, its knowledge would be at least escalated to level 9. In this way, the requirements start changing and getting more mature. The catastrophic situation would occur when the employer level significantly overtakes the contractor leading to the project failure. To survive the project, the contractor must align with the customer's requirements in a step-by-step manner and cannot simply stick to its initial requests when signing the contract. Such step-by-step manner intensifies the usage of methodologies with dynamic scope known as the agile category."

–PMO

4.2.3.6 Managing Cost, Risk, and Change

In the new methodology, specific measures have been considered to cope with the cost, risk, and change terms associated with MIDRP. Precisely, although the agile part of the proposed hybrid methodology deals with a dynamic scope and customers usually like such a flexible approach, the cost management terms are prone to variations. Any significant sort of deviation between baseline costs and actual ones may be accompanied by customers' dissatisfaction. Under this circumstance, an adaptive framework methodology seems to be a crucial remedy when the project scope and cost are set to be variable and constant, respectively. In the newly employed methodology for MIDRP, it has been tried to lessen the dependency of the cost terms on the project scope. In this way, a fixed amount of cost is set and then the requirements would be completed by providing the potentially shippable product increment that fits the budget.

Moreover, another important driver toward framing a specific methodology for a project is dependent on the available constraints stemming from the appetite for change and risk. It would be very crucial to deem the appropriate way of enacting processes in order to minimize the underlying risks and propel the teams' fitness in dealing with a particular methodology. In fact, capturing the involved risks should be the prime concern of the decision-makers when designing/selecting a methodology for running the project. The potential risk in the initial methodology of MIDRP was to complete the development process and try for satisfying MIDHCO's requirements without considering the details in practice. In this regard, the new methodology is designed in a manner to mitigate such risk by leaving nothing to chance. Clearing responsibilities and roles besides forming effective committees have been helpful risk-averse maneuvers being laid in the proposed hybrid methodology.

Furthermore, in the context of the new methodology, dealing with the changes of the project has been structured in the context of the issue management framework. In that respect, any sort of malfunction in the software performance is first reported to the corresponding product owner by MIDHCO. The product owner justifies the issue and determines whether it can be considered an interrupting problem or not. In case of approval, the resolving plan of the issue is put into the ongoing sprint agenda regarding a threshold of ten issues per sprint. In the case of disapproval, the product owner argues to persuade the customer about the lack of the presence of any error or non-conformity associated with that issue. If there are, either dissonance between both parties about the issue or the issue is a time-consuming one, the matter will be discussed in the Change Control Board (CCB). The board is composed of the influencers of FANAP, MIDHCO, and POSCO, respectively. CCB, in fact, discusses the issue in detail and determines the way of handling it. A broad range of decisions may be set by CCB, e.g., neglecting the issue, holding it, postponing it to the next phases, and considering a high priority for resolving it.

4.2.3.7 Capturing the Consequences of the Deployment Step

For the sack of a flawless deployment, the new methodology prescribes the much more active contribution of the business analysts throughout the whole production process. Accordingly, their responsibilities are not limited to the implementation step and have to be extended when it comes to deploying the products at the business units. Now, business analysts become conscious of the prevailing deployment problems stemming from deficiencies at the early stages of the product analysis. Taking such a lesson learned into account, they do attempt to hedge against the occurrence of similar problems in the next series of deliverables that are going to be developed. Moreover, the presence of business analysts could enhance the information and skills of the deployment team over the correct functionality of the corresponding product leading to a smoother deployment. Another new maneuver at the deployment step concerns constituting a technical support team at the customer sites. This team is to resolve specific sorts of issues that do not need to go through the development process. Such issues include simple debugging, report making, navigating, and stuff like that. In doing so, the technical support team responds to the issues in a more agile manner and hedges against intervening in the development team by such minor errors.

4.2.4 A Process-Based Perspective Over the MIDRP Methodology

Here, a process-based perspective over the different steps of the MIDRP methodology is presented. In fact, the activities and necessary actions associated with the accomplishment per step of MIDRP are discussed in detail. In the rest of this section, the implementation step is first introduced and then the deployment step is explained.

4.2.4.1 Implementation Step

The implementation step endeavors to operate the following nine processes in a sequential manner as depicted by Fig. 4.11. These items embrace defining scope, analyzing the system, preparing the instructions and processes, designing the software, testing and developing the software, performing integration tests, carrying out pre-deployment, and providing the pedagogical content.

4.2.4.1.1 Scope Definition

As discussed earlier, the aforementioned consultant (i.e., TEC Company) has specified the required features of the MIDRP which have been enclosed in the existing contract between MIDHCO and FANAP. Now in this process, the implementation team of FANAP explores the scope of that product group according

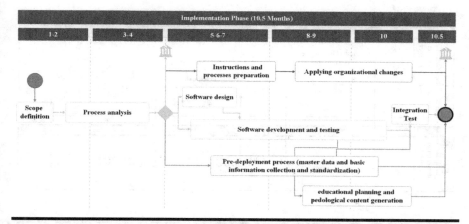

Figure 4.11   Detailed process-based perspective of the implementation phase.

to the TEC standard. Concurrently, the project manager of POSCO delegates the product responsible while its business expert provides the Process Hierarchical Diagram (PHD) and the structure and communication framework of the third process level. FANAP assesses the PHD and conducts planning to prioritize the detail of the fourth level. In response, the business expert of POSCO prepares the big picture and the detailed draft of the fourth level of the process model. The aggregated documents are sent to the expertise team to perform the As-Is analysis. The As-Is analysis is, in fact, an evaluation framework to demonstrate the current functionality and workflow of a business process (Bouafia & Molnár, 2019; Lamine et al., 2020). In the MIDRP project methodology, such analysis is finalized whenever the expertise team unanimously confirmed it. By doing so, the scope per product group is realized and documented. The implementation team also updates MIDRP Big Picture of levels 0 and 1. Actually, MIDRP Big Picture clarifies the integration, scope and complexity of such a tailor-made ERP product. For an in-depth and crystal-clear understanding of the level of integration, the Big Picture is depicted in four layers, including the Satellite (level 0), Bird (level 1), Magnify (level 2), and Human (level 3) views. Further, the business expert of POSCO finalizes the fourth level of the process model. Fig. 4.12 compares the initial and new methodologies in terms of the process of the scope definition. It can be observed that in the initial methodology the As-Is analysis was exclusively done under the supervision of FANAP causing serious problems as described earlier.

4.2.4.1.2   Analysis

The business expert of POSCO provides benchmarking proposals and process models of best practices ranging from level 1 through 4 being accompanied by charts and accustomed to MIDHCO's procedures. To proceed further, the

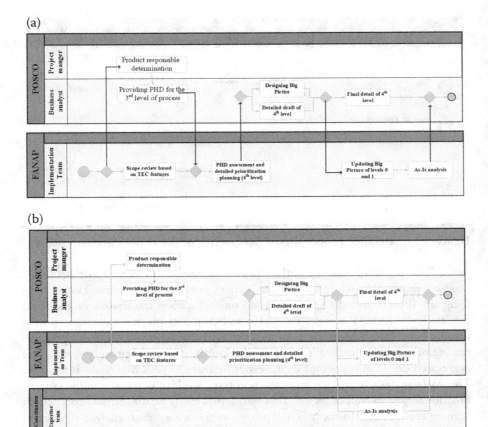

Figure 4.12 Comparing scope review process between (a) initial and (b) new methodologies.

initial draft of the To-Be business process model and related charts are prepared by the FANAP implementation team. Now, it is the expertise team's turn. The members are supposed to finalize the To-Be business process which highlights the ideal workflow related to the associated product group. Additionally, the expertise team determines the MIDRP Big Picture at levels 2 and 3. These schematic illustrations border the interconnection among different functional units provide and a perfect framework for the FANAP implementation team. Accordingly, this team could create the systematic To-Be functional model coupled with underlying roles, data, and processes.

Then, the expertise team is responsible for evaluating the systematic process model by focusing on the provided charts and official forms. Besides that, in terms of each datum and role, the team casts doubt on its necessity to be considered in the corresponding process. In a recursive manner, the FANAP implementation

(a)

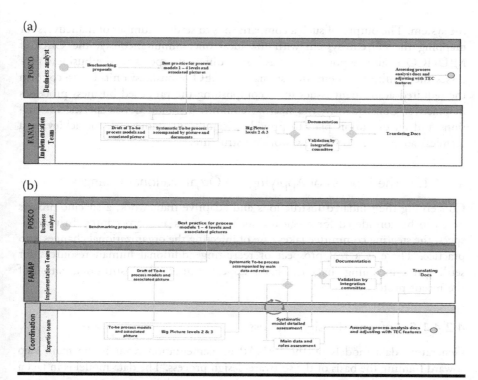

(b)

Figure 4.13 Comparing analysis process between (a) initial and (b) new methodologies.

team is also engaged to resolve the problems until satisfying the expertise team's notifications. The output documents of the systematic To-Be model is recorded based on the quality control procedure by FANAP. By receiving validation from the integration committee of the system analysis, those documents are translated. Eventually, the expertise team assesses the adaptation of each business process with the given TEC features and grants the final approval in case of non-conformities. Concerning the analysis process, Fig. 4.13 combs through the statuses of the initial versus new methodologies. Simply, in the initial methodology, FANAP directly derives all the necessary specifications except studying the benchmarks and best practices while completely ignoring the MIDHCO's comments bringing about noticeable ramifications.

4.2.4.1.3 Instructions and Processes Preparation

The implementation team of FANAP compares the existing state with the ideal one in order to explore the key requirements to conquer the future functionality of the system. The output of such a comparison is to settle a number of maneuvers for mapping the current system with the ideal one. Simultaneously, the CEO of MIDHCO is also responsible for assessing different aspects of the business processes and confirming them. In response, the CEO of business units has to confirm the required adjustment issues for accomplishing the proposed business processes in practice. Consequently, the steering committee should devise specific instructions and an execution plan to provide a significant framework for achieving a seamless adaptation to the new working structure.

4.2.4.1.4 The Process of Applying the Organizational Changes

Concerning the validated instructions and adaptive framework, a specific process needs to be considered for executing such new rules and procedures. In that respect, the steering committee takes care of injecting the organizational changes into practice. There is a real prospect of recruiting additional human resources for settling the upcoming challenges being appeared under the institutionalization of the recent protocols.

4.2.4.1.5 Software Design Process

Generating data models by the FANAP implementation team is the main step toward framing the basis of the software design process. The data model is in fact a specific tool to demonstrate the relationship among different entities of a system through the digestible structure of the software engineers. Then, the quality control documentation of the software design is stored. These documents are also translated into a general form that is digestible for all targeted audience and not only the computer programmers. The translated docs are sent to the information and communication technology (ICT) sector of MIDHCO Company. This sector is in charge of assessing and arguably confirming the documents of the software design process.

4.2.4.1.6 Software Development and Test Process

Presumably, the FANAP implementation team is at the core of deploying the software. Intermittently, the quality of the software and its fitness of functionalities with the pre-specified requirements are assessed by the steering committee. The interval checking period of testing the performance of the software is determined on the basis of the corresponding sprints of the project management plan as well as coordinated meetings. In terms of non-conformities between the test-based performance and the customers' expectations, the necessary feedback is sent to developers for removing the drawbacks. Considering this cyclic cooperation, the FANAP implementation team firms up the software development and test process.

4.2.4.1.7 Pre-Deployment Process

The initialization stage of the pre-deployment process is associated with the identification of the master data and its configuration. The data collection pattern should also be prepared in advance. The initialization stage, in fact, steps into the database design procedure. The FANAP implementation team sends the appropriate data collection pattern to the ICT sector of the MIDHCO Company. As MIDHCO ICT receives the pattern, it would be distributed among the corresponding data collectors. Meanwhile, the steering committee takes over the data standardization for the product configuration. In response, the standardization committee is to provide a systematic structure to consider the devices. Additionally, the committee standardizes all available commodities and services as another grounding step for leading to a flawless deployment phase. The next activity of the committee is to detail the document associated with the standardization framework.

The standardized package is sent to the information technology manager of the company for constituting the data collection team and assigning specific expert employees. The manager schedules the timetable for the purpose of data collection. Afterward, the team begins with gathering the master data across the holding level while the basic information is exclusively brought together in terms of each business unit. On the one hand, the output of the master data is directed toward the standardization committee aiming at integration and confirmation. On the other hand, the committee releases the history of the collected data to the IT manager regularly. However, the IT manager periodically (e.g., every two weeks) reports the status of the data collection to the MIDHCO ICT. Further, the manager disseminates the completed data file to the FANAP implementation team base on the output of the received basic information. Such a file provides the skeleton for the data migration. Under the migration procedure, the generation of the new information is accomplished through the basic and master data and the designed entries' forms.

4.2.4.1.8 Process of Educational Planning and Pedagogical Content Generation

The FANAP implementation team determines the execution requirements of the pedagogical program. Next, the educational content and user guidelines are provided further. By observing the educational requirements, the head of the human resource of the MIDHCO introduces the users of the new system. Taking the users into account, the educational plan is made available by the FANAP implementation team. The educational committee in MIDHCO is supposed to confirm the plan along with the associated content being supplied by the FANAP implementation team. The educational plan coupled with the appropriate content is sent to the human resource of the MIDHCO Company for the executive coordination of the program.

4.2.4.1.9 Integration Test Process

Arguably, there are different possible approaches to be defined in order to carry out the integration test. Considering the prospective scenarios, selecting the appropriate one is the first step to initiate the integration test. This scenario is transmitted to the steering committee to test the software. Then, it passes into MIDHCO for testifying different features in practice. The necessary changes are announced to the steering committee indicating that some of the business processes are not fully realized yet. Accordingly, FANAP adopts the required modifications and cyclically, such a procedure would be repeated until satisfying all MIDCHO's needs.

4.2.4.2 Deployment Step

According to Fig. 4.14, the deployment phase of the proposed methodology is composed of 11 processes being coupled with the software development cycle and pedagogical maneuvers. This phase encompasses mapping the data, initial adjustment, data migration, fulfilling the customer's requirements, dual adjustment, education, customization, non-functional test, installation, and initialization test, installation, and initial running of the system. In the next paragraphs, these processes are described.

4.2.4.2.1 The Process of Data Identification, Collection, and Mapping Data

The FANAP deployment team takes action to identify the reports and printable forms owing to their importance in leveraging the new system across the MIDHCO's business units. Next, the hardware requirements of the users are assessed and specified to be listed and sent to the customer aiming at upgrading the devices. The

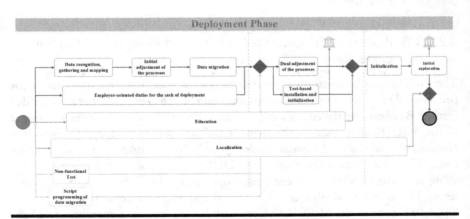

Figure 4.14 Deployment framework of the proposed project methodology.

pre-requisites of the hardware-based relationship among different processes of the new system should also be explored. The existing software located in business units is double-checked for storing useful data. Furthermore, FANAP deployment team is in charge of updating the master data and basic information to facilitate configuring the system specification in practice.

4.2.4.2.2 Initial Adjustment of the Processes

The proposed confirmed business processes have to be streamlined to maximize the possibility of flawless software deployment. To do so, the non-systematic and manual tasks are detected in advance due to hedge against the asynchronous performance of the software during this phase. By identifying the non-official organizational units (OU) on the basis of each product skeleton, the specified roles in the underlying processes are mapped into the organizational structure. Considering the aggregated results of the manual tasks and roles' adaptation, alternative ways of accomplishing the upcoming parts are prepared. Meanwhile, to configure the system specifications, a number of sites and workstations are required for recording the necessary data as well as carrying out a process in a standardized way. Thus, another concern is related to determining the layout of the workstation within the business units. Subsequent to taking the aforementioned steps into account, the customized principle per process is documented in terms of each business unit. Moreover, recognizing the users, assigning the roles, and regulating the level of access are prescribed here. Finally, an identification document is provided to demonstrate the history of the initial adjustment process.

4.2.4.2.3 Data Migration Process

The FANAP deployment team and project management of the consultant company besides the deployment committee of MIDHCO are interactively involved in the data migration process. The FANAP deployment team receives the updated master data and basic information as the cornerstone material of this process. Prior to the data entry, there is monitoring over the available information being supposed to be recorded. The latest version of the master data and basic information is now entered into the new system. FANAP team issues a detailed report on the status of the master and basic data entry and gives it to the consultant project manager. The consultant assesses the report and forwards it to the MIDHCO in case of validating the result. When the deployment committee assures the accuracy of the data entry, this process would be finalized and confirmed.

4.2.4.2.4 Hardware Requirement Satisfaction Process by the Customer

The critical practitioner of the hardware requirement satisfaction process is MIDHCO ICT. In fact, FANAP notifies the hardware-based pre-requisites of setting up the system in the business units and announces to the MIDHCO. MIDHCO ICT updates the instructions as a grounding step to organize the upgrading plans. The procurement of the essential hardware associated with each process is another action that should be provided as the foundation for running the enterprise solution. Further, the existing computers of users in the business units may be subjected to a hardware-based promotion according to the FANAP deployment team's notifications. In terms of the educational plan, some specific locations, as well as corresponding facilities, have to be considered in each business unit to propel the training of the employees. However, the FANAP deployment team demands a particular working space that should be accurately satisfied by MIDHCO. Furthermore, MIDHCO must supply the master data and basic information to the FANAP team to easily get involved with the migration procedure.

4.2.4.2.5 Non-Functional Test Process

The business expert of the consultant designs the integration test scenario. Both performance and security aspects of the test are also bordered by the consultant. Based on the recommended scenario, the FANAP deployment team undertakes the integration test by measuring those aspects, rigorously. The consultant monitors how FANAP has operated its proposed protocol over the non-functional test. The CCB of MIDHCO assesses the issues and asks for necessitous changes. FANAP team resolves drawbacks, and the process is completed until the satisfaction of MIDHCO's overall requirements.

4.2.4.2.6 Dual-Adjustment Process

Regarding each business unit, the underlying procedure of the confirmations is customized while the modifications associated with each business process are taken into account. Additionally, the FANAP deployment team ties up the reports and printable forms that are used at the operation level. By aggregating these items, the final adjustment report could be published. Then, the project managers of the consultant and deployment committee of MIDHCO go through the detail of that report for evaluating and confirming it, respectively.

4.2.4.2.7 Installation, Initialization, and Test Processes

At this stage, three main activities are simultaneously triggered by FANAP and MIDHCO. On the one hand, MIDHCO ICT installs the hardware equipment associated with the new system besides initializing the computers of users. Complementary, FANAP deployment team installs and initializes the server. The next task is to set up the software and authorizes its accessibility to the users. Then, it comes to the test phase of the software under the supervision of the FANAP team.

4.2.4.2.8 Pedagogical Process

The pedagogical terminology must be unified by the FANAP deployment team. The terminology should detail the curricula of such a plan during both elementary and advanced courses. Initially, the users are taught in the context of the elementary course by mentioning the basic concepts. Next, general and professional classes in relation to the business processes are provided for the targeted audiences. Afterward, the use and functionality of the system's framework are addressed by the trainers of FANAP. Meantime, the associated managers of the MIDHCO are trained and separated from the rest of the employees. The educational committee of the MIDHCO evaluates the quality of the performed classes and marks the employees. Further, the users' skills are examined in practice. In case of encouraging performance, the corresponding certificate is issued, and the report of the assessment is forwarded to the steering committee of MIDHCO. Based on the results, the professional users are adopted and consequently, the human resource manager of MIDHCO updates the educational records of the employees.

4.2.4.2.9 Initialization Process

Different units and complexes of the MIDHCO should provide a basis for sharing new and modified data with the FANAP team. The latest status of the information based on the variations in data besides the prevailing information, being transmitted as the data related to the beginning of the deployment period, is delivered to FANAP team. FANAP validates the received information and updates data in terms of the present condition of any business unit/complex. Data on the system's configuration is further migrated and sent to the business units/complexes for assessment and confirmation. By publishing the related version and concerning updated data, the preparation for running the system is announced.

4.2.4.2.10 Localization

When the MIDHCO's employees have become accustomed to working with the MIDRP system, the sole intention of the localization process will be realized. Thus, the localization demands long-term planning and is almost lengthened from the beginning to the end of the deployment process.

4.2.4.2.11 Initial Exploration Process

By installing hardware devices and preparing the users' computers, the exploration of MIDRP parallel with the existing software is instigated over MIDHCO's business units and complexes. Thenceforth, CCB assesses the cases and calls for applying the modifications via FANAP deployment team. FANAP issues with the required version on the test server and reports the release note. CCB examines the new version and puts it into action if it satisfies the prescribed criteria. As a result of such interaction, the validated version is located on the main server and the exploration is met.

4.3 Project Collaboration

To efficiently handle the proposed project management methodology, special maneuvers are required to enhance the collaboration within MIDRP. Generally, collaboration implies the process of two or more individuals or organizations working together to accomplish a mission or to achieve a goal. Project collaboration is a way for managers and team leaders to coordinate, control, and monitor the project in which they are involved. Today, with the expansion of communication systems and the development of the teamwork concept, collaboration has become an integral part of organizations. Project collaboration tools are pieces of software that help project managers and teams simplify their tasks and achieve better results. These tools offer a wide range of functions to assist with core tasks such as knowledge management (KM) and task management. These methods and tools strengthen communication, idea sharing, and transparency for different work teams.

To understand project collaboration, since it is a new topic in project management, we must first examine the project management style in the organization. Traditional project management is the process that aids each person involved in the project to plan, monitor, and report different tasks over a specified period of time. This planning involves scheduling tasks to achieve a specific result, all of which are led by a project manager. This traditional top-down process, then, can prevent collaboration and the sharing of ideas, and destroy communication. In fact, this method does not encourage collaboration and there is no opportunity for people to expand their knowledge. But in new approaches, a separate tool is provided to individuals to present their most significant asset, the knowledge gained from the project to the system. In the following, opportunities for cooperation and participation of individuals in the MIDRP project will be mentioned.

4.3.1 Knowledge Management System (KMS)

Acquired project knowledge and experience is beneficial in terms of both time and cost. The logging and use of this acquired information and lessons learned will move the projects of the company forward and avoid the recurrence of unpleasant experiences in projects. KM and project experience documentation is a vital approach in organizations in start-ups or those who have running unique projects. Project managers and experts are producing managerial and technical expertise every day, the results of which can be transferred to other colleagues as lessons learned resulting from project successes and failures. Organizational knowledge was traditionally spread through the guidance and conversation with experienced people with new employees and did not have a specific structure. But this approach faces the challenge of forgetting and not fully transmitting project knowledge.

Knowledge management (KM) is the systematic process of creating, maintaining, and cultivating the talents of a company through the effective use of expertise to achieve sustainable competitive advantages and high efficiency (Alavi & Leidner, 2001). Other benefits of KM include significant improvement in personnel performance and increased competitiveness. KM is inherently interdisciplinary and is derived from the integration of topics such as strategic management, organizational theory, and information systems management. Therefore, KM is an emphasis on an integrated and formal approach to the management of intangible organizational information assets, the main components of which are organizational mechanisms, information technology, and software (Dalkir, 2017).

KM software has grown tremendously in recent years. Today, choosing the right KM software for small- and medium-sized organizations has become a serious challenge due to the increasing growth of various software products, the difficulty of differentiating product types, rapid changes in technology, and economic conditions. In recent years, there has been significant growth in access to KM software. Market research predicts sales of about $5.4 billion in 2023 for KM software worldwide (Market Research Future, 2020).

There is a wide range of KM technologies and software, such as content management, document management, enterprise interactive, intelligent tools, databases and knowledge repositories, knowledge directory and classification of knowledge types, portals, expert search systems, and data mining. It is considered that companies use a systematic process to select their software. This is important because of the large and varied number of software applications and the urgent need to integrate them with existing systems. One of the most popular tools for managing organizational knowledge is SharePoint, which is also used in the MIDRP project.

4.3.2 SharePoint-Based KMS

SharePoint is a Microsoft product that uses .NET framework technology and SQL Server database. It has been used since 2007 to control and record documents. Due to changes in management standards in 2015, the ISO 9001: 2015 standard focuses on documented information and organizational knowledge. Hence, the use of SharePoint in management systems can play a very critical role in establishing documented information and organizational knowledge.

The SharePoint-based KM system allows people in the organization to interact with each other, stay in touch, and be constantly updated with information related to their field of work. But there are some challenges, including finding and communicating with experts, the lack of highly uncategorized information, security issues in sharing information, as well as different insights into information. To address these challenges, you need a way to manage expertise and make it easier to access. It is essential to have a secure and definable resource, as well as a system that facilitates referral and retrieval and ultimately enables interaction between defined groups and individuals. In addition, the system should be able to provide access to classified information for defined groups. Therefore, such a system has been developed in the FANAP Company for KM of the MIDRP project.

The most common use of SharePoint in management systems is in document management and KM. Some of the features of this system are as given below.

4.3.2.1 Documented Information Must be Approved Prior to Publication

The use of SharePoint in management systems leads to the creation of a document library and the process workflow for document approval. In some cases, customization is done to achieve document approval through the design of the workflow.

4.3.2.2 Documentary Information Must be Reviewed/Updated

SharePoint automatically provides information management policies such as the information flow of each document within the specified folder.

4.3.2.3 The Latest Version of the Document Will be Available to Users

SharePoint has a number of options here. The draft of the Document Library for document owners will be used before publication. The history of documents can be viewed and accessed in each edition. Basic or minor editing can be defined each time the document is created. Only authorized users will be able to access all edits, and other users can access the final version.

4.3.2.4 Identify the Status of the Latest Document Edition

The latest status of the document is available along with a history of document changes. Comparing documents and their history with the ability to compare the document with previous edits can be defined for the user. For example, the user can see what changes have been made to previous versions and the location of the changes and the modified words are clear.

4.3.2.5 Prevent Unwanted Use of Obsolete Documents

Many of the features of SharePoint mentioned above can be used for this purpose. Only defined users have access to the latest version of documents. SharePoint Information Management Policies help archive and destroy documents in accordance with specified rules.

4.3.2.6 Preservation and Usability of Documents

Documents remain legible and easily identifiable.

4.3.2.7 Development of Organizational Knowledge

This is addressed in the ISO 9001: 2015 standard and using SharePoint and providing intra-unit and organizational portals can greatly help develop organizational knowledge.

The most important features of SharePoint-based KMS in the MIDRP project include the following:

- Edit office files and integrate easily with other Microsoft products such as Outlook.
- Ability to compare files with previous versions.
- Versioning feature, major version number, and minor version number can be defined for created or updated documents.
- Create a workflow, for example, for folders, you can specify the creator and the approver.
- Advanced search with the ability to search the contents of the file.
- Notification: By sending an SMS or email to specific users.
- The ability to control records can be determined by the life cycle of the time it takes to transfer records to archives.
- Creating a wiki will help develop organizational knowledge.
- Advanced reporting with a variety of charts and tables.

4.3.3 Lessons Learned Collection System

"NOT Again!!" Or *"We made the same mistake again."* We sometimes use these phrases in our lives and work. These are signs that we have not learned from our past experiences. *"Failure is simply the opportunity to begin again, this time more intelligently,"* Henry Ford says (Mueller & Shepherd, 2012). But, how? The answer is the documentation and dissemination of lessons learned. Many organizations either do not capture lessons learned or do not use it when they collect it. Lack of time, resources, management support, clear guidelines around collecting the information, the procedure to capture information, and the knowledge database to store and search information captured for the future are common reasons for this mistake.

Capturing lessons learned is an integral part of every project and serves several purposes. While the finalization of a formal lessons learned document is completed during the project closure process, capturing lessons learned should occur throughout the project lifecycle to ensure all information is documented accurately. The lessons learned document serves as a valuable tool to use by the project stakeholders, including the project manager as well as all experts involving product realization, supporting services, etc. This document should not only describe what went wrong during the project and suggestions to avoid similar occurrences in the future, but it should also describe what went well and how the project or other similar projects may benefit from this information. All logs resulting from this procedure should be communicated to the Project Management Office (PMO) for inclusion in the organizational assets and archives as part of the lessons learned database.

4.3.4 What is a Lesson Learned?

Lessons learned is a lesson that is derived from an event, incident, or product realization activity or implementation and evaluation of a system, process, or software that is used to identify strengths and weaknesses. A lesson learned may be derived from an internal or external source and is used to improve systems, processes, or software. An expert of lessons learned is a person in PMO in charge of monitoring (including gathering, logging, and sharing) lessons learned from all units. This expert is responsible to gather all lessons learned and enter the valuable ones in the log form so that a reliable database could be created for future use (Jugdev, 2012).

4.3.5 Procedure of Logging Lesson Learned in MIDRP Project

As shown in Fig. 4.15, the various stages of turning an idea into a suitable lesson learned in the project are as follows.

4.3.5.1 Adopt an Approach

First of all, a systematic approach shall be adopted for capturing lessons learned. Generally, the lessons-learned approach answers two questions:

- How the document should be created during the project lifecycle?
- How lessons should be categorized?

The lessons learned from the project should be used as references for future projects and should contain an adequate level of detail so that the current or other project personnel can use them and so that any other project managers may have

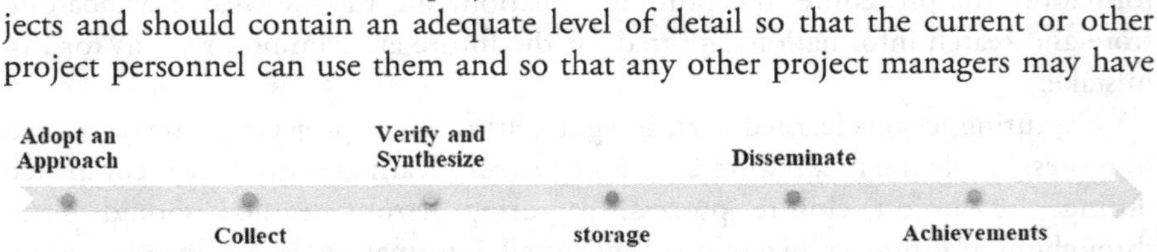

Figure 4.15 Procedure of logging lesson learned.

Table 4.2 A Sample Lessons Learned form in MIDRP Project

NO.	Title:	
Owner:	Date raised:	Status: Success ☐ Failure ☐
Category	Analysis ☐ Development ☐ Deployment ☐ Support ☐ Project management ☐	
Brief description	This summarizes the event or experience that took place in a part of the MIDRP project.	
Result	By observing this event and your reaction to it, what was the result of the event, and what is your analysis of the outcome? For example, compare the effects of the initial approach (in case of failure) and the improved approach (in case of success) according to criteria such as cost, time, and so on.	
Recommendation	In the end, what is your advice for continuing to work on that particular part? Do you have any suggestions for further improvement?	

enough information on which to help base their project plans. Thus, the lessons learned must be communicated consistently. In addition to the categorization and description of the lesson, it is important to state what the impact was and provide a recommendation for a project manager or others to consider for future projects (i.e., analysis and recommendation). Furthermore, it is important to include not only the failures or shortcomings but also the successes. In this regard, valuable information can be given to the people. The lessons learned are mainly categorized by the type of work and then their impacts can be examined based on the project knowledge areas (integration, procurement, risk, quality, time, cost, scope, human resource, communications, and stakeholders).

Table 4.2 illustrates a sample of lessons learned form. These lessons are categorized considering the project knowledge areas that are included in the impact column. Descriptions, analysis (impacts), and recommendations are provided for consideration on similar future projects.

4.3.5.2 Collect

The collection process involves the capture of information through structured and unstructured processes such as project critiques, written forms, personal experiences, and meetings or lesson learned briefings. The collection of lessons may come from as many sources as an organization is willing to solicit. Lessons learned can be based both upon positive experiences that achieve organizational goals and on negative experiences that result in undesirable outcomes. A collaborative lessons collection process can be as or more important as documenting the lessons.

The lessons learned document might also state which historical lessons learned were used on this project. This information not only shows the value of the documentation of such lessons but also shows which lessons are consistently applied by other similar projects.

Personnel who are going to complete the "Lesson Learned Register" form shall bear in mind the following questions:

- What went well?
- What didn't go well or had unintended consequences?
- If you had it all to do over again, what would you do differently?
- What recommendations would you make to others doing similar projects?
- Did the delivered product meet the specified requirements and goals of the project?
- Was the customer satisfied with the end product(s)? If not, why not?
- Was the schedule met? If not, why not?
- Were risks identified and mitigated? If not, why not?
- Did the project management methodology work? If not, why not?
- What could be done to improve the process?
- What bottlenecks or hurdles were experienced that impacted the project?
- What procedure should be implemented in future projects?
- What can be done in future projects to facilitate success?
- What changes would assist in speeding up future projects while increasing communication?

4.3.5.3 Verify and Synthesize

This process serves to verify the accuracy and applicability of lessons submitted. As lessons learned are collected and documented, the organization should approve and implement any process improvements identified. It is important to strive for continuous improvement and this portion of the lessons learned process is an integral step.

4.3.5.4 Store

The storage aspect of lessons learned usually involves incorporating lessons into an electronic database for future sharing and dissemination. Information should be stored in a manner that allows users to identify search lessons by keyword. The lessons learned from the project will be contained in the organizational lessons learned knowledge base maintained by the PMO. This information will be cataloged under the project's name (MIDRP) for future reference by a lesson-learned expert in the PMO. This information will be valuable for all project personnel and any project manager assigned to a new similar project in the future.

The lessons learned knowledge base (database) contains historical information from the current project or previous projects. It is part of the organizational project assets and provides a valuable source of information to be used by similar projects in the future. Most lessons learned knowledge database contains large amounts of information, so it is important that there is a system for cataloging this information.

4.3.5.5 Disseminate

The final element, and the most important, is the dissemination of lessons learned since lessons are of little benefit unless they are distributed and used by people who will benefit from them. Dissemination can include the revision of a work process, training, and routine distribution via a variety of communication media. Lessons can be "pushed," or automatically delivered to a user, or pulled into situations where a user must manually search for them. The lessons learned expert is responsible to determine the access level in SharePoint and or to distribute the documents among the relevant personnel or departments.

Desirable logging and then dissemination of the lessons learned records helps the project team share knowledge gained from experience so that the entire organization may benefit. A successful lesson learned program will help project teams to repeat desirable outcomes and avoid undesirable ones. The lessons-learned expert in PMO shall update the log form at the end of each month and share the log with the project personnel by SharePoint. Project personnel shall keep the lessons learned expert in PMO informed of any possible problems on the lessons learned procedure, process, records, etc.

4.3.5.6 Achievements

If followed well, this procedure provides the current and future project team with information that can increase effectiveness and efficiency and build on the experience that has been earned by each completed project phase. If documented and disseminated properly, lessons learned provide a powerful method of sharing ideas for improving work processes, operation, quality, safety, cost-effectiveness, etc., and help improve management decision-making and worker performance through every phase of a project. They also help validate some of the tougher times endured during the project life and help future project managers avoid similar difficulties.

4.3.6 Task Management

Given the importance of integration and timely exchange of requests by the employer, consultant, and contractor in order to achieve the goals of the project, it is essential to establish a framework to facilitate in-unit and out-of-unit communication. Sending requests, following up and managing personnel tasks, and evaluating and reporting on the activities performed on each unit are among the most important

Figure 4.16 A board view related to the FAMS system.

issues that are considered in any major project. At first, MIDRP project task management was available in the Project Knowledge Management System (SharePoint) which is introduced in the previous subsection. After a while with the development of a new system called FAMS, by FANAP experts, an independent system for task management was designed. A snapshot of the task board related to the FAMS system has been illustrated in Fig. 4.16. As discussed earlier, the sprint is short-term planning for accomplishing the ongoing tasks. These tasks are called user-story which entail features that are going to be attributed to the incremental product.

Planning and management of requests submitted from one unit to another, as well as personnel tasks of each unit, will be done from this portal. Through this online system, tasks can be assigned to certain persons, and the history of the implementation process of each request can be viewed, planned, and managed. There is also the ability to daily, weekly, and monthly activities report based on the content of the desired goal in task management. This system enables each organization involved in the project (employer, consultant, and contractor) to log, perform, and follow up on the requests of other organizations. Also, in this system, it is possible to categorize requests based on different topics and situations.

Other features of the task management system for managing activities related to the MIIDRP project are as follows (Fig. 4.17):

- Based on the agile approach of the project and the definition of sprint and user story.
- Defining the status of tasks as To DO, Doing, Done, Review.
- Sending notifications by email or SMS to assigned managers.
- Break tasks into smaller sections or subtasks.
- Assigning tasks to the desired people.
- User access control in defining, editing, and assigning tasks.
- Establish rules for performing each step of the tasks and checking the correctness of the tasks.

Figure 4.17 A story view related to the FAMS system.

- Prepare reports at each stage of the tasks.
- Create comments by users about each task and determine tips to improve the work and refer the user to it.
- Possibility to enter the expected date, start date, and end date.
- Defining the priority, complexity, and volume of tasks.
- Tagging tasks.
- Determining prerequisites for tasks.
- Check the activity history of users.
- Attaching files to activities.
- Logging time and description of daily tasks.

4.4 Conclusion

This chapter was designed to consider the maturing trend in MIDRP methodology as a worthy experience in a large-scale software-based project. By reviewing the content of this chapter, it could be grasped that switching from the traditional methodology to the hybrid one resulted in significant outcomes for the project's success. In advance of enumerating the main outcomes of such a shift, it would be prudent to respond to the arising questions in the mindset of curious readers. The questions are as follows: "why was the classical predictive methodology adopted initially despite successful experiences with the best practices on the hybrid approach?"; "why were the project deliverables segmented into six phases?"; and "why did a noticeable deviation between actual scheduling and contract-based one exist?" One of the key decision-makers in regulating the MIDRP contract responds to these questions as follows:

"Convincing the customer about the agile and dynamic nature of the development process with adaptive detail was almost impossible at the initialization and preparation steps of the project. When signing the contract, the customer is inclined to acquire a rigid set of detailed information on the necessary activities and corresponding fixed duration for accomplishing the project. At that time, the main concentration centered on the scope definition and system analysis that was inherently predictive-based activities. The skeleton of the necessary infrastructure and instructions was still under development. Consequently, in the beginning, considering something like the current incremental product development planning seemed an improper practice while the scope and analysis were not realized yet.

On the other hand, the customer expectation over such a large-sized lengthy project demanded segmenting its deliverables into a considerable number of phases, e.g., six phases. In fact, the customer mindset was not ready to digest receiving only three deliverables throughout the project, meaning that it approximately took 17 months to have the first package of the software. Similar to the commencement of any other ERP projects accompanied by the shortsighted expectation of customers, MIDHCO envisaged periodically receiving usable deliveries in the shortest possible interval, e.g., sooner than every one year. There existed the same reasoning for deeming an unrealistic interval pertaining to the product development of each phase, namely, 6 months. This time was the maximum possible duration that the customer could put up with it at the onset of the project. As the project progressed, the ongoing challenges instill the too optimistic characteristic of the initial scheduling in the customer leading to come up with re-planning in a more reasonable manner. All in all, the modifications in the basic setting of the MIDRP contract were a matter of enhancing the maturing level of both FANAP and MIDHCO during the project progress. In fact, the normal lifecycle of the project surged us to adopt the initial setting for the methodology and gradually evolve it. If the new resulted settings were considered at the project initiation, MIDRP would be either failed or never signed."

–PMO

Overall, the new hybrid methodology brought about a gradual improvement and expedition in the information flow of the documentation associated with project engineering. Doing so, the achievements of the project in different aspects are certainly under the umbrella of such a change being enumerated as follows. Presenting more and more deliverables to MIDHCO within considerably shorter intervals has been clearly an indispensable outcome of the upgraded methodology. The quality of the deliverables has been certainly escalated by the punctual receiving the customer's comments and applying the necessary revisions. Since MIDHCO perceived itself as the critical player in the development step and obtained whatever that have prudently recommended, its satisfactions with the final product and performance of FANAP were spiked. Another result of enhancing the project methodology could refer to the creation of coherent working teams consistent with professional and up-to-date team-making models being the main tool in advancing the agility objectives. However, regarding the main concern of the top-level managers, the most significant triumph of maturing the MIDRP methodology originated from reducing the development and deployment costs of producing the software. To wrap up the discussion, PMO influencers of FANAP have mentioned in the following comments on the key customer-oriented influential factors on the appropriate methodology formation and working mechanism.

"Generally, methodologies work well when the basic principles of the project management framework (time, cost, and scope) have been logically regulated. In the initiation step of MIDRP methodology, namely contract negotiation, MIDHCO avoided dealing with the financial and scheduling facets in a prevailing business-like manner. This allowed FANAP to adjust the roadmap and advance the project in a systematic and organized procedure. Further, the contribution of MIDHCO in operating the proposed methodology was outstanding when it came to satisfying the rising demands of FANAP at the meetings of expertise teams. Indeed, any sort of FANAP request was never either suspended by the MIDHCO's influencers of the expertise teams or delegated to the higher-level management. All the requirements were fulfilled at the earliest time without the necessity to be burdened by claim management or stuff like that."

–PMO

References

Alavi, M., & Leidner, D. E. (2001). Knowledge management and knowledge management systems: Conceptual foundations and research issues. *MIS Quarterly, 25*(1), 107–136.

Alqudah, M., & Razali, R. (2016). A review of scaling agile methods in large software development. *International Journal on Advanced Science, Engineering and Information Technology, 6*(6), 828–837.

Ambler, S. W., & Lines, M. (2012). *Disciplined agile delivery: A practitioner's guide to agile software delivery in the enterprise.* IBM Press.

Bianchi, M., Marzi, G., & Guerini, M. (2020). Agile, stage-gate and their combination: Exploring how they relate to performance in software development. *Journal of Business Research, 110,* 538–553.

Bouafia, K., & Molnár, B. (2019). Analysis approach for enterprise information systems architecture based on hypergraph to aligned business process requirements. *Procedia Computer Science, 164,* 19–24.

Brenner, R., & Wunder, S. (2015). Scaled agile framework: Presentation and real world example. *2015 IEEE Eighth International Conference on Software Testing, Verification and Validation Workshops (ICSTW)*, pp. 1–2.

Conboy, K., & Carroll, N. (2019). Implementing large-scale agile frameworks: Challenges and recommendations. *IEEE Software, 36*(2), 44–50.

Dalkir, K. (2017). *Knowledge management in theory and practice*. MIT Press.

Ebert, C., & Paasivaara, M. (2017). Scaling agile. *IEEE Software, 34*(6), 98–103.

Ellis, G. (2016). Agile project management: Scrum, eXtreme programming, and scrumban. In G. Ellis (Ed.), *Project management in product development* (pp. 223–260). Boston: Butterworth-Heinemann.

Islam, G., & Storer, T. (2020). A case study of agile software development for safety-critical systems projects. *Reliability Engineering & System Safety, 200*, 106954.

Jalali, S., & Wohlin, C. (2012). Global software engineering and agile practices: A systematic review. *Journal of Software: Evolution and Process, 24*(6), 643–659.

Jørgensen, M. (2018). Do agile methods work for large software projects? In J. Garbajosa, X. Wang, & A. Aguiar (Eds.), *Agile processes in software engineering and extreme programming* (pp. 179–190). Cham: Springer International Publishing.

Jugdev, K. (2012). Learning from lessons learned: Project management research program. *American Journal of Economics and Business Administration, 4*(1), 13.

Kalaimani, J. (2015). *SAP project management pitfalls: How to avoid the most common pitfalls of an SAP solution*. Apress.

Lagerberg, L., Skude, T., Emanuelsson, P., Sandahl, K., & Ståhl, D. (2013). The impact of agile principles and practices on large-scale software development projects: A multiple-case study of two projects at Ericsson. In *2013 ACM/IEEE International Symposium on Empirical Software Engineering and Measurement*, pp. 348–356.

Lamine, E., Thabet, R., Sienou, A., Bork, D., Fontanili, F., & Pingaud, H. (2020). BPRIM: An integrated framework for business process management and risk management. *Computers in Industry, 117*, 103199.

Larman, C., & Vodde, B. (2016). *Large-scale Scrum: More with LeSS*. Addison-Wesley.

Leau, Y. B., Loo, W. K., Tham, W. Y., & Tan, S. F. (2012). Software development life cycle agile vs traditional approaches. In *International Conference on Information and Network Technology*, Singapore.

Leffingwell, D. (2007). *Scaling software agility: Best practices for large enterprises (the agile software development series)*. Addison-Wesley Professional.

Market Research Future. (2020). Global knowledge management software market. Available at https://www.marketresearchfuture.com/reports/knowledge-management-software-market-4193

Mueller, B., & Shepherd, D. A. (2012). Learning from failure: How entrepreneurial failure aids in the development of opportunity recognition expertise. *Frontiers of Entrepreneurship Research, 32*(6), 6.

Paasivaara, M. (2017). Adopting SAFe to scale agile in a globally distributed organization. In *2017 IEEE 12th International Conference on Global Software Engineering (ICGSE)*, pp. 36–40.

Paasivaara, M., & Lassenius, C. (2016). Scaling scrum in a large globally distributed organization: A case study. In *2016 IEEE 11th International Conference on Global Software Engineering (ICGSE)*, pp. 74–83.

Patel, P. M., & Deshpande, V. A. (2015). Application of plan-do-check-act cycle for quality and productivity improvement: A review. *Studies, 2*(6), 23–34.

Saeeda, H., Khalid, H., Ahmed, M., Sameer, A., & Arif, F. (2015). Systematic literature review of agile scalability for large scale projects. *International Journal of Advanced Computer Science and Applications, 6*(9), 63–75.

Shameem, M., Kumar, C., Chandra, B., & Khan, A. A. (2017). Systematic review of success factors for scaling agile methods in global software development environment: A client-vendor perspective. In *2017 24th Asia-Pacific Software Engineering Conference Workshops (APSECW)*, pp. 17–24.

Uludağ, Ö., Kleehaus, M., Dreymann, N., Kabelin, C., & Matthes, F. (2019). Investigating the adoption and application of large-scale scrum at a German automobile manufacturer. In *2019 ACM/IEEE 14th International Conference on Global Software Engineering (ICGSE)*, pp. 22–29.

Chapter 5

Software Architecture

"To produce an ERP system, you must see the system architecture on the ERP scale from the beginning. An ERP cannot be achieved with the approach of producing simple single-purpose software packages."

—**Mohsen Ghasemi**, *Head of Integration Committee of FANAP Co.*

Tracing the storyline and subsequently to clear the project roadmap, the overriding step toward designing the fundamental structure of MIDRP needs to be adopted, now. This step, in fact, pertains to the MIDRP software architecture which provides the required technical functionality for accomplishing the pre-defined mission of the involved parties. The success of enterprise resource planning (ERP) is highly dependent on comprehensive knowledge and a deep understanding of the technical architecture of the system which shows how different components are organized in the system and how they interact with each other efficiently. The concern of organizing the system's components to reach a highly desirable performance using state-of-the-art technologies is the ongoing challenge of this adventurous journey that is unfolding here. Accordingly, in this chapter, we first provide basic definitions and concepts related to ERP architecture. Then, the technical architecture of successful ERP systems in the world is presented. Finally, we introduce and describe the architecture of MIDRP which is designed and implemented by the main executive character of the story.

5.1 Enterprise Solutions Architecture

In the competitive business environments driven by fast changes in today's world, it is very difficult for an organization to operate and survive with silo information

DOI: 10.1201/9781003369806-5

systems. Organizations need to be agile and flexible, and their information systems need to efficiently help them on this path. These systems need to have integrated data, applications, and resources from across the organization. A successful organization will require integrated information systems in order to focus on customers, process efficiently, and help build cross-functional teams that bring employees together effectively for optimized problem-solving.

An ERP system is a comprehensive enterprise solution used to integrate data and processes across different departments and efficiently provide support for the main processes in organizations (Ganesh, 2014). An ERP system can significantly reduce data redundancy and increase flexibility by providing integrated data storage for all information flows throughout the enterprise. When ERP systems take advantage of fast-growing web-based technologies, they have the potential to efficiently integrate information with their external partners, customers, and suppliers. These systems are so popular in the business world and IT industry that the term ERP is even considered equivalent to enterprise systems and well understood in these environments.

An ERP system provides a single unified infrastructure for all departments and functional units across the enterprise to share and integrate information in order to better respond to the business requirements of the functional units. The unified infrastructure facilitates the integration of the business functions in the organization into a central and comprehensive platform working on a single database. As a result, different functional areas, and departments in the enterprise as well as in partners', customers', and suppliers' locations can easily share information and communicate effectively for various business occasions.

A critical requirement of implementing and managing such mission-critical systems is a deep understanding of the system architecture and the interaction of the constituent components. ERP architecture will have a great impact on important business aspects such as cost, ease of use, and maintenance complexity. The architecture demonstrates the essential structure and the communications among various complex information technology components, including hardware, software, and data. It even explains the interactions of such complicated organization components as company structures, business rules, and people. For developing a good IT Plan, the management needs to have a clear vision of the important requirements for infrastructure, training, change management, and business process (BP) reengineering. Understanding ERP architecture will provide enough knowledge for them to go forward with a well-defined plan.

The ERP systems architecture can be analyzed from two different perspectives: (1) the functional perspective where different ERP functional modules, which support organization business areas, are defined and explained; (2) the technical or system perspective, where ERP systems architecture is defined by considering different physical components (such as hardware, software, and networking) which provide technical facilities of the ERP environments. Since the functional modules of the ERP systems are introduced in other chapters of the book, we only address the system or technical aspects of the architecture in this chapter and explain different types of ERP architecture from this perspective.

5.1.1 ERP General Architecture

The architecture of an ERP is actually the main blueprint of the system that determines the main flow of information in the company based on the ERP implementation strategy and expresses the mutual relationships among the system components. Without a well-defined and efficient architecture, regardless of all technological facilities and great expertise, there is no possibility of effective and satisfactory implementation of ERP in the organization. Like the blueprint of a house when the constructors envision their image of the components of the house which is going to be built, such as wiring, plumbing, and furnishings, the architecture of an ERP system demonstrates how individual components are combined together and how their interactions are formed so that the information flow will be efficiently facilitated throughout the organization.

A common practice by most organizations who want to implement ERP systems is to buy them as a software package from famous ERP vendors and deploy it throughout the enterprise department. In such cases, the architecture of the ERP system has been dictated by the vendor design strategy and not by the BP needs and the organizational strategy. This is often referred to as *package-driven architecture* (Motiwalla & Thomson, 2012). Given the competitive market of ERP systems, ERP vendors mostly apply the best practices in the industry's BPs for their system design. Those organizations who want to implement a complete off-the-shelf software package with the required industry standards can benefit from such ready-made systems. For the companies to obtain the highest possible performance and maximize their return on investment (ROI), they need to follow the implementation guidelines pertaining to the software package which they have bought.

Applying a package-driven architecture does not necessarily free the organizations to neglect their organizations' architecture and go forward with "vanilla" or "as-is" implementation. This is a serious mistake made by many organizations as they will not be prepared for the long-term maintenance and subsistence of the system. One needs to consider the fact that the architecture of the system can have significant effects on how the implements can modify or customize the ERP systems so that the organization's policies and procedures, maintenance operations, security, and controls can be supported. Therefore, ERP architecture must be fully understood even after it has been selected and bought as software from any vendor.

Generally, ERP systems architecture can be defined from two perspectives: logical architecture and physical (or tiered) architecture (Markus et al., 2000). As shown in Fig. 5.1, the logical architecture demonstrates how the systems are formed to support end users according to the business functional requirements. At the lowest layers there exist the hardware infrastructure and database systems and after them comes the core business logic, which encapsulates the real-world business rules and constraints. The fourth layer resides on top of the previous three layers to provide the details of business functions aggregated into the ERP system. The client user interface lies between the end users and business applications, providing an efficient way to interact

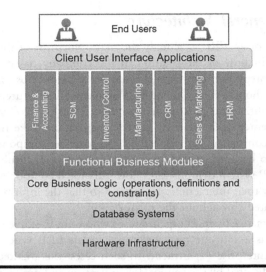

Figure 5.1 Logical architecture of an ERP system.

with the system. Using this layer, the implementation details of the lower layers are hidden from the end user (Motiwalla & Thomson, 2012).

Fig. 5.2 depicts the physical architecture which shows the organization and interactions of different physical components of the system in order to increase performance and reduce costs (Fowler, 2002; Rashid et al., 2002). Usually, the most

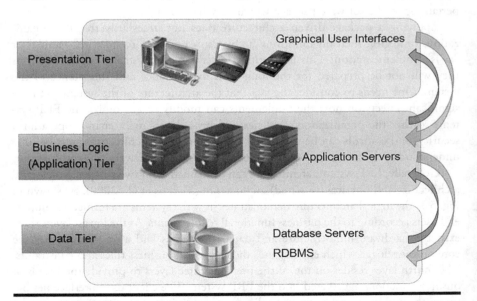

Figure 5.2 ERP systems three-tier physical architecture.

prevalent type of physical architecture is demonstrated in a layered structure, which is also called *multi-tier* or *N-tier* architecture (Buschmann et al., 1996; Jour & Zhaolin, 2013). In this type, ERP system components are organized in layers or *tiers*. An example of this type of architecture is the client-server model. The separation of tasks and resources into multiple tiers can help us manage the complexity of the system providing scalability and flexibility for the business needs. This also provides security and reduces the risk of system failure.

The three-tier architecture is a very common architecture applied in today's ERP software market (Fowler, 2002; Rashid et al., 2002). This type of architecture is the most flexible, scalable, and reliable architecture. As the name suggests, this architecture includes three tiers: data tier, business logic (or application) tier, and presentation (or web) tier. In the following we describe these tiers:

- The *data* tier consists of databases and data storage servers which provide business functions with the tools and space for storing and retrieving the required data. This tier defines the structure of functional data and its relationships with both internal and external subsystems. The data in the first tier are usually stored in relational databases with the ability to handle SQL queries. A database management system preserves the integrity of data transferred to and from the clients and servers. For example, different data about the sales orders, items, and package deliveries are stored and linked in this layer.
- The *business logic* tier provides the functional modules with the application servers and mechanisms to implement the operational logic for the business requirements. In other words, BP rules are implemented in this tier in the form of reusable objects with the capability of being reassembled into many functional applications. The application tier acts as an intermediary between business users (or client software) and the internal implementation of ERP data stores. In fact, the requests arrived from users are handled, the required data are retrieved from the database tier, and these data are then processed according to business function rules.
- The *presentation* tier is aimed at facilitating user interactions with the clients and delivering information in suitable formats. The users of the systems can interact with well-designed graphical user interfaces (GUIs) to have access to the components of the application tier and run the required services. The functionalities of the presentation layer can be implemented internally with the corporate intranet or externally through the web. Thus, this layer can provide its services through web server technologies, hence the name *web tier*. With the web services and protocols, client users can access ERP business functional modules from anywhere outside of the organization.

The three-tier architecture of ERP systems has many benefits for organizations over traditional client-server architectures. Some important performance features such as scalability, flexibility, reusability, maintainability, reliability, and security are provided by this type of architecture. However, it requires more software and hardware resources to support the duties of the business logic layer. It also increases the complexity of operations in development environments as opposed to the two-tier client-server architecture which has a visually simple configuration (Motiwalla & Thomson, 2012).

In general, the advantages of three-layer architecture outweigh its limitations for organizations in the long run. The three-tier architecture is increasingly used by many large-scale distributed systems and enterprise solutions, including e-commerce applications. Two modern component-based technologies, Enterprise Java Beans (EJB) and CORBA Component Model (CCM), support the Application tier to provide powerful frameworks for component-oriented application development (Amini & Abukari, 2020). In addition, this architecture is also applied by most web services based on the hypertext transfer protocol (HTTP) and extensible markup language (XML).

With the emergence and advancement of technologies such as cloud platforms as well as the growing use of the Internet in BPs, ERP modern architectures have also tended to use these technologies. Using the novel technologies, ERP's three-tier architecture has become stronger and more flexible. In what follows, these new architectures are described in detail.

5.1.2 Web Service-Based Architecture

The advantages of web service technologies, including flexibility and scalability, as well as their growing prevalence, have expanded their scope even in the field of ERP systems. ERP vendors have tried to apply these technologies to their architecture in order to use their tremendous benefits and increase their functional performance. As a result, the new resulted architecture is built into four tiers where the presentation layer has been divided into two tiers: the service tier and the browser tier (Sandoe & Boykin, 2007). The Internet technologies and concepts used in web service-based architecture facilitate easy, real-time, and pervasive access to functional modules for the ERP end users. The functionality of web service-based architecture is supported using four elements:

- Web server
- ERP portal
- Back-end server integration
- Browser plug-ins or applets.

Web services offer two critical advantages: (a) ease of integration; and (b) cost reduction. ERP web services can provide easy access to customers, partners, or suppliers without needing any special client software whenever they request information about the business functions such as order status, incident records, or purchase data. Simple access to ERP applications is provided to end users using a web browser over the public network. ERP modules can also be easily integrated with existing internal software or external systems connected with partners and suppliers.

Tarantilis et al. (2008) presented a web service-based architecture. In this architecture, a web portal allows the user to easily log in to the system. Then, an information flow engine navigates the user to each of the defined individual functionalities using object-oriented technology. Each functionality has been developed using a web-based component that can easily be plugged into the system.

In order to provide required services to different business applications, web service-based architecture applies object-oriented technologies which use a mixture of data and functions available in web service methods. Using these technologies, the integration of various vendors' proprietary applications with other tools and services can be facilitated. An example of an ERP suite that applies web service-based architecture profoundly is Oracle PeopleSoft. When web services are combined with ERP systems, they can create malleable application platforms with multiple components that are helpful for different business functions.

5.1.3 Service-Oriented Architecture

A service is a discrete unit of functionality that can be accessed remotely, acted upon and updated independently. It is well defined, self-contained, and does not depend on the context or state of other services. For example, the functionality of retrieving a customer's history record can be implemented as a simple service. In service-oriented architecture (SOA), the important functionalities are designed as individual services and provided to the other subsystems through communication protocols over a network. One of the main features of SOA is the independence from any special products, vendors, and technologies.

In an ERP system, the atomic units of functionalities in the application tier can be implemented as separate services. Collectively, these services are able to offer the business functions of ERP systems. Therefore, any module of ERP in any part of the system can use a service when in need. One important thing in SOA is in strict compliance with design rules and standards for each of the services. Each service has one provider and one or more consumers. The individual services may coordinate some activity for a business function. The SOA services are not dependent on a special platform. Therefore, service consumers from any device with any operating system can use the services offered by the provider only if it used SOA standard protocols and specifications. In the SOA software development model, an agreement is formed between a consumer (client) and a provider (server) that determines some important aspects of the service, which are as follows:

- Service function description
- Service input and output specifications
- The state of the environment before service can be invoked

- The state of the environment after service has been used
- How are errors handled when there is an exception thrown?

One important thing to bear in mind is the difference between SOA and web service-based architecture. Although SOA might be similar to web services in some respects, one must not consider these two the same type of architectures. Web services can be conceived as applications of SOA with web technologies such as SOAP and REST. Nonetheless, SOA includes more than just a set of technologies; it is a standard that defines how to provide functionalities in software solutions independent of any specific technologies. SOA enables the ERP systems to provide agile resources for the business by a set of best practices which help the designer hide the complex implementation of each technology in the system. With SOA, the structure of the different business applications is decomposed and reorganized. Thus, different capabilities can be provided as independent services. As a result, SOA can improve business visibility, reduce the cost of integration, and increase the reusability of services bringing agility and flexibility to an organization.

As an example of a popular SOA ERP, we can name *Epicor,* which is one of the most popular ERP vendors. In the Epicor ERP product, a complete SOA has been implemented and the best practices of service-oriented design have been applied to constructing its solutions.

5.1.4 Cloud Architecture

Implementing ERP in a company's premise involves considering many important issues regarding costs of purchasing and licensing, installation procedures, maintenance activities, and troubleshooting mechanisms. These requirements usually make senior managers and implementation engineers to obtain high budgets and recruit specialized personnel to deal with different types of tasks for the implementation of ERP on-premises. They need to take care of networking, data storage, security, privacy, technical support, and compliance measures related to the ERP modules. These challenges often impose a high amount of expenses and create a lot of working overhead for the organization management, especially in small-to-medium enterprises (SMEs). The solution to these problems in the new century is cloud computing. This emerging and powerful technology can meet the various needs of organizations to access information technology services and reduce their various costs in implementing an enterprise solution.

Cloud computing can be considered as a set of virtualized computing and storage capabilities that are used to facilitate access to services as needed and reduce implementation costs. A more concise definition of this mature technology is "on-demand access to virtualized IT resources that are housed outside of your own data center, shared by others, simple to use, paid for via subscriptions, and accessed over the Web" (Brynjolfsson et al., 2010). Simply put, cloud computing can provide you with high-performance virtualized hardware, servers, and platforms over the Internet for any business needs. Customer businesses can have access to these virtualized resources regardless of the place and the time only using the Internet as a fast and efficient channel. The cloud resources can be located anywhere in the vendors' data centers and the cloud provider manages everything from database systems and network infrastructure to software maintenance operations. Generally, the virtualized resources are offered as a service in three categories: Infrastructure as service (IaaS), Platform as a service (PaaS), and Software as a service (SaaS) (Armbrust et al., 2010).

The cloud computing SaaS model is used for ERP systems to help organizations remove the barriers to implementation and reduce maintenance costs. In a cloud-based ERP system, all required functional modules can be offered as SaaS services and client companies can use them with subscription models. The actual ERP software and its data storage reside on the vendor's premises or at a third-party infrastructure. The end users in the client company can have access to the ERP modules with a remote desktop connection on a computer or even a simple browser on a mobile device with an Internet connection. This model of cloud-based ERP service use can help companies eliminate the ownership and licensing costs associated with a purchased software package and the other installation and maintenance costs of on-premises ERP systems. Additionally, the client companies have the option to select those ERP modules which they actually need for their business and save the expenses for the other unnecessary modules which might never be required.

A good example of a fully cloud-based ERP system can be found in the co-operation of VMware SAP. The former is the most famous vendor of cloud computing services, and the latter is a leader in the ERP market. Together they provide a cloud-based SAP landscape that has many usages in training, development, Q&A, and actual production environments (VMware, 2019). With the benefits of VMware cloud features, the efficiency, scalability, flexibility, and agility of the entire business environment can be improved, and the organizations are allowed to deploy SAP HANA more easily. The SAP cloud-based solution can bring many advantages to the client company: (1) high availability with automated fault tolerance and zero downtime; (2) less time to value with rapid and automated provisioning; (3) reducing total cost of ownership (TCO) through automated data center operations, application provisioning, and infrastructure delivery; (4) better data protection, security, and compliance.

5.2 Architecture of Popular ERP Solutions

In this section, we investigate the architecture of ERP solutions provided by famous leaders in the ERP markets. We present and describe the architecture of the SAP ERP software, Oracle, NetSuite, SAGE ERP products, and Microsoft Dynamics ERP platforms. Considering the significant benefits of cloud computing technologies, as discussed previously, most ERP vendors have shifted to include cloud-based architecture in their product portfolio so that they can attract more customers to their flexible ERP software. Nevertheless, some well-known vendors still provide on-premise deployments in order to cover the requirements of large organizations.

5.2.1 SAP ERP

SAP can be considered the largest and most famous vendor of ERP systems, which has regularly improved its products to meet the growing needs of companies and organizations in the field of enterprise solutions (Gartner, 2019). SAP ERP products have experienced a significant evolution from R/2 and R/3 to ECC, and its database systems have ascended to HANA dB from its traditional RDBMS. This company has also embraced novel technologies in the world of enterprise mobile applications and cloud-based enterprise solutions. One of the SAP ERP products is SAP Business One which is a highly scalable and powerful software to cover all business functional needs of an organization. It helps managers make better business decisions by providing critical data and working modules (SAP Business One, 2018).

The foundation of SAP ERP architecture design is the use of the three-tier architecture described in Section 5.1.1. The following functions are provided by each of the three tiers in the architecture (Kalaimani, 2016; STechies, 2008):

- A relational database and database management system (RDBMS) exist in the database tier.
- SAP functional modules are run in the application tier, which is also known as the *Kernel* layer or *Basic* layer.
- A GUI is provided to the end users by the presentation tier to facilitate their interaction with the functional modules.

SAP systems architecture applies a three-layer architecture (Kalaimani, 2016). A relational database such as Microsoft, Oracle database, SQL Server, or the proprietary SAP native HANA DB can serve as the core component of the database tier storing and providing the required data (Baumgartl, 2016). The application layer consists of some servers to support background processing and request management. In the presentation tier, there are GUIs for allowing end users to access the system using front-end clients.

In the application layer, the main functional modules are provided via a set of application processes. These application servers' processes are executed under the name of a concept called work processes (WP; STechies, 2008; ERPdb.info, 2020). Any specific request that comes from the presentation tier will be processed and executed by a "work processor." In order to watch work processors to process requests, they need to be registered as an individual user in the database system for the entire runtime of the SAP system. The distribution of the workload to the WPs is done by a *dispatcher* which collects different work requests from the presentation layer and divides them into separate work processes.

The SAP has built a modern web-based and open integration platform as a foundation to serve the requirements for many of its applications. This platform is called NetWeaver (SAP NetWeaver, 2020). NetWeaver makes use of SOA in order to integrate enterprise application services. There is runtime environment for the SAP applications which is called "SAP NetWeaver Application Server" (sometimes referred to as WebAS).

The whole business management suite of *SAP* including supplier relationship management (SRM), customer relationship management (CRM), supply chain management (SCM), product lifecycle management (PLM), ERP, and transportation management system (TMS) is executed on SAP WebAS. The SOA-based design allows applications to use web services as a standard method to exchange information in a pre-specified format with a set of other applications.

The SAP NetWeaver is considered as a comprehensive platform for developing, composing, and maintaining enterprise systems. All applications such as business process management, data warehouse, and OLAP reside on the NetWeaver application server. The SAP NetWeaver platform consists of four layers as follows:

- Application platform layer
- Process integration layer
- Information integration layer
- People integration layer.

Using the above four layers, SAP NetWeaver can provide a framework to integrate people, processes, and information. The SAP proprietary products such as SAP native database "HANA," SAP solution bundle, and IS-Solutions, which are capable of integrating people (business) and processes (key business operations), have improved the application platform. The SAP NetWeaver platform has recently expanded its functionalities to support mobile business activities with the *Fiori-based* mobile platform. SAP *Fiori* is a novel user experience (UX) tool for SAP software and applications (SAP Fiori, 2020). The design of the SAP NetWeaver platform was aimed to support non-homogenous software so that it provides more flexibility for a customer's business needs.

SAP NetWeaver mainly acts as a technical layer for all business functions running on top of it. For instance, a Java-based application or any other customer's homegrown application may be run to consume SAP applications via XML. Customers have the chance to develop their own software applications in Java (J2EE) and/or ABAP with customized solutions.

5.2.2 Oracle NetSuite

Oracle NetSuite is one of the best-known ERP vendors which has established its position as an ERP market leader. It is considered the world's largest cloud ERP provider (according to the G2 Grid for ERP Systems, 2020) (G2, 2020). Some of the world's best-known companies and enterprises have trusted this cloud-based ERP system to successfully migrate their financial and operational processes to the cloud (Oracle Netsuite, 2020). NetSuite ERP has attracted more than 19,000 customers running this system in more than 200 countries.

NetSuite offers a full package of cloud-based applications using the SaaS model. Moreover, the NetSuite components have been built in a modular form. The foundation of NetSuite ERP is an amenable, comprehensive, and strong infrastructure called *SuitCloud* platform (Oracle, 2019). NetSuite has been built on top of the SuitCloud platform to enable comprehensive data privacy, data management, security, scalability, and availability for running different functions of ERP. Software developers from the customer companies can use flexible components of this platform to maximize the advantages of the cloud features.

SuiteCloud is essentially a multi-tenant cloud platform that provides functionalities with IaaS, PaaS, and SaaS technologies (NetSuite, 2012). The architecture of the SuitCloud platform has three layers abstracting infrastructure, application, and developer tools. SuitCloud offers *developer tools* in order to interact with NetSuite cloud and customize the applications. Business analysts and software developers can use these tools to quickly extend, customize, and integrate NetSuite features for different purposes, including financials/ERP, CRM, and e-commerce.

SuiteCloud developer tools consist of workflow management, scripting, analytics, web services, and more (Oracle, 2017). *SuiteBuilder* provides tools for graphical customization to efficiently record and manage files and build sophisticated business forms without coding. A workflow engine called *SuiteFlow* can provide easy-to-use, point-and-click tools for users to customize and automate BPs across NetSuite and among other business applications. In order to create flexible business logic within NetSuite, which is tailored to the specific business needs of the customers, *SuiteScript* offers a good set of scripting models and scripting capabilities in a full-featured application level for developers and administrators. The integration of NetSuite with existing on-premise software or third-party cloud applications may be a critical need for businesses. *SuiteTalk* offers web services tools to facilitate just that. Furthermore, *SuiteAnalytics* offers business intelligence (BI) tools to the applications built or customized with SuiteCloud. This will eliminate the need for any third-party BI tools. Finally, the developers can use *SuiteBundler* for a group and package up any customized or built applications on the SuiteCloud platform so that they can easily deploy them in the production environment.

5.2.3 *Microsoft Dynamics*

Microsoft has developed and marketed its ERP and CRM software products under the name Microsoft Dynamics collection. The great advantage of the Microsoft Dynamics suite is that all components designed in the package can be easily integrated with other Microsoft offerings such as Microsoft Office,

Windows SharePoint Services, and Microsoft Outlook (Microsoft, 2019). Recently, Microsoft has presented a new family of enterprise software called Dynamics 365, which has integrated ERP and CRM products with the Microsoft Azure cloud computing platform and Artificial Intelligence products (such as Power BI and Cortana) (Zadeh 2020). Microsoft has organized its Dynamics 365 ERP solutions into two categories (Microsoft, 2020):

- *Dynamics 365 Business Central*: It is a SaaS-based ERP system which is best suitable for SME businesses. It has been created in an adaptation of the previous *Dynamics NAV* ERP product.
- *Dynamics 365 Finance & Operations*: It is a SaaS-based ERP system aimed at large or heterogenous enterprises. Especially, those companies with multiple lines of business, international operations, multi-currency needs, or complex manufacturing processes can benefit from this category. It has been created in adaptation to the previous *Dynamics AX* ERP which was mainly an on-premise solution.

Although the above two product categories will provide the necessary flexibility and efficiency to meet the needs of companies, Microsoft also provides customers with the possibility of installing these solutions On-premise in the case of certain requirements. The Microsoft dynamics 365 ERP solutions with the on-premise architecture pursue the schema of their predecessors. In other words, one can observe that Dynamics 365 Business Central applies an architecture similar to the popular *three-tiered architecture* in its predecessor *Dynamics NAV* (Microsoft, 2017), and Dynamics 365 Finance & Operations mostly is implemented in adaptation with *Dynamics AX* software which also follows *three-tiered* model principles (Microsoft, 2018). The major elements of the Microsoft Dynamics 365 Business Central are web server, server (application server), and SQL database.

5.2.4 Sage ERP Software

One of the major market leaders in enterprise software products and integrated business management solutions is Sage (Sage, 2020). The specialty of this company is in building flexible ERP products for various types of customers depending on the size and the business functional requirements in their processes. Sage provides three major ERP products with a well-planned focus on cloud computing platforms: *Sage 100cloud*, *Sage 300cloud*, and *Sage X3*. Among these solutions, *Sage X3* can be considered a comprehensive ERP system, particularly created to support the demands of enterprises of medium to large sizes. In terms of implementation and deployment, the most important feature of *Sage X3* can be observed in its flexibility. Sage X3's applications can be implemented in various environments, including as a Sage-managed cloud SaaS, on customers' premises, or even in a private cloud environment that they may choose (Sage, 2017).

The Sage's managed full cloud architecture will eliminate the need for installing and maintaining any infrastructure and dealing with the integration, security, upgrade, and backup issues. Users may have access to the ERP modules from a usual web browser, taking advantage of the features residing in a secure and scalable cloud platform on Amazon Web Services (AWS; Amazon, 2020).

Although cloud-based architecture will bring many benefits for customers who desire to use it, there is no obligation for Sage customers to adopt a fully cloud-based solution. Sage will provide this flexibility for customers to take advantage of their existing infrastructure by deploying Sage X3 on their premises or in a private data center. This option is useful for companies, particularly when they need to integrate legacy applications with the newly deployed ERP product and customize their solutions for specific requirements.

In Sage X3 ERP solution, a multi-tier architecture is applied to better structure the functions and services associated with data storage, the application running, and user interactions. The SOA has also been combined with this architecture to ensure that the ERP functions are highly dependable in almost every situation (Sage, 2016).

In order to improve interoperability and increase accessibility, Sage ERP X3 architecture also uses web service technologies using popular languages such as .NET or Java. The web services used in SageX3 will support various standards, including XML, UDDI, WDSL, and SOAP. It is possible for ERP engineers to allocate an external server to Web services and integrate it with the Sage X3 product.

In fact, Sage X3 architecture consists of four tiers. The data servers, application, and client layers are completely matched with the previously discussed three-tier architecture. The new layer added by Sage is the Web Stack layer. It has been created to better make use of modern technologies such as Cloud services and Big Data processing. The technologies used in Web Stack provide scalability and high availability for the ERP services using clusters:

- *Node.js* is a cross-platform, open source, java-script runtime environment applied for server-side scripting and scalable networking applications (Node.js, 2020).
- Elasticsearch is a search platform built on Lucene, an open-source search engine software library. It provides a multitenant-capable, distributed, full-text search engine using a RESTful web interface and schema-free JSON documents (Elastic, 2020).
- MongoDB is a scalable NoSQL database for big data storage and retrieval in the form of documents with load balancing and data replication features over multiple machines (MongoDB, 2020).

In Table 5.1, a summary of the main ERP vendors' applied architecture has been presented. What is notable here and will have an accelerating trend in the future is

Table 5.1   Main ERP Vendors' Products Architecture

Vendor	ERP System	Type of Architecture
Oracle	NetSuite (OneWorld)	Cloud (SaaS)
SAP	S/4 HANA	On-Premise three tiers with NetWeaver and SOA
	Business One	Cloud (SaaS), three tires + SOA for On-premises
Microsoft	Dynamics 365 Business Central	Cloud (SaaS), Three tiers for On-premises
	Dynamics 365 Finance & Operations	Cloud (SaaS), Three tiers for On-premises
Sage	Sage X3	Cloud (SaaS), Multi-tier + SOA for On-premises
	Sage 100cloud	Cloud (SaaS)
	Sage 300cloud	Cloud (SaaS)

that the use of cloud technologies will have a significant role in the establishment of ERP systems.

Concerning the adopted approach of the popular vendors, how FANAP is going to design the MIDRP architecture? Particularly, FANAP has to decide whether to exactly borrow one of the existing best practices or design a hybrid one? In case of the latter, is any sort of innovative measure required to be injected into the architecture to fully customize the product? The next subsection goes through responding to these inquiries.

5.3 MIDRP Architecture

Along with the proposed mission, the MIDRP architecture has been designed according to modern ERP architecture styles and technologies in the world. It has been formed in a layered structure similar to other well-known ERP architecture styles and applied a hybrid of other modern architectures such as SOA, micro-service architecture (MSA; Open Group, 2016), and event-driven architecture (EDA; Richards, 2015). In this section, we first present the layered architecture of the MIDRP system and then elaborate on the details of the components in each layer. We naturally focus on the new ideas and innovative approaches applied in the architectural design.

5.3.1 MIDRP Multilayer Architecture

The MIDRP architecture is an extension of the traditional three tier architecture composed of five layers. Fig. 5.3 illustrates the five-tier architecture of MIDRP system. In this architecture the *data tier* and *presentation* tiers have the same functionality as their corresponding tiers in the three-tier architecture. There are two layers named *business logic* layer and *service bus* layer which are responsible for providing the most functionality of the application tier in the traditional three-tiered architecture. They implement the core business logic of the ERP system and execute the BPs originated by the end user from the presentation tier. For better managing the communication with the databases in the data layer, a new layer called *data access layer* was added which provides a high-performance accessibility to the database for the domain objects that are manipulated in the business logic layer. The technologies and tools for building the MIDRP architecture were provided by the FANAP platform unit. Each of the architectural layers was developed using a special framework with a specific set of tools. The name of each framework is chosen from the ancient Persian names.

The interactions between the tiers can be described as follows: when an end user initiates a BP, the presentation layer will send a request to the *Service Bus tier* to receive a service that performs the tasks for the BP. The request includes the information related to the BP that is to be executed within a particular

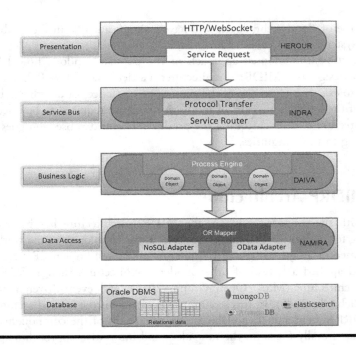

Figure 5.3 The tiered architecture of MIDRP system.

MIDRP product. In the service layer, the request for service is stored as a message, transformed, and routed to a proper processing engine in the lower layer (business logic layer) so that the BP related to the request is executed. The processing engine in the business logic layer decomposes the BP into its atomic components and runs the tasks related to each of the components. The business logic layer interacts with the *data access layer* in order to store and retrieve the data-related BPs. It sends/receives the BPs' data to/from the data repository via the data access layer. The data access layer acts as a middleware between the business logic layer and the database layer getting the data from the databases and delivering them in a proper format to the processes in the business logic layer. The data layer is in direct interaction with the data access layer and provides the data which are requested from the data access layer and stores the data that are coming from the above layers into the databases.

5.3.2 Database Layer

The data layer is mostly designed to use relational databases such as Oracle database and Microsoft SQL Server. As the MIDRP system grew over time, the capability of using NoSQL databases such as MongoDB (MongoDB, 2020) or ArangoDB (ArangoDB, 2020) or even some search platforms such as Elasticsearch (Elastic, 2020) was added to the data layer. The databases are configured for implementing the data models of the ERP modules and storing the data that relates to BPs. The relational databases are managed and controlled using a DBMS.

5.3.3 Data access layer

The data stored in the data layer (databases) is defined to be in a particular standard format based on the rules and restrictions in the DBMS. In order to access the needed data and communicate with the databases, the software components in the application layer need to use the SQL language and take into account the database configuration and restrictions. For example, the developers need to know the relational structure of the data entities stored in the database tables and understand in what format the data fields are stored. As a result, they are dependent on the database schema, the relational models, and data configurations in the data layer. Since the software components in the application layer may be developed in different languages, mostly with the object-oriented model, communicating the data directly with the databases is burdensome. This problem is resolved using object-relational mapping (ORM) (Roebuck, 2011).

ORM provides an automated method for connecting an object model, sometimes referred to as a domain model, to a relational database by using metadata as the descriptor of the object and data (Mehta, 2008). In other words, ORM is a design pattern that helps convert the data stored inside a relational database into objects in a way that they can be accessed and processed within an object-oriented language (Roebuck, 2011). Using ORM, the logical representation of the objects can be translated into an atomized form that is capable of being stored in the database while the properties of the objects and their relationships are preserved so that they can be reloaded as objects when needed. Since the main language used in the development of MIDRP functional modules is Java, there was a need for Java-specific ORM to perform the data management tasks with the data stored in the databases.

There are many ORM libraries developed for the Java language, including Hibernate, EclipseLink, Ebean, TopLink, etc. However, given the customization needs, we felt in this project, we decided to design and develop our own ORM called "NAMIRA" so that we could easily create new functionalities wherever and whenever any special requirements come into existence. The other important reason to develop our ORM was the performance and memory usage. The data access layer with NAMIRA also allows access to the OData. It has an OR mapper that can connect to MySQL, Oracle, and so on with the main focus on the Oracle database. NAMIRA also provides a method to connect to NoSQL databases and the Elasticsearch storage repository.

5.3.4 Business Logic Layer

The business logic is at the heart of the MIDRP system where the processing engines can execute the BPs and implement the business functions required for each product. The engines are able to execute BPs which have been designed using BPMN 2. The BP models have used the OMG specifications. Due to the specific functional and performance requirements for executing processes, the business logic layer was completely developed by the FANAP platform team. It is actually one of the great achievements of the MIDRP project. This layer is built using the DAIVA platform which provides a set of process engines (or process engine pool) to execute the codes of the BPs that have been generated from the upper layer based on a model-driven architecture (MDA) approach. Each process engine can run a series of BP codes related to a particular product.

The DAIVA platform provides the ability to run the BPs as services. In fact, the service request is sent from the Service Layer (INDRA) asking to run a particular BP. The BP is then decomposed into the TPs and RBPs. Each RBP is also decomposed to its TPs. The set of resulting TPs is placed in a layer called *transactional service*. The transactional service is responsible to implement TPs as a form of a complete database transaction with persistent data. In order to run each TP, it is decomposed into a set of individual tasks that show the atomic activities with business logic. These tasks are then executed by the process engine as a form of *micro-service*. The results of the micro-services are aggregated and sent back to the transactional service layer for completing the transactions. When all TPs are run and their data are stored in the database, the BP is completed, and the related output is sent to the upper layer.

5.3.5 Service Bus Tier (message broker)

The Service Bus tier includes mechanisms to receive, store, transform and route the requests which are generated in the presentation layer. These requests ask for executing one or more BPs in a particular product or product group. The Service Bus tier is implemented as a message broker (Hohpe & Woolf, 2004) so that the requests coming from the above layer be stored in the format of messages in special queues. Since the messages may have different formats according to the protocols in the presentation layer, each message is transformed to an appropriate format for the lower layer protocols and routed to the appropriate engine in the business logic tier to be executed. In order to satisfy all the software requirements and tackle the challenges of BP handling, a custom service layer called "INDRA" was developed for MIDRP using advanced messaging and queuing technologies and tools such as Apache ActiveMQ, Apache Kafka, and RabbitMQ (Apache, 2020). The message broker allows the system to coordinate the process executions and provides flexibility and persistence for request handling.

When a request for executing a BP arrives in the service bus layer, it is first analyzed, and business-specific information is extracted from the request. The information includes the organizational unit of the end user who has sent the request, the set of rules, variables, and criteria for the BPs involved in the request. Then, the *service gateway or API gateway* finds the appropriate engines in the business logic layer which can execute or run the BPs in the request. Next, the BPs included in the request are extracted and each BP is sent to the designated engine in the lower level. When the BPs are executed in the engines the result is sent to the service gateway. The service gateway then merges the results from different engines and sends complete results as a message in reply to the end user's request in the user interface layer.

5.3.6 Presentation Layer

The user interface of the MIDRP system was designed to be accessed by the end users through web browsers. So, there is no need to install any client desktop application on the end users' desktop systems. However, the UI is accessible anywhere in the organization and the users can log in to the MIDRP web portal with different operating systems such as Microsoft Windows, Linux, and MAC OS. The presentation layer is responsible for displaying the information about BPs and workflows in a structured way, according to the UI design of each BP, product, or product group. In addition, the users can interact with the system using dashboards, menus, forms, and pages in the UI and send their requests to perform any BP or related task. It also offers the users a mechanism to search the information about their daily tasks.

The main component in the presentation layer is called "Herour" which is a framework specially designed for running the user interface for the various BPs.

Inside Herour, there are protocols to send and receive the end users' requests and relay them to the service layer. The end users' requests from the web browsers are made with popular protocols such as HTTP and Web Socket. The Herour framework has been built specifically with JavaScript language and useful technologies such as React.js and JSON Schema being used for rendering form and generating dashboards. The requests received from the users are transformed by the presentation layer into the JSON message format so that they can be sent to the service bus layer and stored in the message queue.

All in all, the proposed multi-layer design for MIDRP architecture has completed another piece of the story. It has also stepped into puzzling out the rest of pieces by providing an efficient and robust framework for the implementation engineers. The executive character along with the other parties are now confident that the developed software modules can be performed well in interaction with the involved components yielding satisfactory results. In particular, such results are sensible when it comes to the system analysis and development stages which are the subject of the next coming chapters.

References

Amazon. (2020). Available at https://aws.amazon.com/

Amini, M., & Abukari, A. M. (2020). ERP systems architecture for the modern age: A review of the state of the art technologies. *Journal of Applied Intelligent Systems and Information Sciences*, *1*(2), 70–90.

ArangoDB. (2020). Available at https://www.arangodb.com/documentation/

Armbrust, M., Fox, A., Griffith, R., Joseph, A. D., Katz, R., Konwinski, A., Lee, G., Patterson, D., Rabkin, A., Stoica, I., & Zaharia, M. (2010). A view of cloud computing. *Communications of the ACM*, *53*(4), 50–58.

Apache. (2020). Available at https://www.cloudkarafka.com/blog/2020-02-02-which-service-rabbitmq-vs-apache-kafka.html

Baumgartl, A., Chaadaev, D., Choi, N. S., Dudgeon, M., Lahiri, A., Meijerink, B., & Worsley-Tonks, A. (2016). *SAP S/4HANA: An introduction*. SAP Press.

Brynjolfsson, E., Hofmann, P., & Jordan, J. (2010). Cloud computing and electricity: Beyond the utility model. *Communication of the ACM*, *53*(5), 32–34.

Buschmann, F., Meunier, R., Rohnert, H., Sommerlad, P., Stal, M., Sommerlad, P., & Stal, M. (1996). *Pattern-oriented software architecture, volume 1: A system of patterns*. Wiley.

Elastic. (2020). Available at https://www.elastic.co/elastic-stack. Accessed 10 March 2020

ERPDB.info. (2020). Available at https://www.erpdb.info/sap-system-architecture/. Accessed 14 March 2020.

Fowler, M. (2002). *Patterns of enterprise application architecture*. Addison-Wesley Longman Publishing Co., Inc.

G2. (2020). Available at https://www.g2.com/categories/erp-systems. Accessed 7 March 2020.

Ganesh, K., Mohapatra, S., Anbuudayasankar, S. P., & Sivakumar, P. (2014). *Enterprise resource planning: Fundamentals of design and implementation*. Springer.

Gartner. (2019). Available at https://www.gartner.com/doc/3913449. Accessed 7 March 2020.

Hohpe, G., & Woolf, B. (2004). *Enterprise integration patterns: Designing, building, and deploying messaging solutions.* Addison-Wesley Professional.

Jour Jinjin, H., & Zhaolin, F. (2013). The design of ERP in the multi-tier architecture. In *2013 Fourth international conference on digital manufacturing & automation* (pp. 1441–1444). IEEE.

Kalaimani, J. (2016). *SAP project management pitfalls: How to avoid the most common pitfalls of an SAP solution.* Apress.

Markus, M. L., Tanis, C., & Van Fenema, P. C. (2000). Enterprise resource planning: Multisite ERP implementations. *Communications of the ACM, 43*(4), 42–46.

Mehta, V. P. (2008). Getting started with object-relational mapping. *Pro LINQ Object Relational Mapping with C#, 2008,* 3–15.

Microsoft. (2017). Microsoft documentations. Available at https://docs.microsoft.com/en-us/dynamics-nav/product-and-architecture-overview. Accessed 10 March 2020.

Microsoft. (2018). Available at https://msdynamics.net/dynamics-ax-updates/microsoft-dynamics-ax-architecture/. Accessed 10 March 2020.

Microsoft. (2019). Available at https://dynamics.microsoft.com/

Microsoft. (2020). Available at https://docs.microsoft.com/en-us/dynamics365. Accessed 9 March 2020.

MongoDB. (2020). Available at https://www.mongodb.com/. Accessed 11 March 2020.

Motiwalla, L. F., & Thompson, J. (2012). *Enterprise systems for management* (p. 245). Boston, MA: Pearson.

NetSuite. (2012). Available at https://www.netsuite.co.uk/portal/common/pdf/ds-suitecloud.pdf

Node.js. (2020). Available at https://nodejs.org/en/. Accessed 10 March 2020.

Open Group. (2016). Available at https://publications.opengroup.org/w169

Oracle. (2019). Available at https://docs.oracle.com/cloud/latest/netsuitecs_gs/NSSCP/NSSCP.pdf

Oracle. (2017). Available at https://www.netsuite.com/portal/assets/pdf/ds-suitecloud-platform-development-tools.pdf

Oracle Netsuite. (2020). Available at https://www.netsuite.com/portal/assets/pdf/ds-netsuite.pdf. Accessed 7 March 2020.

Rashid, M. A., Hossain, L., & Patrick, J. D. (2002). The evolution of ERP systems: A historical perspective. In *Enterprise resource planning: Solutions and management* (pp. 35–50). IGI Global.

Richards, M. (2015). *Software architecture patterns.* O'Reilly Media.

Roebuck, K. (2011). *Object-relational mapping (ORM): High-impact strategies-what you need to know: Definitions, adoptions, impact, benefits, maturity, vendors.* Tebbo.

Sandoe, K. C., & Boykin, G. (2007). *"Enterprise integration"* (pp. 79–81). New York: John Wiley & Sons.

Sage. (2020). Available at https://www.sage.com/en-ae/erp/. Accessed 10 March 2020.

Sage. (2016). Available at https://partnerportal.sagex3.com/sites/default/files/sage_x3_partner/storage/architecture_guide_v11.pdf. Accessed 11 March 2020.

Sage. (2017). Available at http://www.tangerinesoftware.com/documentation-SageX3-version7/Sage-X3-V11-Technology-and-Architecture.pdf. Accessed 10 March 2020.

SAP Business One. (2018). Available at https://www.sap.com/uk/products/business-one.html?pdf-asset=2e4955be-937c-0010-82c7-eda71af511fa&page=1

SAP Fiori. (2020). Available at https://www.sap.com/products/fiori.html. Accessed 15 March 2020.

SAP NetWeaver. (2020). Available at https://www.sap.com/uk/products/netweaver-platform.html. Accessed 14 March 2020.

STechies. (2008). Available at https://www.stechies.com/types-of-work-process-in-sap/

VMware. (2019). Available at https://www.vmware.com/solutions/business-critical-apps/sap-virtualization.html. Accessed 4 March 2020.

Zadeh, A.H., Zolbanin, H.M., Sengupta, A., & Schultz, T. (2020). Enhancing ERP learning outcomes through Microsoft dynamics. *Journal of Information Systems Education*, 31(2), 83–95.

Chapter 6

Business and System Analysis

"The business process analysis of MIDRP is framed based on the stakeholders' requirements from top-level managers to shop-floor experts by considering the process architecture of the best practices. The challenges of the proposed framework are met when it comes to persevering the integration among different domains besides surmounting the end-user's incompatibility with the specialized functionality of BPMS."

—**Amir Arsalan Safari**, *Member of Business Analyst Committee of FANAP Co.*

The plot of the MIDRP story has been broken by the MIICHCO's requirements being hinted at in the exposition of Chapter 1. Thenceforth, this term has been intermittently implied and can be regarded as one of the central keywords throughout the previous chapters. In Chapter 3, the requirements have been generally presented in a hierarchical manner. However, that was only a simple introduction and the detailed aspects behind the adopted approach are going to be covered here. The system analysis is at the heart of the implementation step of MIDRP and thereby plays a critical role in the mission of the main executive character. In fact, one of the main thrusts of the pre-defined mission is to maximize the MIDRP performance. To do so, the essential unit of MIDRP that provides full systematic functionality for the end-user needs to be identified and extended in order to embody the corresponding requirements. In what follows, the way of handling this new challenge is going to be revealed.

DOI: 10.1201/9781003369806-6   137

6.1 Overview

The foundation for MIDRP development is formed by understanding, identifying, and categorizing all business processes that need to be automated throughout MIDHCO Company. Actually, the two most important stages of the software development life cycle (SDLC), for developing any type of software, are requirement analysis and system analysis. In order to design a successful ERP system, the business functional requirements of the organization must be identified correctly, and the system properties have to be analyzed so that those business requirements are satisfied in the best and most efficient way.

Therefore, a thorough analysis has been done to understand the required business processes in the systems and define the organization, structure, and interoperability of those business processes as individual components within the whole ERP system. For the MIDRP project, the business and system analysis stages are started with *requirement gathering* and continue with two important processes: *scope definition* and *business process analysis*. Fig. 6.1 illustrates the business requirement and system analysis stage in the implementation phase of the MIDRP project.

LESSON LEARNED 6.1

"Grasping the appropriate reasoning behind a specific requirement helps the business analysts to provide a better and more efficient solution pertaining to the system. For the sake of a crystal-clear understanding, let's focus on a particular requirement of the purchase module. The officer of the purchase unit issues a request associated with observing the list of users that have ordered different types of goods in the purchase form. In this certain case, the true reasoning behind the request of that officer is to only let the authorized users apply for a purchase requisition. Neglecting such reasoning may deceive the business analyst into considering a simple view feature of the users that ordered goods, previously whereas the accurate issue is to define the authorization level for the system's users. This perception against the backdrop of a requirement is yielded by being in touch with frontline officers of the industrial units."

by Amir Shiri

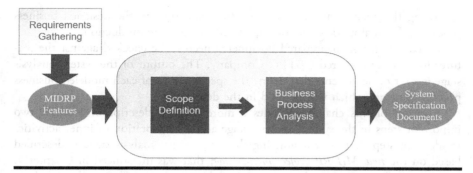

Figure 6.1 The MIDRP business and system analysis process.

As stated in Chapter 4, a consulting company (TEC) was responsible to provide the required features for a successful ERP system in the Mining and Steel industry. A feature is a capability or service that an enterprise system can offer. Considering TEC's expertise and experience in this field, it was ensured that they can prepare a comprehensive list of ERP features according to MIDHCO business requirements. Thus, the requirement gathering is mostly done by TEC and the output of their activities is a preliminary list of features that should be implemented in the MIDRP system.

The features list developed by TEC Company was used by the FANAP implementation team as an input for the analysis stage. The first step in the analysis defines the scope of the MIDRP system by identifying the business processes that provide those features and categorizing the business processes into a number of products and product groups. In this step, the processes and products were analyzed from a business perspective to meet the needs of the customer. The hierarchical structure of products and processes is also determined and verified with the cooperation of POSCO as a consultant company. Further, an *As-Is* analysis was done on the whole MIDHCO Holding to understand the current state of the business processes and workflows in the Holding. It would help to identify the existing processes and detect the areas which need careful attention for designing business processes.

The output of the scope review step is a complete list of defined business processes organized in products' hierarchical structure along with the results of the *As-Is* analysis. The next step is the process analysis where the required business processes (To-Be processes) for the organization are designed and modeled according to the benchmarking proposals, best practices of the business process modeling, and the requirements of the organization which are documented in As-Is analysis results. After To-Be processes are designed systematically by FANAP analysis teams, they are validated and verified by the expert teams. Then, they are documented in business process specification (BPS) and business process models (BPM) documents. As stated in Chapters 3 and 4, some expert teams have been formed with representatives of MIDHCO and its subsidiaries, and members of FANAP and POSCO business analysis working groups. These teams are responsible for reviewing, analyzing, and approving the analysis artifacts so that after validating all the designed business processes, the final models could be approved for software production.

Of course, the final prepared documents need to be checked against the features list already prepared by TEC Company. The output of the system analysis stage is a set of documents that define the specifications of each modeled business process in detail, which will be used in the design stage.

The rest of this chapter includes a more detailed description of these two important steps in the system analysis stage and an elaboration of inner activities inside each step. It is worth noticing that the system analysis stage is described based on the *new MIDRP project methodology* that was introduced in Chapter 4. For more information on the new methodology and its different phases, please refer to the aforementioned chapter.

6.2 Scope Definition

The first step in developing enterprise software is to gather and understand the customer's needs. The Scope Definition in the MIDRP project is the equivalent of the requirement analysis in SDLC (Langer, 2016; Innovative, 2020). The preliminary requirements were prepared by TEC Company as a list of features that the MIDRP system should provide to solve the problems of the operation and business management of MIDHCO Holding. These features were used in a *scope review* activity to define business processes that are necessary to improve the business performance of the companies and organizations within MIDHCO Holding. In fact, every process has to pass a number of features. Then, the *hierarchical structure* of the processes was defined, and the *big picture* of the system was designed in different levels. In order to have a good understanding of the required business processes for the MIDPR system, the FANAP expert teams performed a thorough *As-Is analysis* to investigate the current state of existing and needed business processes in MIDHCO Holding and all the subsidiaries. In the following Fig. 6.2, we elaborate on each of the steps taken for scope definition.

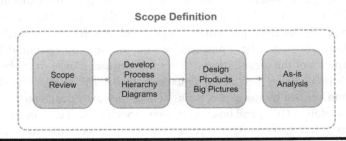

Figure 6.2 Scope definition steps.

6.2.1 Scope Review

As mentioned in the introduction section as well as in Chapter 4, in order to understand the requirements of the customer, the aforementioned Consultant (i.e., TEC Company) has specified the required features of the MIDRP which have been enclosed in the existing contract between MIDHCO and FANAP. Eventually, more than 5,600 features were identified by TEC Company. In addition to the features presented by TEC, FANAP also identified about 200 more features according to the gathered requirements in MIDHCO Holding. A feature is a well-defined capability that an ERP module should provide in order to manage, automate, or improve a certain area of business processes. Therefore, the needed features are identified regarding each subsystem of an ERP module (called source system by TEC). In addition, a priority number (in the interval of 1 to 10) is defined for each feature that shows its significance and importance for the final MIDRP implementation. For example, the Warehouse Management System (WMS) in Supply Chain Management (SCM) module should provide the following features:

- Warehouse Configuration
- Bin Location Setup
- Inventory Management
- License Plate Tracking
- Receiving
- Put-away
- Picking
- Packing and Shipping.

The important question that needs to be answered is "How do we design a system that is able to offer the required features?" To answer this question, it is worth noticing that the cornerstone of the MIDRP project is the business process (BP). Therefore, the first thing that should be clear is what business processes are going to be available in the system and what capabilities (features) can be provided by running and automating these business processes. First, let us define a business process clearly:

> *A business process is a collection of related, structured activities or tasks in which specific service or product is produced in a sequence to serve a particular business goal.*

> (Weske, 2012; Von et al., 2014)

In MIDRP, a business process (BP) is the main unit of the system that creates a complete systematic functionality for the end user. For each business area in MIDHCO Holding and its subsidiaries, there are some BPs required to be included in the MIDRP system. Therefore, we needed to identify or define the required BPs that satisfy the business requirements of any business units covered within the MIDRP scope. In this stage, the required BPs were identified according to the list of features already developed by TEC. In other words, each BP is a major component that offers a set of features from the list. The BPs can be categorized based on the business areas for which they are defined. Furthermore, each BP was named according to the feature categorizations in the TEC feature list and the related business areas in which it is implemented. Eventually, a total number of 238 BPs were identified to serve the requirements of the customer.

One of the most important things to consider when identifying and organizing the required BPs is the level of importance and complexity of each BP, as far as implementation is concerned. This is especially critical for planning the delivery phases for MIDRP products. To deal with this challenge, a special weight is assigned to each BP. This weight is proportional to the number of features the BP is responsible to make available.

6.2.2 Process Hierarchy Diagram

After the processes are identified, it is necessary to organize them into an appropriate structure tailored to the business functions of the organization. A *process hierarchy diagram* (PHD) or *functional decomposition diagram* provides a graphical view of the functions of a system and helps you decompose them into a tree of sub-processes (SAP, 2020; Sybase, 2020). The PHD is commonly used during the analysis phase of an ERP project to identify all the processes in a system by name and decompose them into multiple levels of sub-processes. Moreover, a PHD allows us to divide business processes into multiple levels, identify the problems in each level, and associate problems and analysis techniques with specific levels (Harmon, 2019).

The PHDs were originally prepared by POSCO, the consultant company, to define and clarify all the processes performed in the scope of MIDHCO business functions. It helped us recognize and enumerate the necessary BPs, decompose them into sub-processes up to desired levels, and display the hierarchy of all defined business processes in a single tree diagram. The PHDs for all business processes of the MIDRP were developed up to the third level according to the best practices and standards of the business process management in the steel-making industry.

LESSON-LEARNED 6.2

"The FANAP and POSCO ICT collaboration on reaching out to a significant level of joint awareness about the accurate system analysis of MIHCO business was very critical. Particularly, both parties should convince each other over the special business processes of MIDHCO that are certainly tunned based on the corresponding

cultural, governmental, and geographical restrictions. Among the others, one could refer to the domestic laws associated with tax calculation, and financial and human-resource-based terms which completely obey customized regulations of the target region. In this regard, these items demand a higher level of assessment to become truly digestible for both FANAP and POSCO ICT."

by Mahsa Kashkooli

Fig. 6.3 shows a sample process hierarchy diagram for the Quality Management Process. As can be seen, a PHD is drawn in three levels by default. The first level shows the *mega process* which is under the main umbrella of all the business processes implemented in a distinctive business functional area (Quality Management). The second level includes *major processes*. Each major process is a grouping of the main business processes according to the best practices in this domain. These groups are also called *process chains* as they include the business processes that are related to each other and are run in a pre-specified sequence. The third level shows each of the individual impartible business processes that form the process chain in the upper level. Along with the main PHD, for each process at any level, a description of the process is presented, its components are introduced, and a graphical map is drawn including its inputs, process components, and the resulting outputs.

After the PHDs were delivered to FANAP, the analysis team performed an assessment of the diagrams, evaluated them against the already defined business

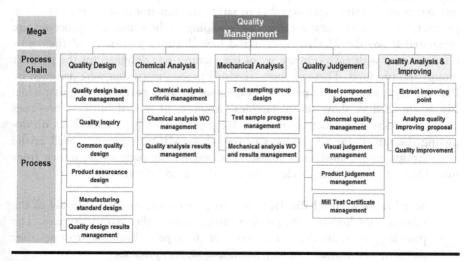

Figure 6.3   A process hierarchy diagram for the quality management system.

processes, and determined the ambiguities in the PHDs. After the PHDs are analyzed according to the requirements, the details of the processes at the third level are examined. For those hierarchy diagrams that need to be more clarified, the FANAP team requested POSCO to present the fourth-level diagrams so that the ambiguities about the details of their hierarchy would be removed. In response, the business experts at POSCO prepared a detailed draft of the process hierarchy at the fourth level.

At the end of this stage, the MIDRP scope was defined completely. This means the landscape of the MIDRP system was designed on three levels, including product groups (13 product groups), the products in each product group, and the individual business processes inside each product. In the MIDRP structure, each product is mapped to a certain *mega process* in PHDs to serve the requirements of a specific business area. In each product group, there are some products that were created according to the process chain or *major processes* that separate the business processes of a specific business area into well-defined logical classes.

Using the PHDs and the requirements analysis, the structure of MIDRP was clearly defined by the FANAP analysis team. The MIDRP scope was presented in a tabular content diagram for documentation and future use.

6.2.3 Big Pictures

MIDRP is an integrated enterprise system consisting of multiple functional modules called product groups. Each product group is an equivalent of an ERP module and includes a number of subsystems that work in a certain business area. These subsystems are called products. Inside each product, there are several business processes that work together to satisfy the functional requirements of the product. In order to have a clear understanding of how business processes are integrated inside the MIDRP system and how different products and their processes interact with each other, a set of big pictures was designed for the product groups and products. These pictures are visual process maps that were designed by POSCO regarding the best practices in the domain. It is worth noticing that while PHDs are used to show the hierarchical structure of related business processes inside a particular product group (or a Mega process), big pictures focus on depicting the integration of products in the whole MIDRP system as well as the relationships among business processes if necessary. Big pictures are drawn from four different perspectives or view levels, as described below:

- **Satellite view (level 0):** This view focuses on the *conceptual model* of the relationships between the product groups within the MIDRP system. The product groups are divided in terms of the type of business processes they support: *core processes, Management, and support processes.*

- **Bird view (level 1):** In this view, an overall map of the system components is displayed at the *total system integration level*. With the focus on the products, the macro relationships between all products of the system within and outside their product groups are presented.
- **Human view (level 2):** This view is defined at the *product integration level*. It is presented for every product of the system with the focus on macro data relationships between a product with other products from *the same or other external product groups*.
- **Magnified view (level 3):** This view displays the *process integration* level in which data relationships between the business processes of one product with other business processes are presented. This view is also defined for every product of the system.

Fig. 6.4 depicts the satellite view of the MIDRP system with its 13 product groups divided in terms of the type of business processes they implement. This picture shows an overall perspective of the system and will guide the rest of the analysis activities. Fig. 6.5 shows the bird's view of the MIDRP focusing on the products and their relationships inside or outside their product groups.

Also, Fig. 6.6 shows a sample human view of the Transportation Management System and Fig. 6.7 displays a magnified view of this product with all its business processes as well as their internal and external relations.

After the big pictures were delivered to the FANAP analysis team they could modify and update them according to the scope review analysis, MIDHCO requirements, and PHD assessments.

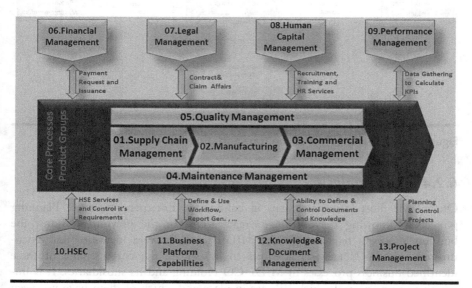

Figure 6.4   The satellite view of the MIDRP System.

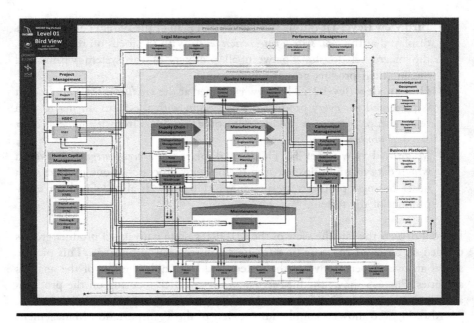

Figure 6.5 The bird view of the MIDRP System.

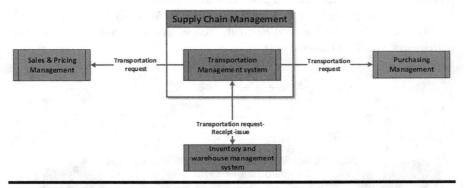

Figure 6.6 A human view of the transportation management system.

6.2.4 As-Is Analysis

One of the most important steps in conducting Enterprise Resource Planning projects is knowing the customer organization. In the previous sections, the business processes required for the MIDRP project were identified and documented. The As-Is analysis attempts to investigate the current state of these identified business processes in MIDHCO Holding and its subsidiaries. It is imperative to understand which BPs are in place and which of them have not been

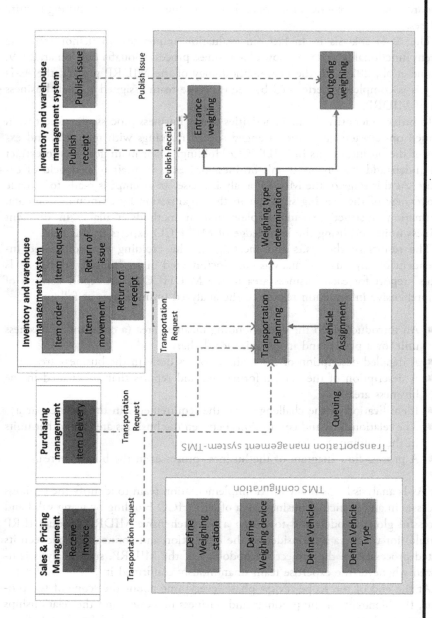

Figure 6.7 A magnified view of the transportation management system business processes.

implemented yet. In addition, for the existing BPs, it is necessary to determine the structure and the implementation details to check if they comply with the latest standards and best practices that were defined in the scope review and big-picture analyses.

The As-Is analysis is, in fact, an evaluation framework to demonstrate the current functionality and workflow of a business process (Bouafia & Molnár, 2019; Lamine et al., 2020). In the new methodology of the MIDRP project, the As-Is analysis is completely performed by the expertise team assigned to each business area of MIDRP.

In order to identify the main activities of any business process, the expert team planned on-location visits and arranged special meetings with managers and experts of the business units in MIDHCO Holding. Their main goal was to extract and understand the organization's business processes in their related field of expertise. At this stage of the MIDRP analysis phase, an attempt is made to provide an overview of the existing situation in the organization by examining the data, information, instructions, and implementation methods available in different business units and using the knowledge of MIDHCO experts in this field.

The results of the visits and meetings in the Holding were organized independent of any business analysis and documented in an "Identifying the As-Is Status" report for each business area in the MIDHCO. Each report consists of comprehensive information related to the analyzed business area as follows:

- An introduction to the corresponding business area (a company, a business unit, or a plant), and its organizational chart
- A detailed description of the main activities done in the business area
- A description of the data, information, and reports that are created in the business area
- Identification of the challenges and the requirements in the business area
- The relationships and connections between the business area and other units in the holding
- A process flow diagram of the business processes in the business area.

The As-Is analysis helps the MIDRP implementation team to identify the business processes in any particular business area of MIDHCO Holding by using valid and successful global models and to design a comprehensive MIDRP product (ERP module) for that area by considering the integration and connections between its related processes. In the project methodology of the MIDRP, such analysis is finalized whenever the expertise team unanimously confirmed it.

At the end of the scope review phase, everything about the scope of the products, the hierarchy of the products and business processes, and the relationships between products and business processes have been clearly defined and documented. In addition, the integration, scope and complexity of the tailor-made ERP products have been clarified. With an understanding of the current existing processes in the Holding, the requirements, and challenges, the next stage is to define and model the business processes that are going to be part of the MIDRP functional modules to satisfy the business requirements of the MIDHCO Holding.

6.3 MIDRP Business Process Analysis

The business process analysis stage is the most critical part of the analysis phase since it is analogous to the system analysis in the software development life cycle. This is exactly where the system components are determined and evaluated to produce an efficient and high-performance complex enterprise system. As the main focus of MIDRP is on business processes, the system analysis is performed at the business process level. In fact, by defining and modeling all the business processes in the system and the integration framework, the MIDRP system analysis is finalized. The output of this stage is a comprehensive set of business process specifications (BPS) documents that describe all the required business processes in the final MIDRP system.

LESSON LEARNED 6.3

"Amid designing business processes, there are several peripheral factors that need to be identified prior to entering the development step. For instance, the performance of the processes, being interpreted as the rate of requested inputs as well as the transacted outputs, is critical to be highlighted in the documents of the system analysis. In this regard, the developers could conduct the necessary measures to satisfy the prerequisites of such processes and hedge against any impracticality that may arise at the Go-live stage in advance."

by Saman Sarafraz

In general, business process analysis can be described in two important recursive stages: (a) business process modeling, and (b) validation and assessments. One of the great achievements in the analysis phase of MIDRP was the development of an Analysis Management System (AMS) which helps to facilitate the analysis tasks, automates the analytic document creation, and ensures that all the analysis activities throughout the project are consistent and error-free. AMS is especially very effective to provide a good integration among the products of the MIDRP system. We will discuss this system at the end of this section to better present the capabilities provided by this novel-developed solution. Fig. 6.8 shows

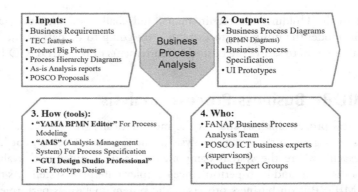

Figure 6.8 A view of business process analysis for the MIDRP project.

the inputs and outputs of business process analysis as well as the tools and people who participate in such activities. We discuss more of the steps taken for business process analysis in the following subsections.

6.3.1 Business Process Modeling

After the initial scope determination and business process identification as well as an understanding of the current situation with As-Is analysis, it is now time to completely specify the business processes which can satisfy the business requirements in MIDHCO Holding. This set of business processes is called *To-Be* Business Processes.

The business process models for MIDRP were defined with the BPMN 2.0 (OMG, 2011) standard as well as best practices in this domain. In order to design the To-Be models, the knowledge of the scope definition phase is specially used as the major input. The To-Be process models describe the details of each newly defined business process both on the internal activities and the external relationships with other business processes and products.

The expert teams play a significant role in the business process modeling as they are responsible to use their knowledge and expertise as well as the As-Is analysis reports to assess, modify and finalize the first drafts of the To-Be business processes. The expert team, which has been assigned for each product, reviews and adapts the business process requirements in the product committees and refers the feedback to the analysis stage to improve the process model. Additionally, the expertise teams develop and update the MIDRP big pictures at levels 2 and 3 for each product and its business processes.

6.3.1.1 Business Process Diagrams

After the approval of the To-Be business processes models by the expert teams, the FANAP implementation team could create the systematic To-Be functional models coupled with underlying roles, data, and processes. *The systematic models are created with a customized business process modeling tool called YAMA which was designed specifically by the FANAP platform unit in order to provide well-customized business process models.*

In the MIDRP project, business process modeling is done in an organized, principled, and uniform manner based on the standard *business process modeling document* which has been developed by the management of the Business Analysis Unit. This standard includes all the required methods, guidelines, and practical tips for using the BPMN modeling language in business process modeling. It is necessary for FANAP analysis and development teams to comply with this standard for the analysis and design of business processes of all products in the MIDRP project. In addition, all the necessary components and capabilities for the execution of instructions and process modeling guidelines have been implemented by the software platform of the infrastructure unit.

Business process modeling for the MIDRP system is performed with a focus on some fundamental concepts described below:

- **Business Process (BP):** A set of interconnected transaction processes (TPs) that have a specified beginning and end can be initiated independently (Triggered). BPs in the MIDRP are the main components of a product and provide complete systematic functionality for the end user.
- **Transactional Process (TP):** A set of activities performed by one person at a time when one or more transactions occur and change the data in the database. If there is a need to continue these activities with another person, another TP needs to be created.
- **Non-Transactional Process (NTP):** A set of activities performed by one person at a time when no transaction in the process data occurs. The execution of an NTP does not change the data in the database.
- **Reusable Business Process (RBP):** A process that cannot be triggered independently, but can be invoked (called) by other BPs and run as a part of the main BP. RBPs are also drawn independently similar to BPs.

6.3.1.2 Business Object and Messages

One important component of any business process model is the *business object* definition. In MIDRP, a business object is an entity that contains the needed information for the process or is influenced by the process when it is executed. For example, accounts, requests, customers, and suppliers are some major business entities in the MIDRP system. A business object is usually mapped to a data entity in the design phase so that the data related to a business process can be organized, stored, and updated in the database. The business objects are categorized according to the level of access and management of the processes in the MIDHCO Holding organizational structure. There are three levels of business objects in MIDRP:

- Holding: the business entities that can be accessed and controlled by the processes throughout MIDHCO Holding. The business object that is at the Holding level is called *master data.*
- Company: the business entities that can be only accessed and controlled by the processes inside a specific company within MIDHCO Holding.
- Business unit: the business entities that can be only accessed and controlled by the processes inside a specific business unit within a company or organization.

The business entities are identified for all the business processes (BP) and their underlying components (TPs and RTPs). Each business object includes some information fields which show the type of information that needs to be stored or manipulated by the business process. These data fields are defined meticulously so that every necessary information is ensured to be available during the process and data consistency is assured among all the business processes that work together. For each field, a number of attributes are defined which show the type of information that is displayed by the field. Generally, these attributes include English and Persian title, name, and type (numerical, text, categorial, etc.). They also involve some Boolean attributes that show whether the field is mandatory or optional, computational or not, list or not, has a search capability and has a default value.

It is important to understand that when a business process is executed it can change the data fields in multiple business entities. The business entities in an ERP system may have similar data fields with the same type of information. The similarities of shared data fields create relationships between different business entities inside a system. When a business process is run and changes the data fields in a particular business object, this change can be propagated to other business entities through the shared fields. Another important thing to consider is that for some data entities that are related to other data entities using them as a reference (e.g., a person that starts a request from a customer organization), there should be a data field that displays this reference. In MIDRP, for each data entity that contains such a reference, an additional structure called *Fields From Other Entity* is defined that exactly has the same attributes as the referenced business object. Table 6.1 shows the specification structure of a business entity and the description of each attribute.

LESSON LEARNED 6.4

"Concerning the general specification of a business object, the emphasis on recording the history of previous versions is to shed the light on the subsequent influencers of the project. This fact is not going to be restricted to the developers. Precisely, the trend of modifications within different versions of any product should be documented and reported to the deployment team and thereby the end-users as well. Sometimes, the fundamental discrepancies between the previous version and the new

one could lead to end-user confusion while disturbing the system functionality. Hence, by sharing the docs with the deployment office, the corresponding team could raise the awareness of end-users about such changes and the reasoning behind them."

by Mehrnaz Loloei

Using the above concepts, all the business process models (BPMs) are built according to the required features of each process, the integration methods defined in the big pictures, and the analysis done in the previous sections. The BPMN 2.0 standard will provide all the rules and symbols for process modeling so that the built process models are understandable by all business process users, including business analysts, software developers, business process managers, and supervisors. Therefore, BPMN is a bridge between the business process designers and implementers.

Table 6.1   The General Specifications of a Business Object

Attribute	Description
Business object title	A title for a business object according to naming conventions for business entities.
Business master object	The name of the master entity for this object.
Change history type	For each business object, it should be stated how the changes of this entity are recorded. The options for this attribute are as follows: 1. Log history: it needs to maintain change history 2. Version: it needs to maintain versioning 3. Log history& versioning; it needs to maintain both change history and versioning 4. Null: it does not need to maintain its change history
Business object level	The entity level in the MIDRP system can be one of these options: *Holding, Company, and Business unit.*
Reference object	The name of the parent object that this object inherits from
Object description	A short description of the entity in the business process

The business process modeling standard document provides guidelines on naming conventions for BPs, TPs, RBPs, NTPs, Task, and Pools as well as the used symbol for these concepts. Additionally, everything about the details of the business process diagrams, such as events, data entities, Lanes, Roles, gateways, tasks, throwing, and catching is presented in the document.

One important thing in the business process modeling of MIDRP is the interconnections between BPs inside a bigger process or product. The interconnections are important from the integrated perspective since the integrated BPs can provide complete functionality in a product. Defining the right connection types can tremendously increase the integration efficiency of the system. Creating connections between two BPs is possible using several methods:

- *Sending a message or signal:* This method is used for calling a process from the starting point or the middle of the process. When the message is sent to the invoked process, the main process may continue in parallel with the invoked process or wait for the response from the invoked process to continue with the new results.
- *Using call activity:* Reusing the RBPs is done by calling them with the call activity symbol. The use of call activity can also happen in special cases for calling BPs and TPs.
- *Providing services:* It is possible that some BPs need information from other BPs or products to perform their tasks. In such cases, they can ask for this information as a service request, and the information is provided for them as a service from the BP or a product that has such information.

The specifications of the messages that are communicated between BPs are documented in tables. For each message, there are several attributes to describe the message, including message type, sender BP, receiver BP, the name of the data fields in the message, the object or process that receives the message, the object or process that sends the message, the mappings of the data fields in the message to data fields in the destination entity.

Fig. 6.9 shows a sample business process model using BMPN for a BP named *HSE Inspection Management* which is a business process from the Health, Safety, Environment, Community (HSEC) product in the MIDRP system.

In order to show the details of the business process models, the BPMN diagram is drawn for all TPs and RTPs that are used inside a BP. Fig. 6.10 shows a sample diagram for a TP with the title "Need to Inspection Plan" in the *HSE Inspection Management* BP.

6.3.1.3 User Interface Prototypes

One important step in designing the business process models is the detailed specification of the internal activities or tasks inside BPs. In order to clearly understand

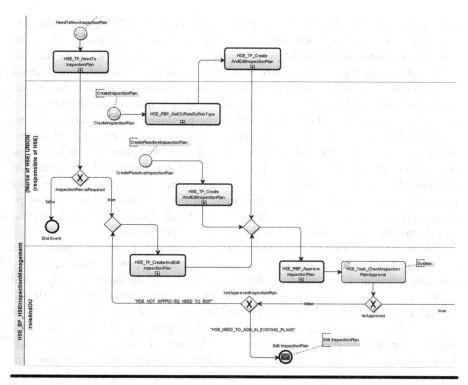

Figure 6.9 A part of the BMPN process model for "HSE Inspection Management" BP.

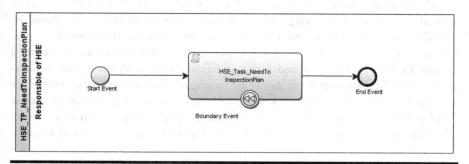

Figure 6.10 A BPMN process model for "Need to Inspection Plan" TP.

what a certain component of a BP does and how it works according to the user's needs, the user interface prototypes are used for each task or TP inside a BP. Prototype design with the help of user interface design software is one of the most powerful techniques in software development, especially in agile and iterative methods. A prototype is an early sample, model, or the release of a product built to test a concept or process (Hartson & Pyla, 2018). In the MIDRP project, the user interface prototype design was used during the analysis and design phases of the software development life cycle. With this technique, a prototype of the user interface for a business process is created in which the end user or customer needs are at the center of focus. The prototype can display the image of the system from the end user's perspective and describe how they interact with the system in order to execute a certain business process. The preparation of the prototype creates effective and efficient communications between different units for the production and development of the products and make a better understanding of the customer's needs for review and delivery phases. One of the key features of this technique is the simplicity of understanding for all stakeholders, its comprehensiveness, and its abstract view of the issues. Therefore, the design of the prototype for the user interface by a prototype design software is a good bridge between different levels of stakeholders' expectations and the software requirements from the developers' perspective.

In order to create a uniform structure for user interface prototype design in the analysis and design teams and the preparation of business process models, a set of standard procedures and guidelines has been prepared by the business analysis and infrastructure teams and approved by the project management of the MIDRP project. In addition, the efficient commercial software *GUI Design Studio Professional* (Carreta, 2020) was chosen as the main tool for UI prototype designs. The prototypes for the business processes are prepared to be presented to the customer and get their approval about how a certain task is performed before the final development of the software. They can also help the development team to design and develop the software components of each business process and act as a benchmark for the testing phase when the implemented BPs are to go under quality control mechanisms.

The user interface prototype for the TP and tasks inside all the BPs have to be created and documented along with the business process models. Each prototype includes the forms, fields, and the interactive environment that should be presented to the end-user when he or she wants to work with the system to execute a certain TP or BP. The designed forms and fields must conform to the business process specification document as far as naming, default values, titles, and other attributes are concerned. Fig. 6.11 shows a sample user interface prototype for the *Need to Inspection Plan* TP which is a component of incoming item quality control BP. The prototypes are typically prepared in two languages: Persian and English.

6.3.2 Assessment and Validation

Basically, all the business process models, and their related artifacts, have to be examined and approved by the expert team which is specialized for each product. As stated in the previous section, each expert team is responsible to modify and finalize the first drafts of the To-Be business processes.

After the systematic process models have been designed by the FANAP implementation team, the expert team related to each business area is responsible for

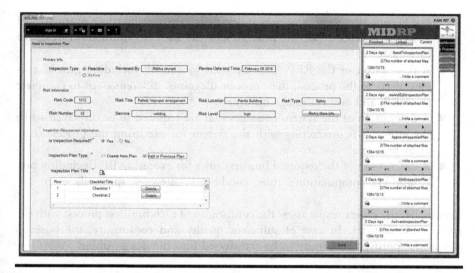

Figure 6.11 A user interface prototype for the "Need to Inspection Plan" TP.

evaluating the systematic process models deeply by focusing on the provided charts and official forms. Besides that, the business process, data, and roles are strictly examined to remove any doubt about considering them in the corresponding process. The results of the assessments are sent to the FANAP implementation team. Recursively, the FANAP implementation team is also engaged to resolve the problems until satisfying the expert team's expectations.

After all the problems in the business process models were fixed and they are approved by the expert teams, the "integration committee" of the system analysis validates the business process models to ensure they can work with other system components. The output documents of the systematic To-Be models are recorded based on the quality control procedure by FANAP. A business process is documented by the FANAP team in a business process specification (BPS) document. The BPS standard format was developed by the business analysis unit and approved by the MIDRP project management. Each BPS document consists of the following components:

- An introduction to the business process (BP) including its goal, scope, definitions, and abbreviations, the related resources, and documents
- A description of the BP including general specifications of the process, BP's BMPN-based diagram, different steps to complete the BP (required TPs, NTPs, and RBPs), and BP's event-message information.
- A description of the business objects that were defined for the BP.
- Detailed descriptions of TPs and NTPs that are part of the BP including general specifications, their process diagrams, the required conditions before,

inside, and after these processes are executed, the user interface prototypes of any related tasks inside the process, and the table of information fields for each task.

- A description of the RBPs that are used by the BP including general specifications of the process, their process diagrams, different steps to complete the RBP, and event-message information.
- A description of the system messages that are required to be displayed while the end-user is interacting with the system for executing the process (e.g., error messages)
- A description of the required business rules for executing BP (including preconditions, computational rules, conditional gateways, approvals, etc.)

Eventually, the expert teams assess the conformity of each business process with the given TEC features. In case of sufficient quality and conformity, the business process is approved and ready to be transferred into the design phase.

6.3.3 Analysis Management System

In the two previous subsections, we discussed the procedure to do business process analysis, including process modeling, BP and TP specifications, business object definition, Big Picture updates, UI prototypes, and so forth. We also presented the assessment and evaluation mechanism of the analysis documents, including BPM and BPS. The MIDRP mega project needed a very large set of analysis activities because the MIDRP system includes a large number of business processes and products that must be integrated correctly and efficiently to work as a system. A very common challenge during the early phases of the MIDRP project was how to make sure that analysis activities are going forward in the right way, how to ensure that business process specifications are developed correctly, and how to avoid mistakes, errors, and inconsistency in the analytic documents that are prepared during the analysis phase.

As mentioned in the previous subsection, in the MIDRP project, it was very imperative that the documents produced in the analysis phase of the business processes and products can meet certain quality standards and follow all the guidelines and instructions. Since a large number of documents would be produced in the MIDRP implementation phase, from analysis up to development and testing, it was very important for the project management to ensure that the documents meet an acceptable level of quality and be compatible with each other throughout the project. For example, the business objects and data field specifications that are defined for BPs must be consistent throughout all products in terms of naming conventions, business rules, and formatting guidelines. On the other hand, preparing the standard documents according to a large set of guidelines and instructions would be a laborious task needing a lot of time and effort. In addition, investigating and evaluating the prepared documents would be difficult and time-consuming for the managers and supervisors.

LESSON LEARNED 6.5

"In different products of the project, business data and entities were used to be generated without following a certain framework. In this way, the documentation could not truly reflect the terms that had compromised what had compromised between customer and analysis teams regarding the requirements of the business processes. To hedge against this, a set of standards and the associated checklists have been designed to provide a unified pattern for controlling the quality of the artifacts. As a result, the documents are now in conformity with the specifications that have been already formed amid the project."

by Mehdi Eyvazzadeh

Finally, FANAP Co. designed and developed an AMS software as a proprietary solution to tackle these problems. AMS is a web-based software platform system that facilitates, automates, and optimizes the creation, edition, and maintenance of all the required documents throughout the MIDRP project. With DCM, the analysis and development teams can create and modify every element of a document according to business rules and standard guidelines ensuring compliance, completeness, correctness, and integrity of the documents. In fact, all business rules, formatting guidelines, and specification instructions for developing analysis documents have been incorporated into DCM. The integration analysis activities can benefit a lot from AMS features because the specification of messages and services between different BPs is determined by *checking criteria* so that no incorrect message is generated. In addition, AMS provides a powerful search capability to find the required documents and their elements as needed. The AMS can provide the following features for the business analyst and software designers at any business process or product level in the MIDRP project:

- Business object management: Creating and modifying all business objects (BO) specifications, including, definition, data field specifications, BO's levels, reference objects, etc. with a standard format.
- Document details management: creating and modifying the specification documents for BPs and TPs with the standard format, including the BPMN diagrams, Big pictures, system tasks, messages, and business rules.

- Glossaries Management: Adding and editing the definitions and abbreviations for all terms and phrases that are used in the analysis and design documents.
- Output file management: Automatic creation of output files (in word format) from the individual elements that are already specified by the analyst, publishing word files for others, retrieving lost files, and versioning management for the output word files.
- Report generation: Generating special reports about the settings, specifications, and status of the process elements that are defined and modified throughout the project, specifically the integration specification.

Fig. 6.12 shows the AMS user interface when specifying the elements of a business object in an HSEC product. It can be seen that some attribute values that are important for an element are controlled so that the specifications are developed easily, safely, and without any error. Fig. 6.13 shows how the specifications of a BP in HSEC are defined. Notice how every element of a BP such as TPs, Messages, System Tasks, and business rules as well as the document details for the BP can be configured with this software system. When all of the elements are configured carefully, they can be assembled into a word file that presents the full standard analysis document for the BP.

The analysis phase is the critical part of the MIDRP implementation phase because in this phase all the conceptual components of the system are identified so that the requirements of the customer are satisfied. In this stage, the MIDRP system is completely defined and the elements are clearly specified. The output of the business and system analysis is a set of specifications for all business processes that form the ERP system functionality. After the system is analyzed, the business

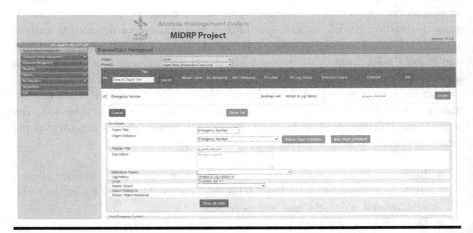

Figure 6.12 Specifying a business object for the HSEC product with AMS user interface.

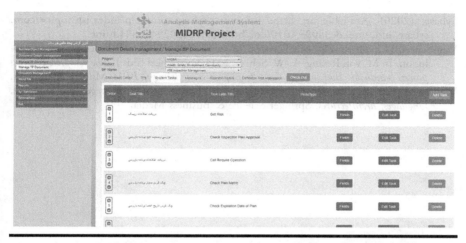

Figure 6.13 **Specifying the HSE inspection management elements with AMP user interface.**

process specifications, including big pictures, business object specifications, BPMN models, BPs and TPs specifications, and UI prototypes are used as input for designing and developing the MIDRP software components in the next stage of the implementation phase. In the next chapter, we elaborate more on the design and development of software components in the MIDRP system.

References

Bouafia, K., & Molnár, B. (2019). Analysis approach for enterprise information systems architecture based on hypergraph to aligned business process requirements. *Procedia Computer Science, 164*, 19–24.

Carreta. (202). Available at: https://www.carettasoftware.com/guidesignstudio/

Harmon, P. (2019). Chapter 8 – Understanding and scoping process problems. In P. Harmon (Eds.), *Business process change* (Fourth Edition). Morgan Kaufmann.

Hartson, R., & Pyle, P. (2018). *The UX Book – Agile UX design for a quality user experience* (Second Edition). Morgan Kaufmann.

Innovative. (2020). Available at: https://www.innovativearchitects.com/KnowledgeCenter/basic-IT-systems/system-development-life-cycle.aspx

Lamine, E., Thabet, R., Sienou, A., Bork, D., Fontanili, F., & Pingaud, H. (2020). BPRIM: An integrated framework for business process management and risk management. *Computers in Industry, 117*, 103199.

Langer, A. M. (2016). *Guide to software development—designing and managing the life cycle* (second edition). London: Springer-Verlag.

OMG. (2011). Available at: omg.org/spec/BPMN/2.0/PDF

SAP. (2020). Available at: https://help.sap.com/doc/saphelp_pd1655_bpm/16.5.5/en-US/c7/e373206e1b1014a8fff94f6f1a7b36/content.htm?no_cache=true

Sybase. (2020). Available at: http://infocenter.sybase.com/help/index.jsp?topic=/com. sybase.infocenter.dc38088.1610/doc/html/rad1232025416831.html

Von Scheel, H., von Rosing, M., Fonseca, M. et al. (2014). Phase 1: Process concept evolution. In M. von Rosing, A.-W. Scheer, & H. von Scheel (Eds.), *The complete business process handbook: Body of knowledge from process modeling to BPM*. Morgan Kaufmann.

Weske, M. (2012). Chapter 1: Introduction. In *Business process management: Concepts, languages, architectures*. Springer Science & Business Media.

Chapter 7

Design and Development

"Simultaneous attention to the high performance of the software infra-structure and the technical complexities of the development activities is critical to building a large-scale enterprise software."

—**Mohammad Bastam**, *Supervisor of Information Solutions Platform Development of FANAP Co.*

In the adventurous series of handling the challenges of the MIDRP journey in a scholarly manner, it is now the turn of design and development. In the previous chapter, we described how the MIDRP system requirements were identified, how different components of the system at multiple levels were defined, and how their detailed structures were specified. The output of the analysis phase is the set of specifications for all components of the system which shows what should be implemented in the system and what the output of such system should be. The created system specifications should be implemented in a software system so that the expected requirements of the customer are realized. Both executive and supporting characters of the story are aware that the development of such a fully fledged enterprise solution could not be simply realized through following the classical approaches. Accordingly, what sort of software development life cycle (SDLC) should be employed to perform as the best fit for the specific characteristics of the project mission? This chapter is to provide a significant yet practical solution for the recent concern.

7.1 Overview

When a large ERP system is to be designed, one should bear in mind that the organization requires a comprehensive software system that defines all processes, workflows, and practices for its business (Sumner, 2014).

It is important to note that commercial ERP products are large-scale, integrated off-the-shelf software packages that support the entire value chain of business functions. Therefore, the main challenge in designing a proprietary ERP system is to fully understand the organization's business processes in order to design the system architecture and provide features which best satisfy its business requirements. No pre-designed module exists and there is not any ready-made product which we hope the standards of our organization's business processes have been regarded in its built-in software modules. Prior to the system design and development from scratch, it is necessary to explore everything about the organization's business processes and functions.

A fundamental difference between designing proprietary ERP solutions and purchasing an ERP product for the business is how the ERP project managers deal with the *business requirements* and the *area of change* in the organization. When organizations purchase a full commercial ERP product from ERP vendors, they go through an *ERP development life cycle* and focus on customizing the software as well as on changing the organization's business processes (Motiwalla, 2012). The ERP project implements should introduce the best practices supported by that ERP system. As a result, some business processes in the organization should be re-engineered in order to fit the newly bought software. However, when an ERP system is designed specifically for a particular enterprise, new business requirements are defined according to the existing business processes, and the ERP software is developed properly to meet these requirements. Therefore, applying the traditional SDLC is more appropriate for this type of situation.

The ERP systems development process includes requirement gathering and system analysis, software design, development and coding, system testing, system deployment, and maintenance. In order to design a custom ERP system, we first need to perform a thorough analysis of the organization's business needs and existing systems. Then, we need to choose a SDLC model (Langer, 2016; Murch, 2012) so that the development process is done based on a well-defined procedure according to the customer requirements and the nature of the product we are building. The first thing that we need to do within any software development model is to perform a requirements analysis. This phase involves specifying the business processes to be supported by the ERP package. For system analysis, all the customer's real needs should be gathered, and a comprehensive requirements list should be organized to determine the complete specifications of the new system. Finally, we must define all the models, processes, and information, which are going to be supported by the system. These activities were described completely in Chapter 6.

In the software design phase, the architecture is defined for the ERP system to show how different software components of the system are organized and interact with each other. Then, the details of each component in the system are described according to the system specifications provided by the analysis phase. Then, the required software and hardware resources are determined. After the system is completely designed, it needs to be developed using the best practices in software development. Proper coding environment and tools must be applied to develop a high-quality software. Once the system has been completely developed, it is necessary to establish proper evaluation methods to test the software performance in the real-world business environment. For testing, we may use integration and end user acceptance test to make sure the system has been properly built and is applicable to the organization's business needs.

The chapter begins with a brief overview of the SDLC with an emphasis on enterprise systems. SDLC provides useful guidelines for the ERP implementation process and shows how we went through the software development journey. Then, we explain what type of SDLC was chosen for developing MIDRP based on the specific needs of the project. Next, we describe the process of designing, developing, and testing the MIDRP software system according to the business process specifications and the product structures that were prepared by the system analysts in the analysis phase (as explained in Chapter 6).

7.2 Enterprise SDLC

Developing a large and complex enterprise information system that may support thousands of business processes for several hundred users both inside and outside an organization can become a complicated and daunting task. Therefore, a well-structured methodology with clearly defined processes should be applied for complex systems development projects (e.g., ERP), to avoid the risk of failure and reduce costs. The software (system) development life cycle (SDLC) is an industry-standard methodology for the systematic process of designing, developing, and delivering high-quality software systems (Langer, 2016; Innovative, 2020).

7.2.1 An Introduction to SDLC

Using a systems approach, SDLC provides a series of stages that create a foundation for the software development process. The phased approach used in SDLC is designed to identify and anticipate errors and pitfalls at an early stage before they are discovered in successive stages imposing redundant rework and huge fixed costs. The SDLC process requires both technical and nontechnical problem-solving skills; therefore, the development team must understand technology, as well as the organization's business processes, culture, and people (Motiwalla, 2012). A newly designed ERP system must reflect the business processes of the organization in a comprehensive and usable format. So, the business processes must be captured and implemented in the ERP modules by a development team that is composed of people with various information technology and business backgrounds.

So far, various models and techniques have been proposed and applied for SDLC. Regardless of the SDLC model, the activities and tasks in this methodology

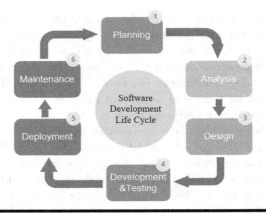

Figure 7.1 Software development life cycle stages.

can be categorized and ordered in six stages (Sommerville, 2016; Foster, 2014; Marsic, 2012; Innovative, 2020) as depicted in Fig. 7.1.

7.2.1.1 Planning

The first stage is focused on defining the scope of the project, requirement gathering, deciding on the functions and operations of the intended software application, and understanding how it is going to meet the business requirements of the customer organization. This phase is especially important as it aims to resolve any uncertainties about the enterprise software or product. The output of this stage is a requirement specification document which includes acknowledged specifications about the required system and may consist of the following information:

■ Functional Requirement Specification
■ Business Requirement Specification
■ Customer Requirement Specification
■ User Requirement Specification.

7.2.1.2 Analysis

The second stage is a crucial part of the SDLC where senior members of the software development team along with marketing and industry experts must analyze requirements for feasibility and validity and understand the essence of the software to be developed and its technical requirements. This stage also includes the identification of the development risks as well as the decision-making about the quality assurance methodology. The outcome of this stage is usually named Software Requirements Specification (SRC) which defines the technical solutions leading to satisfying customer business requirements.

7.2.1.3 Design

In this stage, using the SRS provided by the previous stage, the detailed structure of the software system, its features, and operations are designed. First, the software architecture is defined, and its various components are modeled. Then, all the necessary components including hardware and software specifications as well as data sources and information flow and communication diagrams are described. Different models may be provided for system design by software engineers. These models are evaluated and analyzed based on different criteria such as involved risks, product robustness, design modularity, budget, and time constraints. The best model is then selected for development. The output of this stage is a System Design Specification (SDS) document which specifies the detailed technical design of the software system.

7.2.1.4 Development and Testing

Once the system design documentation is complete, the whole task is divided into modules or units. Now, the actual coding of the enterprise software application takes place. The software developers translate the software design specifications into the source code and the software components of the system are built and organized according to the specified architecture. This phase can be considered as the most important phase of the SDLC for the development teams. Moreover, this is the longest phase of the entire SDLC.

Once the code is fully developed at this stage, the enterprise software application code needs to go through a variety of tests to ensure that it is up to standards and satisfies the specified requirements. During this phase of the SDLC, various types of functional testing, such as acceptance testing, integration testing, system testing, and unit testing, as well as non-functional testing are carried out. The development, coding, and testing procedures often intermingle with each other. In fact, when a module or unit in the system is coded, it should be put to the test. The test might reveal a problem, so the developers try fixing the code or rewriting it.

7.2.1.5 Deployment

This phase is also known as the implementation phase in the software engineering literature. The deployment is carried out right after the successful testing of the software product. It is simply delivering the software to the end user or installing it onto the customer's organization. Now it is up to the customer to try out the software (called beta testing) and see if it matches their expectations and if there are any bugs that developers missed in the testing phase. The required enhancements and adjustments are then reported to the development team working on the project afterward. Once all the changes are complete, the final deployment takes place, and the system will go live.

7.2.1.6 Maintenance

At last, the maintenance phase is executed. This phase deals with resolving the problems and issues experienced by the customers/end users while using the deployed software. The maintenance may include monitoring and troubleshooting the system as well as performing required updates or upgrades in the system components as needed. The maintenance phase can be carried out with the tight cooperation of the development team whenever new versions are released or in situations where more technical details should be taken into consideration.

In recent decades a number of different models and methodologies for SDLC have gained popularity. The software engineers and project managers may choose an SDLC which is best suitable for their requirements. The most popular SDLC models are as follows:

- *Waterfall*: The *Waterfall model* is basically considered the oldest of the structured SDLC methodologies. It is a very straightforward approach that suggests a fixed sequence of activities (as stages) without going back. Each stage relies on information from the previous stage and has its own project plan. Although the Waterfall model is easy to understand and simple to manage, a major drawback is the inflexibility of the steps. Since each step heavily relies on the previous steps, the possible delays in the early stages can cause the whole project to lag behind the timeline. This method gives little room for revisions during the cycle. Once a stage is completed, problems can't be fixed until after the maintenance stage. If the software project is going to be ongoing in a long term and more flexibility is needed, the Waterfall model will not suit the software development managers.

- *Iterative*: The *Iterative model* is an SDCL implementation using small steps with repetitions. In this model, the project team does not start with fully known requirements; instead, they focus on an initial, simplified development of a small set of requirements which then progressively gains more complexity in other iterations and offers a broader feature set until the final system is complete. Incremental development is also a popular term for this model which describes the incremental alterations made during the design and implementation of each new iteration.

- *Spiral*: The *Spiral model* is a risk-driven software development process and is typically used for large projects. This model combines the systematic, controlled aspects of the Waterfall model with the iterative development methods (Sommerville, 2016). The software development project with a Spiral model passes through four phases repeatedly in a spiral: planning, risk analysis, engineering, and evaluation. The iterative nature allows for incremental releases of the product or incremental refinement of the products. One advantage of this model is the ability to handle risks. Each iteration starts by identifying potential risks and finding the best ways to avoid or mitigate them. Therefore, the Spiral model is especially useful for projects with medium-to-high risk and when risk and cost evaluation is important.

▪ *Agile*: The Agile model is another type of incremental software development process in which customer satisfaction and rapid delivery of working software products are the main focus (Ambler, 2002). In the Agile model, "fast failure" is a good thing, and it is important to respond to changes fast enough. Individual and team interactions are emphasized over processes and tools, customer collaboration is preferred over contract negotiation, and working software is given more importance than comprehensive documentation (Sommerville, 2016). In this model, the software system is developed in incremental rapid cycles ended with delivery to the customer called "release." Each release features small, incremental changes from the previous release. Each iteration involves a team working through a full SDLC, including planning, requirements analysis, design, coding, and testing before a working product is demonstrated to the client. In order to ensure that software quality is maintained, each release is thoroughly tested.

▪ *Lean*: *Lean model* for software development is mostly an Agile framework inspired by lean manufacturing practices and principles (Womack, 1997). Lean development can be summarized by seven principles: eliminate waste, amplify learning, decide as late as possible, deliver as fast as possible, empower the team, build integrity in, and optimize the whole. The lean process suggests that the development activities must be focused only on necessary tasks at the time, therefore eliminating the possibility multitasking.

▪ *DevOps*: The *DevOps* methodology is the newest one in the SDLC landscape. It emerged from two trends: the application of Agile and Lean practices to operations work, and the general shift in business toward seeing the value of collaboration between development and operations staff at all stages of the SDLC process. On a DevOps model, development and operation teams work together closely—and sometimes as one team—to accelerate innovation and the deployment of higher quality and more reliable software products and functionalities.

7.2.2 Custom ERP Development Best Practices

Custom ERP system development is considered one of the most challenging development tasks and it requires a consolidated vision of your company's growth strategy. In order to develop the right piece of enterprise software for our business, avoid failure and prevent common pitfalls, we need to strictly follow and apply standard processes and best practices used in the area of custom ERP software development. There are many software developments companies which are specialized in developing custom enterprise systems for various customers. By reviewing the development processes and best practices used by these companies, we can grasp a foundational understanding for building our own custom ERP systems.

In this section, we summarize the most important steps taken by well-known ERP software development providers (SDCR, 2020) to review the common development processes and best practices in this area.

7.2.2.1 Define Goals and Expectations

Identifying the goal for the enterprise software will help us determine how to approach the development process. Although the business objectives are known to business analysts, the developer team helps you refine these goals and, ultimately, bring them to life. Before starting an ERP development process, the organization needs to understand and clearly define the goals and the related objectives that the system must reach in a specified timetable. We need to express why we need the system and what business needs should an ERP product satisfy for our organization. Clearly defined goals and objectives can act as a single point of reference with all the important decisions to come, like choosing the core functionality, prioritizing, and so on (Reshetilo, 2018). To bring value to your project, the stated objectives have to be aligned with the business strategy, based on goals, and they should have the SMART[1] quality set.

It is also a good practice to consult both major company stakeholders and IT experts when preparing the objective and requirements list for the enterprise resource planning system. This will ensure the organization set realistic, achievable expectations (Clockwise, 2020).

7.2.2.2 Check the Availability of Resources

Another important thing to decide on is if the company host the expertise required to develop an ERP or hire a dedicated team via an outsource provider (Clockwise, 2020). The available resources (both human and financial) should be estimated. It is a good practice to gather a team of professionals who have enough experience in developing enterprise software (Webcase, 2020). A group of employees that have been working for the company for a while is a good candidate to attend requirement gathering and planning meetings. The business and technology requirements for the Minimum Viable Product (MVP) should be documented (Tabbaa, 2017).

7.2.2.3 Designing the Application

In order to design the ERP software, it is important to conceive the overall system and its layout. A blueprint describing how the ERP software should be designed. When designing an ERP for a large organization with multiple departments, it's important to involve representatives of every department in planning (Clockwise, 2020). It would be best to include the heads of different departments in the discussion (Webcase, 2020). During this stage, the functions of each ERP module should be clearly defined. Another important decision to make is whether to use cloud services or on-premise deployments (SDCR, 2020). The best practices involved in the design process are as follows (Webcase, 2020; SDCR, 2020; Reshetilo, 2018; Tabbaa, 2017: Anadea, 2020):

- The system is decomposed into layers so that the maintenance and management become easier.
- The major building blocks including their responsibilities and interfaces should be defined.
- The user stories, visualized data models, third party constraints, and business rules are determined and documented.
- The software architecture should be visualized for shared understanding using unified modeling language (UML) diagrams.
- The databases must be designed since they are the most important elements for fast and effective data exchange.
- The running platform is determined. The system may run on desktop, web, or mobile. If it's desktop, you may build it in Windows, Mac OS, or perhaps Linux. However, for mobile, you have Android, iOS, and a few others.
- A foundation should be created in order to be used as a skeleton for any new features to be added.
- The user interface (UI) should be created as simple as possible because this system should be able to be used by everyone. This way, we avoid spending hundreds of hours teaching end users how to work with it.
- The required features are added to the system's main structure while paying particular attention to the service function of the software (security, response time, etc.).
- The size of the team working on the project is determined and the resources required for the development team are provided.

7.2.2.4 Creating Wireframes and Prototypes

When a preliminary list of features is prepared, the business and development team will have pictures in the mind of what your system should look like. It is imperative to unify these two visions into a single one, and visualization may be the best way to do this (Reshetilo, 2018). Building a prototype of UI and MVP concepts can give the developers a basic idea of what the software should look like and where everything goes. It is a good practice to create clickable prototypes and discuss them with all the stakeholders (SDCR, 2020). The feedback received from end users and stakeholders will definitely help to perform necessary modifications and improvements in the design of the product. Those wireframes that gain the approval of the stakeholders can later be used for interface design.

7.2.2.5 Developing the Software

When the business analysis and development teams have agreed on some version of the ERP system, the development team can eventually begin programming. There are some best practices in this are as follows (Webcase, 2020; SDCR, 2020; Reshetilo, 2018; Tabbaa, 2017):

- Choose the right development mythology that fits the software development requirements and challenges. The most common methodology used for ERP software development is agile because it is flexible and fast and allows the software to be released in iterations. Other methods such as Waterfall, Spiral, and Rapid Application Development (RAD) are helpful only when the objectives and requirements are clearly and appropriately defined.
- It is critical for ERP development that the system development be divided into small parts and each part is delivered when completed. The development can be started with the most important feature set or even a single feature of the software. When a part is developed, it should be tested with the other previously built subsystems as soon as possible.
- Choose the right technology stack for the development process. It includes choosing the proper type of cloud computing services and choosing relational/SQL databases for small businesses or NoSQL/document-based databases for large complex data infrastructures.
- Decide on the right coding language depending on the structure of the enterprise software. The usage of languages such as Python, Java, C#, and JavaScript is popular among software development companies.
- It is a good practice to allocate separate environments for development, test, and production.
- Properly use the automation tools for the builds and deployment processes, such as VSTS, Chef and Puppet, Octopus, PowerShell, bash, etc.

7.2.2.6 Testing and Quality Control

It is important to know any developed pieces of software can satisfy the expected requirements and predetermined standards. Therefore, testing the enterprise software applications throughout the entire development life cycle is a necessity. This especially means during the coding phase, before delivering each completed software component, and also in the deployment phase (SDCR, 2020). There are some best practices to ensure the development software possesses the expected qualities (Tabbaa, 2017; SDCR, 2020; Clockwise, 2020; Anadea, 2020):

- Review the design documents before coding and review the code before deploying the product. The review is done to make sure the system matches initial security, integration, and functionality requirements.

- Plan and define extensive tests for the correctness of the codes, integration, performance, security, and UX.
- Define automated unit tests such as MSTest, NUnit, jUnit, or RUnit.
- Employee focus groups to test dedicated modules and module sets. For example, the HR department will likely work with some combination of modules designed around payroll recording, human capital management, and personnel records.

Finally, one important thing that may create a significant impact on the quality of any enterprise software is regular and efficient communications between the involved people during the design and development process. It is important to make sure everyone understands the importance of the project and knows what's expected of them (Reshetilo, 2018).

7.2.3 Selecting the Right SDLC for MIDRP

Choosing the right SDLC model for the software development project will require careful thought. Developing a custom ERP software for a large organization involves complex issues to resolve and great challenges to face. Because the time needed to build an enterprise software can be lengthy, customer needs are likely to change during this time and you need to be prepared to meet those needs. There are also other challenges and problems, including changing economic conditions, declining budgets, and management change. Thus, a proper SDLC should be carefully chosen to satisfy the various requirements in diverse conditions and respond to changes that might happen during the project.

Generally, the software process used in a company depends on the type of software being developed, the requirements of the software customer, and the skills of employees in handling the software. According to the nature of the MIDRP project and the challenges that arose during the journey, we selected three SDLCs for developing the systems: *Waterfall*, *Iterative*, and *Agile*. The reasons to use this hybrid of SDLCs are as follows:

- At the beginning of the project, the requirement analysis had to be done for up to two years for some products (subsystems). Considering the significance of accurate requirements gathering and analysis of such a large system, no design or development phase was initiated so that we ensure the requirement analysis has been done properly and reached a good level of maturity. In addition, the design and development of the systems needed a large infrastructure that was not available at the time. Therefore, the Waterfall model suited the conditions and challenges we faced at the beginning of the process.
- After the infrastructure became ready for product development and the analysis of requirements had reached sufficient maturity, we shifted our SDLC to use an *Iterative* model. The Iterative model would allow us to start

designing and developing simplified software products with a portion of requirement specifications gathered until then and provide the initial versions of the software for the customer. Then, the system would incrementally evolve to a more complete software system as more components would be added to it in each iteration.

■ After a while, the customer organization states its readiness to make a greater impact on the project output via reviewing and confirming the outputs (mostly reconfirming the requirements by observing them in the software). In addition, as the size of the system would grow large, the need for more effective collaborations to build complex products was felt seriously. The SDLC model that best suited the new condition was the *Agile* model. Therefore, the company shifted to using an Agile model on the *Scrum* framework with two-week sprints.

Detailed documentation has been prepared in the project control unit regarding the latest software development process, which is an Agile model. These documents have been agreed upon by the supervisor and the project customer. A detailed description of the scrum methodology has been presented in Chapter 4.

Regardless of what SDCL model we used in the software development process for the MIDRP project, there are some key steps that must be taken in developing any component of the system. As described in chapter 6, an extensive requirement gathering and system analysis were done by the FANAP implementation team, POSCO, and the expert groups from the MIDHCO with a special focus on business processes as the main building blocks of the system. For the rest of this chapter, we focus on the design and development activities that translate the analysis documentation into working software components. For simplicity, we elaborate on each task in the design and development phase individually. However, note that all of the design and development activities for a certain component in the MIDRP system might be done concurrently in a scrum sprint leading to a final release.

7.3 System Design

After all required business processes were designed by the analysis team and approved by the expert team assigned to each product, the complete specifications of the business processes for each product were ready to be used as the main input in the design phase. The design phase includes a process-centered procedure which starts with creating conceptual data models for all business processes and continues by designing the system entities and data models for each business process according to the approved design patterns and standard structures. In addition, a system architecture is defined for the ERP software so that all the hardware and software components of the systems are organized in an efficient manner according to the latest design patterns and state-of-the-art technologies. Fig. 7.2 shows a

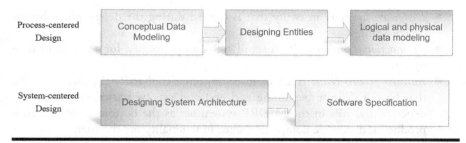

Figure 7.2   Software design activities for MIDRP system.

high-level sequence of the design activities for the MIDRP software design. The design activities can be divided into two streams: process-oriented design and system-oriented design. We elaborate more on each of the activities in the following sections.

7.3.1 Conceptual Data Models

The most important thing for designing any software system is understanding what data is needed and how it should be organized so that it can support business processes, record business events, and track related performance measures in the organization. Therefore, we need to devise *data models* for representing the data objects in the system, the relationships among them, and different business rules and policies which are to be enforced on the data for supporting business functions.

The *conceptual data model* is a high-level description and structured business view of the data needed to support business requirements independent of any software or data storage structure (Batini et al., 1992; Sherman, 2014). This model represents the overall structure of data by focusing on identifying the data used in the business, but not the processing flows or physical characteristics. The conceptual data model is a map of concepts and their relationships which forms the foundation for database design. Using a conceptual data model, we can describe the semantics of MIDRP products and represent a series of assertions about their nature. In particular, we identify the significant things to an organization (entity classes), about which it is inclined to collect information, and characteristics of (attributes) and associations between pairs of those things of significance (relationships).

The conceptual data model is the prerequisite for designing data models of business processes. It provides an overview of the products' data concepts and relationships for the data designer and is used as a reference document for the detailed design of data logical and physical models related to each business process. Before we go any further, we need to define the main concepts used in our data models:

■ *Business object*: It is an entity that is identified at the system analysis stage by the business analysis team.

- *Design entity*: It is an entity that is created during the design phase by the design team.
- *Transactional process (TP)*: A set of activities performed for a period of time by one person.
- *Business process (BP)*: A set of interconnected transactional processes (TPs) that have a definite beginning and end and can be started (triggered) independently. BPs in the MIDRP system act as the bottom layer of a sub-product and provide complete system functionality for the user.

Conceptual data modeling or designing *conceptual schema* was done on a per-product basis so that we could understand the important data entities and their relationships within the product and with the entities in other products driven by designing business processes. In order to model the conceptual schema, the *entity-relationship* approach was used because it is the most advantageous data modeling approach and the most appropriate one to reflect our natural view of the business objects and information structure within the business process components (Chen, 2011). For any conceptual design, the related approved specification document from the system analysis stage must be taken into consideration. Other guiding documents, such as *design specification standard for product conceptual data model* and *design standard for entity classes* were to be used. These standards were developed by the design team and approved by each product manager and finally by the project manager.

In the first step, the design entities are defined according to the business objects in each product. Those entities which are important to the designer in terms of introducing the product are selected to be incorporated into the conceptual model. To describe each entity, their defining attributes are also introduced. For example, in the Item Management System (IMS) product within the Supply Chain Management (SCM) product group, there exists a business object named "Item" which can be mapped to a design entity named *Item* with two identifying attributes called "identityCode" and "title." Then, the product conceptual model is drawn using the defined entities. For entities in a product conceptual data model, the name of the BP, which is the owner (creator) of the entity, is specified. In order to avoid the complexity and incomprehensibility of the model, *not all* entities need to be represented in the conceptual model and there is no need for *all* BPs to be present in the product data model. Fig. 7.3 depicts an exemplary entity-relationship model for the product WMS (Warehouse Management System) and the inter-connected BPs from the two other products, IMS and PJS (project management). The *Enterprise Architect* (EA) software (Sparks Systems, 2020) was used for creating data conceptual models. This software is a multi-user, graphical tool with powerful document generation and reporting capabilities for designing and modeling software systems; designing business processes; and modeling industry-based domains.

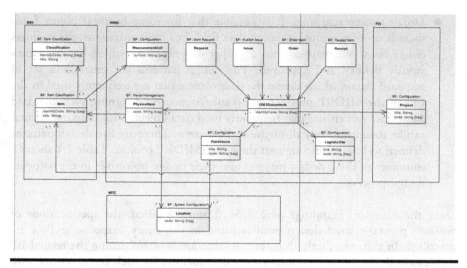

Figure 7.3 Entity-relationship model for the product WMS and inter-connected BPs with the two other products, IMS and PJS.

7.3.2 Design Entities

Each design entity is a class of data objects defined to reflect a characteristic or functionality of a business object according to its related BPs. For a particular business object, one or more entity classes may be defined depending on how a designer distinguishes different information components of a business object. Then a mapping is displayed between the analyzed business objects and their designed entity classes. There is also a mapping between a business object's attribute fields and entity class data fields. The entity class definition is done for every BP in any particular system product. For this purpose, for each of the business objects that have been analyzed for a particular BP process, three important mappings must be defined as follows:

- *Entity mappings*: A series of entity classes are defined for each business object according to information needed in the TPs being inclusive of business objects. For each BP, the business objects, their defined entity classes, and the related TPs are then documented in a table.
- *Field mappings*: Each business object has a set of attributes or fields which characterize the object's features and role in a business process. Therefore, these attributes need to be mapped into a set of data fields in the corresponding entity classes. A table of field mapping is designed for each BP in which the name of all business object fields (in Persian and English), their defined data fields, and the name of related entity classes are inserted.

■ *Design pattern mappings*: It is possible that for some business object fields there is no corresponding design data field. For these situations, the business object fields are mapped into a proper *design pattern* which has been previously defined and approved. The design patterns are generally a set of standard classes which define the data objects that are frequently used in the BPs of the MIDRP product group subsystems. By designing such standard classes, we can ensure that frequently used data objects with the same format can be used uniformly throughout the system. There are five design patterns defined to be used throughout the entire MIDRP project. Table 7.1 shows a summary of these design patterns and their design objectives in the software design process.

Once the necessary mappings were defined and organized, the specifications of business process-related design entities listed in the entity mapping section are described. In this stage, only those entities that are *modified* during the related BP are described. A table of specifications is documented for each design entity with the following information items:

■ An English name for the design entity
■ A short description of the design entity
■ The primary key for the design entity
■ An alternate key for the design entity (if one exists)
■ A list of candidate keys for the design entity
■ Some design rules for the design entity which may not have been mentioned in the analysis phase

Table 7.1　Class Design Patterns and the Purpose of Using Them

Design Pattern	Design Purpose
Category Element	Grouping discrete, constant, and finite values
Objective Category Element	Grouping a number of records of an entity
String Value	Keeping a list of strings
Long Value	Keeping a list of long integer values
Entity Attribute Value	In the cases where an entity has a large number of attributes, and for each of the records, only a number of attributes are valued and the result is null, or where the domains of the variables vary in different industries.

- The level of the design entity: It is defined based on where the entity is used in the organizational structure of the MIDRP system. This level can have one of the three following values:
  - *Holding*: The level of an entity that is defined and used throughout the whole MIDHCO organization. The entities in this level are considered as *Master Data*.
  - *Company:* The level of an entity that is defined only in one of the companies in MIDHCO holding.
  - *Business unit:* This level is used for the entities applied inside a particular business unit of a company.

One important thing that is to be defined after the entity specifications is the possible relationships between the entities in each BP and *other products*. These relationships are defined and documented using a table in which the name of the design entity, the name of the other product, and the *foreign key* in the current entity which is associated with a data field in the other product are inserted.

In order to design entity classes and the related mappings properly, all the analysts and designers must follow a set of *rules and contracts* for defining entity classes and consider the *naming conventions* for entity classes and data fields. Generally, these rules ensure that design entities and mappings are defined in a standard and uniform format throughout the system and documented appropriately. The business objects and attribute fields defined in the analysis document, as well as the classes and data fields created by the designer in the EA, are recorded in the Analysis Management System (AMS), and the designer must create mappings between these two entity's types in the AMS system.

7.3.3 Logical and Physical Data Models

Data models ensure that all data objects required by the database are accurately represented. They help system designers to provide a clear picture of the main data and can be used by database developers to create a physical database. They also help us to ensure consistency in naming conventions, default values, semantics, and security while maintaining the quality of the data. In order to present the structure of data entities and their relationships in each BP, two types of data models were developed by the designers: *logical* data models and *physical* data models.

The logical data model defines *how* the system should be structured, regardless of the implementation details or DBMS type (Olivé, 2007). In the system data architecture, the logical model is a representation of the details of organizing data, which is independent of the technology or limitations of different types of databases and expresses the data structure for entities and relationships among them in more detail compared to the conceptual data model. Using the logical data models, we can identify individuals, locations, objects, rules, and the relationships between them by determining all the characteristics of the entities, the relationships between the entities, and all the information fields required in each entity. Since a conceptual data model is typically defined for each product, it is certainly associated to many logical data models depending on the various BPs used in the product. To build a logical model, entity classes with their fields, their relationships to each other, and existing constraints per BP must be created in an EA software environment.

 # LESSON-LEARNED 7.1

"Concerning the way of structuring data in a system that is composed of multiple distinctive modules, the consideration of a centralized design is a must. If different modules of a system are designed distinctively, there will be islands of modules that are only able to satisfy their own requirements. To remedy this, a committee including a number of key individuals of the system should undertake the responsibility of designing the modules in a holistic manner. The committee members should have a general knowledge of the whole requirements and aspects of the system. This guarantees the ideal design of each module which logically interconnected to other ones."

by Saman Sarafraz

The Physical Data Model describes the specific implementation of the data structures regarding a particular database management system (DBMS) or any data storage technology (Olivé, 2007). The logical data model of any BP is provided for database developers or DBAs so that they can build physical models according to the specific internal implementations of the database system. This model creates a visualized database structure and helps generate the schema which is going to be used to store data records related to each BP. After building physical data models, all the table columns, keys, constraints, indexes, triggers, and other RDBMS features are defined and ready to be developed. Therefore, the real data structure for each BP is now available for implementing the BP and can be used for defining other components of the software.

7.3.4 System Architecture

In order to design a robust and efficient ERP software, a good architecture needs to be defined based on which the required components of the system are implemented. Defining a good architecture requires a good understanding of the system requirements, expected functionalities, and available resources. In addition, the well-known architectural styles are good models to follow since they have experienced a long journey of development and have strong academic and industrial backgrounds. The architecture designed for the MIDRP was described in full detail in Chapter 5. In this section, we summarize the most important concepts of the architecture related to the design and development process of the MIDRP.

The MIDRP architecture follows the principles and methods of the famous three-tier architecture (Fowler, 2002; Rashid et al., 2002). However, the central concept of the business process is maintained throughout the whole software structure playing an important role in the organization of the software components. The architecture was designed in a way that the business processes can be executed in the systems in an efficient and effective manner. In order to make the architecture more efficient with business processes and create flexibility and scalability for the development phase, two other tiers were added to the three basic tiers creating architecture with five tiers. Fig. 7.4 shows the general architecture of the MIDRP software system. A summarized description of each tier is presented as follows:

- *Presentation layer*: The presentation layer is responsible to display the information about business processes and workflows in a structured way, according to the UI design of each BP, product, or product group. In the presentation layer, a framework was designed specially to run the UI for the various BPs. This framework applies some protocols to send and receive the end users' requests and relay them to the service layer. The end users' requests from the web browsers are made with the popular TCP/UDP protocols, HTTP, and WebSocket. The requests received from the users are transformed by the presentation layer into the appropriate message format so that they can be sent to the service layer and stored in the message queue.
- *Service layer*: This layer includes mechanisms to receive, store, transform, and route the requests generated in the presentation layer. When a request for executing a business, process arrives in the service layer, it is first analyzed, and business-specific information is extracted from the request. Then, the *service gateway* finds the appropriate engines in the business logic layer to execute or run the BPs in the request. The service layer is designed as a message broker on top of an Enterprise Service Bus (ESB) and uses queueing technologies to store and route requests. The service bus is responsible for unifying and managing the flow of information between enterprise software subsystems with an asynchronous approach. One of the most important tasks of the ESB is to support and convert different protocols to each other. The service requests which come from the representation layer components are stored in a queue structure. The ESB is where all the requests for the BP execution are received and stored. The queue structure ensures persistency and fault tolerance for data management.
- *Business logic layer*: In this layer, there is a series of processing engines that execute the business processes (BPs) and implement the business functions

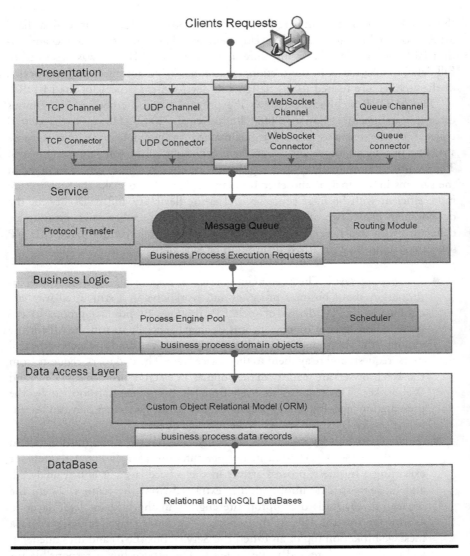

Figure 7.4 MIDRP multilayer architecture.

required for each product. Thus, business logic is at the heart of the MIDRP system. The engines execute BPs which have been designed using BPMS 2. The design of this layer was completely performed by the design experts in FANAP because we needed to consider BPs as a central concept in the business logic layer.

■ *Data access layer.* This layer acts as a middleware between the data layer and the above layer (i.e., the business logic layer). In this layer, an object-relational model (ORM; Mehta, 2008) is implemented so that the relational data in the data layer can be converted into domain objects in a way that they can be accessed and processed within a component written with an object-oriented language in the business logic layer. The main language used in the development of MIDRP functional modules is Java. Therefore, a Java-specific ORM was needed to perform the data management tasks with the data stored in the databases.

■ *The database layer*: This layer is mostly focused to use relational databases such as Oracle database to store the data related to business processes (BPs). The databases are configured to implement the designed physical data models for the BPs. However, the possibility of using NoSQL databases and big data support has been anticipated.

7.3.5 Software Specification (Programs and Procedures)

After we design the elements of the software system, it is now time to specify how the data flow inside the system and how different components of the software work together. We summarize the software specification in three important parts: UI, components interactions, and business process execution.

■ *The user interface*: The graphical UI (GUI) of the MIDRP system was designed to be accessed by the end users through web browsers regardless of where they are. There is no need to install any client desktop application on the end users' desktop systems. It was imperative that GUI is accessible anywhere in the organization and the users are able to log in to the MIDRP web portal with various operating systems including Windows, Linux, and MAC OS. In addition, the GUI allows the users to interact with the system using dashboards, menus, forms, and pages and send their requests to perform any business process, manage workflows, or related tasks. It also offers the users an efficient search platform to find information about their daily tasks. The users' requests from the GUI are translated to HTTP and WebSocket requests and sent to the presentation layer to be processed and handled. The user interaction with the UI is performed by the multi-window support and back and forward handling. The interface of the MIDRP system has also provided a large set of features such as Geo Map, Gantt chart, Tree view, Barcode and QR code, etc. The personalization capabilities are offered through dashboards, menus, and tasks. The GUI of the system also provides multilingual support for users' interactions with the MIDRP subsystems.

■ *The interactions*: The interactions among system components are done over the central concept of business process (BP). In fact, the system components are organized in a way that the BPs within different MIDRP products can be executed efficiently. The interactions between system components can be described as follows:

- When an end user initiates a business process (BP) the presentation layer will send a request to the service tier through *HTTP* or *WebSocket* protocols to ask for performing the tasks related to the BP. The execution of a BP is designed as a service that will give the results back to the presentation layer after BP is executed. The service request includes the information related to the BP that is to be executed within a particular MIDRP product.
- In the service layer, the request for service is stored as a message, transformed, and routed to a proper processing engine in the lower layer (business logic layer) so that the BP related to the request is executed.
- The processing engine in the business logic layer decomposes the BP into its atomic components (RBP, TP, business logics) and runs the tasks associated with each of the components. In order to store and retrieve the data-related BPs after the business processes are run, the business logic layer interacts with the data access layer (DAL).
- The BPs' data are sent/received to/from the database system via the DAL. The DAL acts as a middleware between the business logic layer and the database layer. It implements an ORM for getting the data from the databases and delivering it in a proper format to the processes in the business logic layer. The data layer is in direct interaction with the DAL and provides the data which are requested from the DAL and store the data that are coming from the above layers into the databases.
- *Business process execution*: Business processes (BPs) are the major building blocks of the MIDRP system, and the system functionality is focused on the business process execution. Therefore, the most critical part of the design is to specify how business processes are executed in the system to perform the end users' expected functions. The BPs, which are generated by the user in the presentation layer, are routed to a proper business process engine (BPE) in the business logic layer. A BPE is a software framework that enables the execution and maintenance of process workflows (CioIndex, 2020). It provides business process interaction and communication between different data/process sources. The process engine will process each BP and execute it to satisfy the user's request.

Fig. 7.5 depicts how BPs are executed inside the business logic layer. Any BP may include several RBPs and TPs. Therefore, a BP is first decomposed into its RBPs and TPs, and each of these components are executed in their specific environments. RBPs are stored and managed separately since they might be used by many BP throughout the system. The TPs are managed in a container called Service, where TPs are considered *Trace Service*.

In order to execute each BP, it will be mapped a set of atomic services that perform a business logic (e.g., entering a list of goods in a warehouse, or checking the balance of credit and debt). Each business logic is implemented as a microservice (Opengroup, 2016). The usage of microservices would help us structure the

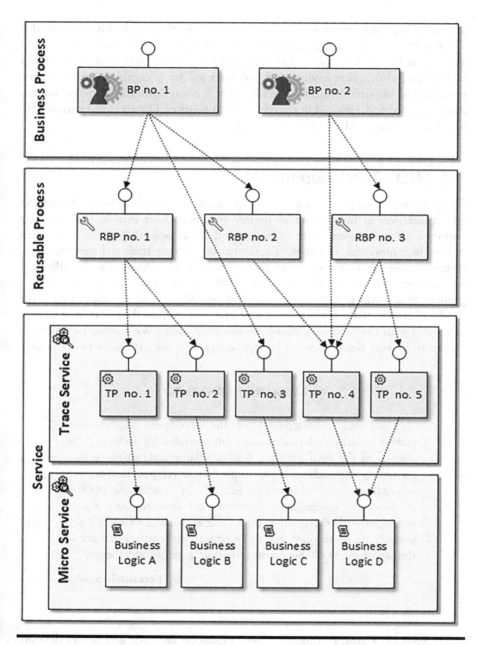

Figure 7.5 BP execution in the business logic layer.

business logic applications as a collection of services that are highly maintainable and testable, loosely coupled, and independently deployable. In addition, they can be organized around business capabilities and owned by a small team. TPs are at a higher level than microservices and are executed by a combination of atomic services. The important feature of a TP is that it always commits a transaction (its data are stored and persisted in the database). A series of TPs are called within a BP based on the designed BPMN-based model.

7.4 MIDRP Development

ERP software development is a very complicated and complex process. It requires an organization to invest a lot of money and man-hours into it. Developing a custom ERP may involve a lot of pitfalls and could potentially cause millions of dollars in unforeseen expenses. Therefore, developing such a huge enterprise system requires a lot of knowledge about the tools, technologies, and methods as well as careful planning and control. In MIDRP system design and development, a great emphasis was placed on the standard procedures and methods so that the products can be easily extended at the lowest cost and the bugs can be removed easily and with the least code changes when they occur. We wanted our software system to be very flexible against change, easier, and less expensive to maintain.

LESSON-LEARNED 7.2

"It's not an overstatement that the developers, as the main players of the development step, can considerably influence the efficacy of the final product. Actually, large-scale software programming demands multiple numbers of developers that need to be gradually involved in the project. The key underlying point is to provide a streamlined framework for synchronizing a new developer with the existing ones. The realization of such a framework passes through designing educational courses that are so similar to the workable environment and go beyond theory."

by Fereshteh Saadat

In FANAP, a great emphasis has been placed on fast code generation, development automation, high degree of customization, performance increase, and reducing the dependence on commercial tools. In order to satisfy these requirements, FANAP has developed an integrated and comprehensive set of tools and technologies called the MIDRP development platform for supporting the development and testing of the software components of the MIDRP system. This platform has been completely built by the FANAP software developers and engineers to respond to the specific needs of the MIDRP development. Moreover, in order to improve product quality, achieve codes with higher reliability, and better maintenance, the MIDRP development standards have been prepared by development unit management and approved by the project manager. These standards are a set of documents which describe the standard structure and packaging of products and the key points that should be considered in the development of products leading us to produce software with testability, and proper performance.

In this section, we elaborate on the MIDRP development phase, including the development platform, programming languages, and coding environment, products development process as well as the standards and rules defined in the software development process.

7.4.1 Development Platform

In order to provide a comprehensive, flexible, and favorable environment for developing the ERP products, and in response to the specific *customization* and *localization* needs of the MIDRP project, a huge set of building tools and technologies were provided by the *infrastructure unit* in the MIDRP project. The infrastructure unit was responsible to develop and provide all the required tools and technologies in an integrated framework for the development teams so that the development tasks are done easily and rapidly with standard procedures and reliable components. This integrated set of tools and technologies was called a *development platform*. All the subsystems in each MIDRP product were produced based on this platform and their development would not be possible without it. This infrastructure was created gradually as new needs came into existence while the MIDRP project was progressing.

The reason why FANAP developed such a comprehensive development platform can be expressed from two important aspects:

■ *Technical aspect:* Increasing efficiency and performance was a great concern in the MIDRP project. In the field of BPE, which is the executor of the business processes, the solutions available in the market are based on reflection and include complex internal codes. They did not meet the expected performance needs of the MIDRP system. In addition, the FANAP project management wanted a solution in which the designed business process models would be automatically converted directly to code, and such a feature did not exist in the world. Therefore, it was decided to develop a proprietary BPE platform that provides powerful process engines for the developers to run their deployed processes in the MIDRP *business logic layer*. There was a similar reason for the DAL. The existing ORMs in the world are proxy-based, creating a proxy for the domain object to connect it to database records, which wastes memory resources. Therefore, to prevent memory leaks, it was decided to develop ORMs internally. In the benchmarking process, FANAP's proprietary ORM gave better performance compared to other similar ORMs such as Hibernate and EclipseLink in terms of completed transactions per second (TPS) measure. Another important technical reason was to provide integration (in terms of coding system, structure, and methods) for the platform modules with the subsystems of the MIDRP that are built internally. The maintenance of components, bug fixes, and the introducing new features to the system would naturally be more efficient with the in-house developed infrastructure than external solutions.

■ *Non-technical aspect*: The more realistic reason for the internal implementation of such an infrastructure was the issues of localization and reusability. Because in the field of software infrastructure components, very little localization has been done in Iran. Considered as one of the largest and most capable companies in Iran, FANAP Company decided to implement such infrastructure components in a local way to be able to widely use them in all future projects or programs and to reduce the dependence on external tools.

Each of the platform components was designed specifically to help develop a certain part of MIDRP products according to its place in the software architecture layers. The main components of this infrastructure are as follows[2]:

■ *YAMA*: It is a customized integrative development environment (IDE) that allows business process analysts to design the process models using BPMN 2.0 diagrams. YAMA offers the capability of managing the business processes in the BPE using a management panel. The developers can deploy or cancel a BP to see how it works. When a BP is deployed, YAMA automatically generates code from BPMN diagrams. This is the most important software tool in the project which gives us the ability to convert BPMN-based designed business into executable codes for programmers. In other words, this software infrastructure is one of the important communication bridges between business process analysts and software developers. Furthermore, YAMA offers a process simulator and the ability to produce some reports about process executions in the process engine.

■ *ANAHID*: It is an infrastructure for developing UI and visual forms design. Allows developers to design forms graphically so that they can design the form based on a default schema. For example, they can create layouts, add or remove keys, and change colors and sizes. An innovation made in Anahid is the ability to write scripts. If designers have coding knowledge, they can write JavaScript scripts that are mostly used to manage events.

■ *HEROUR*: A software framework for running and displaying the web-based UI for the business processes as a part of the presentation layer. It is completely created based on javascript and offers tools for the end user's cardboard management and performing actions, defining search and creating dashboards. Form Rendering is based on Jason Schema that comes from the server. It can also connect to other modules.

■ *NAMIRA*: This is a software framework that can implement a middleware for establishing connections with databases, data access management, and implementing ORMs. As mentioned previously, the ORM is able to convert the java objects into database records. The ORM built by FANAP has been developed completely in-house and customized according to the MIDRP-specific data storage and retrieval needs. The advantage of the NAMIRA's ORM over external equivalents such as Hibernate or Eclipse Link is that the proprietary model does not create a dynamic proxy and has improvements in the field of memory management.

■ *INDRA*: It is a lightweight ESB designed with an asynchronous approach to support the integration and management of information flows, service request routing, and protocol conversion (e.g., WebSocket to JMS). It is designed to help develop the components in the service layer of the software architecture.

■ *DAIVA*: It is a process engine pool for executing the business process components. When a business process is designed and created as a process instance, the process code can be executed using a proper engine in the business logic layer. DAIVA is also responsible for workflow management and transaction management. The data relating to the executed business process are sent to the DAL components.

■ *AZHI*: It is a piece of software used for process simulation and test automation. Process simulation helps to illustrate the steps of executing processes or the path on which processes proceed. The simulations are done according to test cases.

■ *MARTA*: It is a software framework for managing the organizational chart. The developers can define OUs, roles, persons, and views with a tree structure. In the MARTA module, a new syntax is defined for lanes called lane query. It is possible to write specific queries on BPMN lanes and perform a search on the organizational charts based on these queries. This is a simple and new syntax that is parsed with ANTLR technology and converted to Arrango DB queries.

■ *DIRANA*: It is a file management platform for data and information sharing between different modules in the development process.

LESSON LEARNED 7.3

"Early in the project, there was an attempt to move to a type of BPMS which generates code and does most of the software production work (e.g., execution of process, domains and domain objects, creating user interfaces, controlling business rules, etc.)

through the development platform. Intis regard, the developers just would add more details to the relationships between business processes by performing CRUD operations. Although many efforts were made to design good software, the fundamental focus on the platform had made everyone in the various layers of software production think that it was the platform that had to solve all the problems. Whereas, in the continuation of the work, we realized that the development domain itself has its own problems and complexities. It took just as much focus and time for the development activities, and given the size of the MIDRP, it needed to be seen more widely. As the project went on, the development domain was given more concentration, the people's attitude was changed and most of the problems were resolved."

by Mohammad Bastam

It is important to note that despite the many benefits brought by the development platform to the development process of the MIDRP project, one should understand that the infrastructure services in the world are considered tools and they could not and must not dictate the software architecture. Designing the software architecture and its components must be done in a separate independent process in advance and all the possible problems and bottlenecks for the software development must be anticipated. Naturally, the use of the platform placed restrictions on doing things. For example, a form created by the Anahid platform has less flexibility and capabilities than a form generated by a programmer from scratch. But over time, these problems were solved by adapting to platform tools.

7.4.2 Development Environment

Developing the software modules and components in the back-end (engines, services, and data access components) was carried out mostly using the *Java* programming language in the JetBrain *IntelliJ* IDEA software (Jetbrain, 2020). The main language used for developing the UI modules was JavaScript. There were also some scripting languages that were developed by the infrastructure unit to satisfy some particular requirements.

Creating and managing databases was done in the Oracle Database DBMS software. As we mentioned earlier, the EA was used for designing logical data models. The database management tools were provided by the project *data management unit* for the development teams. Logical data models designed in EA are converted to Java codes using a proprietary tool called the *object builder*. When the java codes are executed, they generate some Data Definition Language (DDL) statements of SQL code that produce the physical data. Providing various capabilities, including programming environment, testing, production, and maintenance of databases, this set of tools was one of the most important services of the data management unit to the development unit.

7.4.3 Development Process

As discussed in the design section, the main concept behind the MIDRP product development is the business process (BP). Therefore, each product is built by a group of implemented BPs in the system. In this section, we describe the steps to develop a software component which implements a BP using the software modules provided with the development infrastructure. There are two important inputs to the development process of a BP implementation. First, the relational data models associated with BP, which were designed by the *EA* software as described in the design phase. Second, the file of the BPMN diagram associated with the BP was designed with the YAMA environment by the business analysis teams according to the customer needs and best practices in the world.

After getting the inputs, the development team which is designated for the product in which the BP is implemented begins to develop the software component of the BP. Generally, the development process for each BP includes the following steps:

- Converting the BMPN diagrams of the BP to java codes that show the internal implementation of a BP (Using YAMA IDE).
- Developing the data access components to send and receive transaction data to the database (using NAMIRA).
- Developing the internal implementation of the TPs and using the reusable modules developed for RBPs (using Java in the IntelliJ IDE).
- Configuring the process to make it run using the process engines with YAMA.
- Designing the UI components (i.e., forms and layouts) for the BP (Using ANAHID).
- Generating and deploying the implemented BP in YAMA to see the results (using DIAVA and HEROUR).

The aforementioned process applies a full integration of different development tools in the various software layers. Fig. 7.6 depicts the process of implementing a BP using the development infrastructure. The business process implementation is started with YAMA which has the BMPN diagram of a particular BP. The YAMA environment provides a comprehensive set of tools to build a BP as an active software component. It allows the developers to connect each of the BP transactions to the database and use the entity classes designed in the data models. YAMA is connected to a set of tools called *development manager* for process code generation. The BPMN diagrams in the YAMA can be converted to a set of Java codes

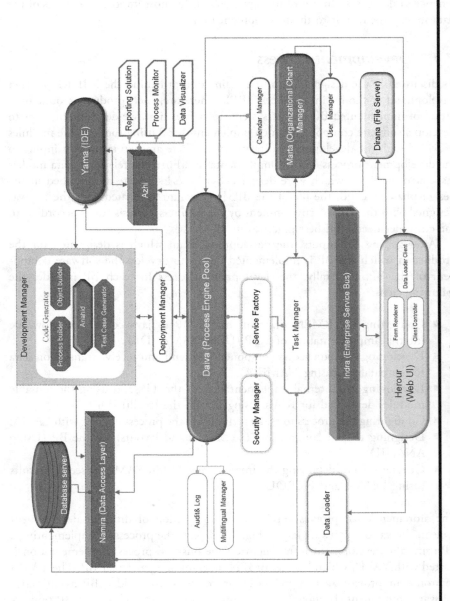

Figure 7.6 Development of BPs using the MIDRP development platform.

with which the developer can implement and modify the BP software components in the product package using the IntelliJ IDE. Code Generator has two parts: process builder and object builder. ANAHID and test case builder are also parts of the *development manager*. After the implementation codes were written in the IntelliJ IDE, the process is ready to be deployed. The deployment is performed in the YAMA environment using the process engine management tools, which are selected according to configuration rules for each product. YAMA includes all the commands needed to run or change business processes in the engines. Managing the interactions of the end user with the system while executing a BP through a UI is implemented by the Herour. Herour is responsible for rendering the BP forms and connects the interface to other modules to load related data and perform needed actions.

7.4.4 The Products Structure

The software products[3] in the MIDRP system must be developed based on standard patterns and structures approved by the development team manager. These standard patterns have been prepared according to the SOLID principles of object-oriented design (Millington, 2019). Considering the size of the enterprise system, SOLID design principles help developers to create more maintainable, understandable, and flexible software and ensure scalability with fewer costs and challenges. Implementing products according to standard patterns, according to SOLID principles and rules, prevents duplication of codes and coupled classes and helps produce testable codes using unit tests.

For building the software products in MIDRP, a standard structure and packaging method were devised which must be considered in the development of products to create software with high quality, testability, and proper performance. The overall structure of the MIDRP software products should consist of the following three general sections (or layers):

- *Controller*: It acts as a gateway to the business functionalities of a product. In this layer, all Service classes and Service methods that are called in the business processes are defined.
- *Business*: In this layer of the product, business rules and information flow associated with business processes are implemented. Information validation, all calculations, and data manipulations, including the creation and updating of information according to the existing business rules, are performed in this layer.
- *Repository*: This layer of the product is responsible for communicating with the DAL. All calls related to DAL and database session generation are done on this layer.

Fig. 7.7 shows the relationships and communications between the three layers. In the displayed direction of the arrows in the image, the layers are organized in such

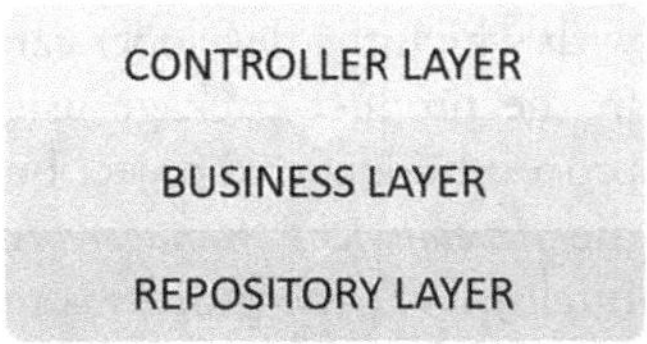

| CONTROLLER LAYER |
| BUSINESS LAYER |
| REPOSITORY LAYER |

Figure 7.7   Relationships between the three layers of a software product.

a way that the upper layers can be dependent on the lower layers. However, the opposite is not allowed. That is, the Controller layer depends on the Business and Repository layers, and the Business layer depends on the Repository layer.

In the coding environments (i.e., IntelliJ), each of the above layers is implemented as a package and inside each package, a set of generic packages are defined. This packaging structure is preserved in all products by the development teams to maintain a unified structure throughout the system. Each of these standard sub-packages can include other packages that can be defined by the product's technical manager, depending on the product features and its requirements.

7.5 Testing and Integration

After developing each software component in the MIDRP system, we needed to conduct comprehensive, standard, and efficient evaluations of built products to make sure developed software products work exactly as expected based on the specified requirements. To ensure good quality, a systematic testing procedure was designed to perform tests in developing software components in different levels of integration. The testing procedure has two main purposes: the first is to make sure that the implemented system meets the software requirements; and the second is to ensure that the software system can function well in real-world environments with different characteristics, conditions, and work time pressures considering diverse people with different abilities and skills.

As a great portion of the SDLC for the MIDRP project used the Agile approach, programming and testing the produced software components were often done concurrently. After a series of sprints have passed and some products are developed, they are tested and integrated with the MIDRP system in the production environment in the form of new version releases. The version issuance process (VIP) and integration procedures were devised meticulously in FANAP to ensure that the least amount of error caused by misconfiguration between different versions of products and infrastructure and backup systems occurs.

In this section, we first describe the testing procedure used after the development of each product or BP in the SDLC. Then, we explain the integration process for adding the new products to the production system.

7.5.1 Testing Procedure

An important part of any software development process is the testing phase where a thorough investigation must be conducted to provide stakeholders with information about the quality of the developed software product or service (Lewis, 2016). MIDRP testing procedures involve the execution of a software component or system product to evaluate if the newly developed product meets the following retirements:

■ It provides the functionality exactly according to the required specifications or user story designed for the product or system.
■ It can work and function within an acceptable time.
■ It can perform well under different circumstances and responds properly to various possible inputs.
■ It can be run and engage with other parts of the system to support the whole business requirements.

There are many perspectives on how to look at software testing. Generally, tests can be categorized as *static* and *dynamic* based on whether we simply check the source codes and review the statements or execute a generated piece of code with already defined test cases (Graham et al., 2008). In MIDRP software development, the formal testing procedure mostly has emphasized the dynamic tests with the execution of the developed products according to well-defined test scenarios and test cases. The static tests are done naturally inside development teams while coding and collaborating.

The dynamic tests designed for MIDRP products generally follow the *black box* or *specification-based* approach (Limaye, 2009) because the main focus while testing the software components is on the functional requirements defined in the user stories or test cases. This type of test does not oblige the tester to have any special programming knowledge or know the specifics of written codes. In fact, it places more emphasis on being aware of the business functions and a better understanding of the business requirement specifications.

The black-box approach usually requires thorough test cases to be provided to the tester, who then can simply verify that for a given input, the output value (or behavior), either "is" or "is not" the same as the expected value specified in the test case. Regarding the importance of the business requirements checking and strict evaluation of the products, the tests in the MIDPR project are carried out *manually* by the designated testers who are responsible to do the tests and evaluate the results according to detailed test cases.

Regardless of the type of test, there are some levels for testing depending on where, when, and/or what type of software component we perform the testing procedure. These are called the testing levels. Generally, there are four testing levels: unit testing, integration testing, system testing, and acceptance testing (Machado et al., 2010; Lewis, 2016). The testing levels in MIDRP software development were slightly modified (customized) according to the internal requirements of the quality control unit and the nature of the development modules. As a result, the quality control and test management defined four levels for testing the software products:

- *BP level*: The test includes the examination of an individual BP such as a single-step price calculation or an object configuration by executing it based on an already defined test scenario.
- *Product level*: This test includes evaluating the integration and interactions of the implemented BPs inside a particular MIDRP product. For example, the test scenario may include registering and confirming a purchase invoice, registering and confirming extra service invoices, etc.
- *Integration level*: The tests at this level involve the interactions of multiple BPs inside a product with other external products in MIDRP. For example, it can include a scenario with registering and confirming a purchase invoice.

All the tests in the above levels are performed whenever a new piece of software has been developed and the related sprint is going to be finished. It should be noted that there is a mapping between our testing levels and the common testing levels in the literature. The BP level testing corresponds to unit tests. Of course, the BP implementation codes can be divided into some smaller components, such as TPs or even the internal tasks of a TP. In the early days of the system development, when software modules were not yet so large and only a number of business processes were implemented, TP-level testing was performed. But as the system grew and more BPs were created for each product, testing all TPs became very time-consuming and costly. Therefore, the unit tests were transferred to the BP level. Testing the BP as a unit has the advantage of reflecting a business-oriented vision. In addition, if a BP test is passed successfully, it shows that its constituent units (TPs) are working well. The product level tests correspond to the integration level in the common classifications since they can test the integration of the various BPs inside a product. However, the integration level in the MIDRP tests is analogous to the *system level* testing in general because the interoperability of the BPs from different products in the system is evaluated. All of the three levels described above can be done as a *user acceptance test* whenever a new release is going to be published during the development process.

The tests are carried out according to a standard document named "Release Test Scenario and Test Cases Development Procedure" prepared by the Quality Control and Test Management unit. Based on this standard, two important documents are defined and used in the test procedures as follows:

- *Test scenario*: A high-level categorization of the basic system requirements that test important system capabilities. In fact, a test scenario determines the main and important paths in any business that represent high-level business requirements to be tested without going into details. Each scenario can be prepared for a BP or a product or an integration of products.

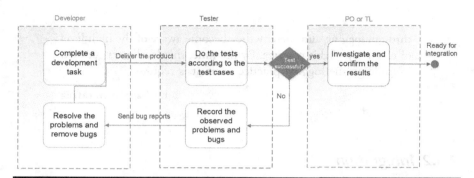

Figure 7.8   Testing procedure during a sprint.

■ *Test case*: Low-level activities that determine how tests scenario are performed. A test case is a set of steps that measure the expected outputs according to different inputs and includes the precondition, input data, and expected conditions or output data. Test cases are created in the test design phase and are strictly used as the basis for testing products by the testers. The testers are independent of the development teams and are familiar with the business processes as well as the specification of the MIDRP products.

Fig. 7.8 shows the testing procedure during one sprint in the software development process. As shown in the figure, the procedure starts when a developer (or team) completes a development task to write a piece of software and delivers the software component (which is usually a BP) to the tester. The tester will do the tests according to a set of test cases defined based on the user story. If the test is successful, both the developing task and testing task will be done and the results will be sent to the technical leader (TL) or product owner (PO) to investigate and confirm the test results. If the test is not successful, the observed bugs are recorded by the tester, and a new task is defined for the developer to remove the bugs and resolve the problem in the software code. The tester task will be in the "doing" status until the modified component is delivered by the developer.

LESSON-LEARNED 7.4

"Logging is a crucial practice for debugging within the production environment. However, production teams usually conduct debugging in the context of test-server and ignore recording the associated logs. This makes the process of problem-solving so complicated. In response, test conditions in the development environment should be simulated according to the production basis. In doing so, developers are supposed to solve the bugs

> through logging and thereby they become aware of the high level
> of efficiency of this practice. By the time, the developers get used
> to undergo the logging practice when it is required."
>
> **by Saman Sarafraz**

7.5.2 *Integration*

Integration is a very important part of the system development because the developed components are to attach to the working production system and go live. Therefore, it is imperative to carry out rigorous testing to make sure everything has been set up well and works properly. In addition, we need to ensure that all the integrated components can work together without any defect or failure so that the ERP system can serve the end users as a unified coherent system in the organization.

The integration of developed software products with the existing production system is done through the VIP. The VIP includes all the activities that integrate the final developed products in scrum sprints (when a release is complete) into the production EPR software running on the main server. In order to do this process, two separate servers are dedicated to testing the new versions of the products before they go into the production environment. The process starts when the beta version of each developed product is delivered by the development team. Then, the integration of the product's beta versions is tested on an *integration test server* and a *master* version is created if the tests are successfully passed. Next, the master version is tested on a *test server* to make sure the integrated system can work in a totally different environment. Finally, the master version will be installed and run on the *main production server* if the tests on the test server are successful.

Fig. 7.9 shows the detail of the VIP implementation. This process generally includes four distinct stages, which are described in the following sections.

7.5.2.1 *The Beta Version Release*

In this stage, the developed products are tested on the internal server by the implementation team and the Beta versions of the products are released after the PO approves the correct functionality of the product. In summary, the following activities are done:

■ The specifications of the product release and other related products as well as required infrastructure, which should be considered in the development process, is determined and finalized through the interaction of product, TL with the person in charge of the product or PO in the Agile model and the final specifications are notified to PR.

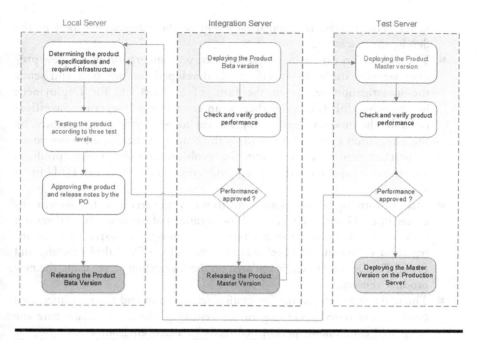

Figure 7.9 A high-level view of the version issuance process.

- The development team performs tests on the product (according to three test levels described in Section 7.5.4) to ensure the product is working correctly in the system. At this stage, all process lanes must have a syntax based on the standard charts dictated by the PO. A syntax is based on the standard chart when it uses a proper Lane ID and defines the Role & OU which are suitable for the business.
- The PO will approve the product if its performance is fully consistent with the requirements specifications and the prepared release note for the tested product is approved and documented in the task management system.
- After testing the product in the development team and confirming the product function by PO, the *beta version* of the product is released by TL to test the integrity of the product in the real environment.

7.5.2.2 Version Issuance on Integration Server

In this stage, the following activities are performed to implement the beta version on integration server:

- The PO issues a request in the task management system regarding a new update on the MIDRP system version which is running on the integration server. This request is automatically sent to the integration expert in the development team.

■ The integration expert investigates the correct integration of the new product versions using the specific tools developed for this unit and sends the investigation results in the form of a POM file for Deployment Engineering Unit (DEU). If there is an error in the integration investigations for the products before they are sent to, an error report is created by the integration expert and is sent to the sender of the original integration request to inform them about the problem aroused. Other products which can be updated without any problems should be sent to DEU in an *update list*.

■ After performing the necessary steps to set up the server, a deployment engineer in DEU sends the technical specifications of the new MIDRP version in a form called *product installation on the integration server report* to integration expert in the development team, TLs, POs, DEU officials, and PMO. Finally, the system is updated on the integration server using the new product version.

■ The updated system on the integration server is run and the new integrated products are tested according to the testing guidelines to make sure the integrated components perform correctly in a new environment.

■ The PO of each product follows the version testing on the integration server, verifies and confirms the expected operation of the product on the server. If needed the BPMN diagrams are updated by the development team.

■ If the PO does not confirm the right operation of the newly integrated product, the development team will be responsible to fix the critical bugs and resolve any disruptive issue. After fixing the bugs and updating the products the new beta version is released and a new request to place this version on the integration server will be registered in the task management system.

■ After testing the product and confirming the product operation by PO, a new master version for the product is issued by the TL. The master version is going to be installed and tested on the test server.

7.5.2.3 Version Issuance on the Test Server

The test server is a dedicated server for testing the final products located at the customer premises. It is similar to the real production server of the MIDRP and has the complete ERP modules which have been developed so far. It is the ultimate place to test the products before they go live and be used by the end users. So, it is critical that everything is carefully observed and evaluated before they are finally installed in the production environment. In order to place the master version on the test server, the following steps are taken:

- Similar to the previous stage, the PO sends a request in the task management system regarding a new update on the MIDRP system version which is running on the test server. This request is automatically sent to the Integration expert in the development team.
- The integration expert receives and checks the request forms for installing the master versions on the test server from the DEU, investigates the correct integration of the new product versions and sends the result back in the form of a POM file to DEU.
- If there is no problem about the integration, the necessary measures to set up the test server are performed *separately* for each company by the deployment engineers and all interested stakeholders are informed. The product is then installed on the test server.
- After launching the test server, for each company, the end user support specialist in each site configures settings of the new installed version in accordance with the site condition (including approval cycle, necessary changes in BPMN Lane syntaxes, and so on).
- After configuring the products settings, the functional tests are performed in the testing environment by the user support team and the results are presented to the process support team. Then, the testing results are sent to the PO.
- In this step, the PO will check the test report and if all the functionalities are consistent with the specifications, then he or she confirms the correct operation of the master version. If the software does not work properly, the issues and bugs will be deleted and the development team will take the steps to fix the critical bugs and create another beta version. The beta version then undergoes the process described in stage 2. Most of the time bugs are not critical and can be removed fast. In such cases, there is no need for another Beta version and the current fixed version is sent to the testing environment.

7.5.2.4 Version Issuance on the Production Server

After confirming the master version on the test server, the necessary coordination is made between the process support team, the deployment team and other stakeholders for installing the new master version on the main production server. The following steps are taken for the final deployment:

- After necessary coordination, the deployment managers provide the permit for running the master version on the production server. The TL controls the update checklist for issuing the master version on the production server.
- The request for installing the master version on the production is sent by PO to the integration expert in the development team.
- The integration expert investigates the correct integration of the new product versions and sends the result back to DEU in the form of a POM file so that the master version is prepared to be installed on the main production server.

- If there is no problem about the integration, the necessary measures to set up the main server are performed separately for each company by the deployment engineers, and all interested stakeholders are informed. The product is then installed on the test server. The steps to setup the production server are performed according to the approved *process for installing and running a product on the test and production server.*
- After launching the production server, for each company, the end user support specialist in each site configures settings of the new installed version in accordance with the site condition (including approval cycle, necessary changes in BPMN Lane syntaxes, and so on).
- If some critical errors are observed when the main server is working with the master version, a report is sent to the PO regarding the bugs and issues so that the problems are resolved, and a new beta version is issued by the development team.

In this chapter, we described the completion phase of the design and development of the MIDRP project. We stated different stages of the MIDRP products design phase as well as the most important concepts and the principle of the design activities. The development phase included many activities for implementing the business processes and product specifications. The in-house built development platform significantly assisted the development and brought flexibility, customization, and localization advantages into the development process. The rigorous testing procedure adopted for verifying the MIDRP software products ensures that all the developed components have been built according to the specifications and can integrate well with the rest of the system. After the system is correctly developed according to the customer requirements and specifications, it is now time to put it into operation by the integration and deployment process. In the next two chapters, we describe how the MIDRP modules are integrated to make the whole system and how to deploy the system in the real-world business environment.

Notes

1. Specific, measurable, attainable, realistic, time bound.
2. The names of the platform components have been chosen based on the ancient Persian names. For example, "Daiva" means the God of Gods.
3. Software products are any software components that are developed according to design specifications and should not be confused with the MIDRP products or modules.

References

Ambler, S. (2002). *Agile modeling: Effective practices of extreme programming and the unified process.* John Wiley & Sons.

Anadea. (2020). Available at https://anadea.info/blog/erp-and-business-management-software-introduction

Batini, C., Ceri, S., & Navathe, S. B. (1992). *Conceptual database design: An entity-relationship approach* (Vol. 116). Redwood City, CA: Benjamin/Cummings.

Chen, P. P. S. (2011). The entity-relationship model (reprinted historic data). In *Handbook of conceptual modeling* (pp. 57–84). Berlin, Heidelberg: Springer.

CioIndex. (2020). Available at https://cio-wiki.org/wiki/Business_Process_Engine (BPE).

Clockwise Official Website. (2020). How to build an ERP system from scratch. Available at https://clockwise.software/blog/how-to-build-erp-system/

Foster, E. (2014). *Software engineering: A methodical approach*. Apress.

Fowler, M. (2002). *Patterns of enterprise application architecture*. Addison-Wesley Longman Publishing Co., Inc.

Graham, D., Van Veenendaal, E., & Evans, I. (2008). *Foundations of software testing* (pp. 57–58). Cengage Learning.

Innovative. (2020). Available at https://www.innovativearchitects.com/KnowledgeCenter/basic-IT-systems/system-development-life-cycle.aspx

JetBrain. (2020). Available at https://www.jetbrains.com/idea/

Langer, A. M. (2016). *Guide to software development—Designing and managing the life cycle*. 2nd edition. London: Springer-Verlag.

Lewis, W. E. (2016). *Software testing and continuous quality improvement*. 3rd edition (pp. 92–96). CRC Press.

Limaye, M. G. (2009). Software Testing. Tata McGraw-Hill Education, https://books.google.com/books?id=VSR2rLJdaF4C.

Machado, P., Vincenzi, A., & Maldonado, J. C. (2010). Chapter 1: Software testing: An overview. In P. Borba, A. Cavalcanti, A. Sampaio, & J. Woodcook (Eds.), *Testing techniques in software engineering* (pp. 13–14). Springer Science & Business Media.

Marsic, I. (2012). *Software engineering, rutgers*. The State University of New Jersey.

Mehta, V. P. (2008). Getting started with object-relational mapping. *Pro LINQ Object Relational Mapping with C#*, *2008*, 3–15.

Millington, S. (2019). Available at https://www.baeldung.com/solid-principles

Motiwalla, L. F., & Thompson, J. (2012). *Enterprise systems for management* (p. 245). Boston, MA: Pearson.

Murch, R. (2012). *The software development lifecycle: A complete guide*. Richard Murch.

Olivé, A. (2007). *Conceptual modeling of information systems*. Springer Science & Business Media.

Open Group. (2016). Available at https://publications.opengroup.org/w169

Reshetilo, K. (2018). How to build a custom ERP system: The 8 step guide. Greenice Official Website. Available at https://greenice.net/develop-custom-erp-software-8-step-guide-business-owner

Rashid, M. A., Hossain, L., & Patrick, J. D. (2002). The evolution of ERP systems: A historical perspective. In *Enterprise resource planning: solutions and management* (pp. 35–50). IGI Global.

SDCR-Top Software Development Companies. (2020). 10 best practices for developing enterprise software applications. Available at https://www.softwaredevelopmentcompany.co/blog/best-practices-developing-enterprise-software-applications/

Sherman, R. (2014). Foundational data modeling. In *Business intelligence guidebook: From data integration to analytics*. Newnes.

Sommerville, I. (2016). *Software engineering*. 10th edition. Harlow: Pearson Education.

Sparks Systems. (2020). Available at https://sparxsystems.com/products/ea/. Top of Form Bottom of Form.

Sumner, M. (2014). *Enterprise resource planning*. Pearson Education.

Tabbaa, B. (2017). Principles, practices, and proverbs of enterprise software development. *ITNext website*. Available at https://itnext.io/principles-and-practices-of-sdlc-5ea8b026b47d

Webcase. (2020). Available at https://webcase.studio/blog/how-create-your-own-erp-software/

Womack, J.P., & Jones, D.T. (1997). Lean Thinking—Banish Waste and Create Wealth in your Corporation. *Simon and Schuster*. https://books.google.com/books?id=2eWHaAyiNrgC.

Chapter 8

Integration

> *"The axiom of integration has been the top priority of MIDHCO since the inception of the MIDRP project."*
>
> —**Mohammad Jafar Ekramjafari**, *CEO Consultant of MIDHCO Co.*

Through sticking to the delineated storyline, one can grasp that the required pieces of the MIDRP development have been put together one by one. Meanwhile, there is a piece of the puzzle that works as an intermediary one which is called integration. As long as the integration piece of the jigsaw has not fallen into the right place, the preceding efforts seem meaningless, and thereby MIDHCO would go back to the era of possessing multiple isolated systems. The current chapter is to highlight the endeavor of the involved parties toward realizing the purpose of integration. The proposed mission inclines the executive character to integrate not only the product groups but also the operational systems of MIDHCO into the body of MIDRP. In the next sections, the adopted mechanism for satisfying the desirable level of integration is explained.

8.1 Overview

A custom ERP system is going to be used in an organization where many other information systems and software applications are running. In order to get the benefits of ERP systems, an organization needs to integrate its ERP system with other existing enterprise systems. Successful implementation of ERP depends on how this centralized system is integrated with other existing systems to improve business operations performance and ensure that consistent information is shared while automating workflows. ERP integration can be defined as the process of designing,

DOI: 10.1201/9781003369806-8

testing, and deploying automated business processes by orchestrating connections between the sub-processes of an ERP system and the sub-processes of other enterprise software applications, web applications, content tools, email/communication systems, social media, and human workflow (Srivatsan, 2019; Johnson, 2010). The integration allows different organizational units to have access to the data and information available in other units that might be needed for their operation.

ERP integration is the key to running a successful business. The business process improvement and operational performance are achieved only when other information systems in the organization, which might be legacy systems, such as old databases or sales order gateways, or modern enterprise applications such as m-commerce, social media tools, or business intelligence platforms, can be connected efficiently to ERP in order to communicate with its various modules. Flexible and efficient communications with ERP can help us streamline the whole organization's processes, augment the information flow in the organization, access data in real-time, reduce human errors, and decrease labor work (Jenkins, 2019; Rosencrance, 2019). It also often helps elevate collaboration among business employees and improve the transparency of activities (Srivatsan, 2019).

Despite all the efforts made in designing and developing a custom ERP such as MIDRP, its tremendous benefits are not evident until we implement it with a correct integration methodology. Therefore, we need to understand the communication needs throughout the organization's processes, software, and platforms, and find an effective strategy to integrate the ERP with the rest of the organization. Integration in MIDRP is important in two aspects: (a) Implementing integrated processes in the system; (b) implementing the integration of the system modules with the business and operational environment. It is critical that business processes in each product are analyzed, modeled, and implemented while considering their interaction and integration as a whole. This means that for each business process model, the incoming messages and information from other business processes as well as its outgoing messages and information to other processes must be accurately defined according to the requirements and best practices in ERP integration. The information and messages that are communicated between business processes must also be implemented properly in the software development phase. Furthermore, for the system design, it is necessary to define the data models in each product according to the identified business objects in the analysis phase. The product design should be done with a comprehensive vision of the integration with other products and processes so that the deficiencies in message passing and information communicated in the system are eliminated.

In this chapter, we first take a look at the most important concepts related to ERP integration, such as integration benefits, common integration types as well as the challenges we face when integrating the ERP with the rest of the organization. We also provide an overview of the most prevalent approaches to implementing ERP integration and the best practices that might help the best implementation of ERP integration. Next, we explain the integration solution provided for the

MIDRP project, the different levels of integration, and the important cases in the integration of the MIDRP with the rest of the organization.

8.2 Background of ERP Integration

Integrating an ERP system with other information systems and applications, such as CRM, HR, and e-commerce systems ensures that data from these applications remain updated in the ERP system. The ERP functions as a single source of truth for a variety of workflows, making it easier to share data and insights across business units. In a nutshell, ERP integration can bring the following benefits to an organization. In fact, ERP integration helps companies streamline their business processes across various departments and workflows, enabling them to operate more efficiently by helping to eliminate human error (Srivatsan, 2019). Moreover, a good integration helps to provide the availability of data in real-time and increases the accuracy of operations through right and error-free data sharing and flexible collaboration (Jenkins, 2019). Integrating all enterprise systems also helps elevate collaboration among business employees and improve the transparency of activities. Additionally, by automating the data transfers between systems, ERP integration would eliminate a great part of manual data entry which is time-consuming and error-prone. This capability frees a lot of time and energy which may be spent on other useful business operations (Johnson, 2010). Furthermore, integrating ERP with the organization's primary business tools, such as project management, enables the centralization of work-related data and helps to better visualize workflows. This will allow employees to see what their peers are working on. It can be beneficial when requesting feedback from a fellow employee or assigning a priority level of tasks and schedule processes (Jenkins, 2019; Miller, 2019).

8.2.1 Most Common ERP Integrations

Depending on the type of business operations, the scope of business activities, and the expected functionalities in an organization, an ERP system may be integrated with numerous possible enterprise systems or software applications. Common ERP integrations with enterprise systems and applications are as follows:

- **ERP-CRM:** Organizations can gain a considerable advantage over their rivals with excellent customer service. Therefore, optimizing their customer communication with a "best of breed" customer relationship management tool is crucial. For this reason, CRM and ERP integration is relatively common and therefore can be one of the most important categories to integrate (Srivatsan, 2019). Integrating a CRM application with an ERP system is highly recommended since there is a critical link between demand (CRM) and supply (ERP). This connection between CRM and ERP is used to streamline the marketing and sales process.

■ **ERP-PoS:** Although processing sales orders from their customers is a regular task in ERP systems, many manufacturers and service providers may have established "trade counters" or deports where customers (trade or retail) can visit. While sales order processing functionality can be quite sophisticated within their main ERP system, something much simpler is sufficient frequently for point of sales (PoS) systems. Therefore, it is usually preferred to implement simplified order entry routines that simultaneously create a dispatch note and invoice, down-date stock, and perhaps even accept payment, all in the same transaction. Then this information is transferred to ERP sales and financial modules for sophisticated processing.

■ **ERP-MES:** The primary function of manufacturing execution systems (MES), also known as shop floor control systems, is to collect production progress data and transmit it, in near real-time, back to the ERP system (ERP Focus, 2020). Depending on the manufacturing environment, monitoring and recording resource usage (both time and materials) and quality data may also be done with these systems. The captured data needs to be fed into the ERP system for evaluation and planning.

■ **ERP-BI:** Business intelligence (BI) software often gives an insight into the business data which can be the launching point for new software implementations. By integrating BI systems with an ERP solution, these valuable insights become easy to access at any time by any authorized employee.

■ **ERP-Project Management:** Project management integration with ERP is so useful because all business tasks, processes, and workflows in an organization can be aggregated in one place. There would be a greater degree of transparency in the project's information (Jenkins, 2019). For example, employees and project managers can see which projects are done, which are in progress, who's working on them, and what projects are coming up at any time. This can significantly help reduce the time spent on project management tasks.

■ **ERP-e-Commerce:** Any business that manages orders can benefit from integrating e-commerce applications largely because of the data collection associated with implementation. Integrating an ERP system with the e-commerce store ensures that data is available to all members of the company who need to work on fulfilling a requirement that arises in the e-commerce store (Srivatsan, 2019). Some of the most essential data that companies collect are related to orders, inventories, customer information, and shipping. When this data is available across the entire enterprise systems, a higher level of efficiency is ensured, the data transfer process is automated and the need for any manual input is eliminated.

■ **ERP-CAD systems:** Computer-aided design (CAD) systems help product designers in the creation, modification, analysis, or optimization of a design (Narayan, 2008). These systems produce and hold information about the materials that go into a particular product. This is just the information that is needed in the ERP system's bill of materials module. Therefore, it is advantageous to connect CAD systems with ERP software so that the data can be transmitted electronically in a flexible manner.

▪ **ERP-External systems:** Integration requirements can be expanded outside of an organization. As an example, our customers may want to send a high volume of orders and expect a quick turnaround. Then, we need to automatically integrate the customer orders channel with our internal ERP order fulfillment systems. We may also want to connect our ERP system to our supplier's ERP so that the purchasing and material delivery processes are automated between the two companies. This is a great capability if implemented correctly using proper integration technologies (Jenkins, 2019). One common cause of ERP integration with external systems is third-party logistics (3PL) systems where a company decides to contract specialist organizations to deliver their products to the customers on their behalf because they realize that such companies can do these tasks more efficiently at that even allowing for reasonable profit (ERP Focus, 2020). In such a case, an integration solution is provided to create data exchange between the company's internal ERP and 3PL system. The 3PL system needs delivery details and normally also shipment dimensions and weight, whilst the ERP system usually receives back a shipment tracking number.

8.2.2 Integration Challenges

Despite all the benefits that ERP integration brings to organizations, the complexity of integration possibilities among enterprise systems along with the fast change in technology always creates big challenges during integration projects. These challenges might hinder the great efforts of integration project managers. In this section we mention some of the most important challenges posed by ERP integration (Jenkins, 2019; Rosencrance, 2019; Stackpole, 2013). Actually, ERP integration needs the support of a coherent strategy. Deciding on an ERP integration solution is an important implementation choice. To determine which software application will be most effective for integration with ERP, it's essential to first consider how the business operates and determine on which points of the business operations there is a need for integration. Defining ERP integration goals is the first and most important step. ERP improvement effects on the organization's business processes are significant only when it is integrated correctly with the rest of the systems. Maintenance and updating of ERP integration is also a challenging issue. Depending on the ERP integration method that is used in a company, there is always a need for maintaining and updating the implementation framework. For example, if a point-to-point integration mechanism is implemented, you will likely need to upgrade and change the structure as new subsystems are added or any existing one is removed. This would likely include an associated cost for updating the applications and is an important factor to keep in mind when selecting an integration approach.

Notably, it can be difficult and costly to integrate legacy applications. There might be some legacy applications in any company which have been in use for many years and cannot be upgraded or replaced by new applications for many technological, cost, and managerial reasons. While in most cases the integration of these applications with ERP would bring a lot of benefits, the challenge is that these applications were not designed to integrate with other platforms. There are middleware software solutions available that can deal with some of the issues, but they can be costly and require huge amounts of customization and manual processes. Meanwhile, Structural and technological heterogeneity imposes intensive planning and development. ERP Systems are usually designed to be deployed on a specific software platform or environment such as J2EE or.NET and run on a specific operating system. However, successful integration of enterprise applications needs to build solutions to enable all systems, including our ERP, to work with all major computing environments and operating systems including Windows, Linux, UNIX, and even IBM i. Designing such assorted integrated solutions for the enterprise needs careful planning and intensive development processes. However, the results would be very beneficial and transformative. Another fact is associated with the lack of sufficient expertise and skills. Today, not only do enterprises have to integrate their ERPs with their internal systems, such as information systems and data centers, but also they should consider a wide variety of external systems and technologies such as mobile platforms and cloud-based applications, which are provided by different vendors. Encountering this challenge requires a specific set of skills, as well as an understanding of the integration process. An organization's internal staff may not possess these skills or knowledge.

8.2.3 Approaches to ERP Integration

Implementing an ERP integration can be done in different approaches. However, the best ERP system integration option for a company depends on the specific business operations and can be influenced by factors such as the currently existing systems, available budget, and whether they use on-premise software, a cloud-based solution, or some hybrid of both. In the following, we describe different approaches to integrating ERP systems with the rest of the software systems in the organization.

In a point-to-point integration, each software or tool is separately connected to the ERP system (Linthicum, 2000). As an example, an organization may need to update a human resources database with information from an ERP system. The difficulty with this method is that you have to conduct a specific communication channel separately for each system that you wish to connect (Miller, 2019). Additionally, the data schema and information formats in any individual system must be translated into acceptable formats defined in the ERP system so that they can be processed correctly and efficiently. This process can become complicated quickly as more and more tools are added. Even in simple scenarios, such as integrating a storefront website into ERP, we see there are multiple reception points within the ERP (e.g., inventory management, accounting, shipment schedule). Since the information must be transmitted from ERP to the storefront, we need to create additional transmission channels. However, the point-to-point approach makes it easy for companies to start integration because it has a reasonably low barrier to entry. Many of the complexities surrounding point-to-point integrations between ERP and best-of-breed systems have been mitigated thanks to technologies such as Web services (Stackpole, 2013). In addition, ERP vendors are fine-tuning their platforms and integration strategies to better support a heterogeneous environment.

Another common approach for implementing an integrated ERP is to build customized applications or *adapters* to integrate various business tools. Custom applications often include solutions for data transfer, but they may be expanded to support more tasks and workflows. In most ERP systems, there exists a library of predefined connections that allows programmers to write customized applications to connect to the ERP system while preserving all the validation and data control rules intact. This approach brings similar issues to the organization as point-to-point integration since it can be challenging to maintain the integrated structure as the company grows and more software tools add to its business operations infrastructure.

As an example, Infor Company offers a middleware cloud platform called *Infor Intelligent Open Network*, which enables companies to integrate their third-party enterprise system (Infor, 2018). Oracle offers a large library of adapters under the umbrella of the *Oracle Integration Platform* (Oracle, 2020) to provide companies with a standardized way to rapidly connect the various protocols required by each application vendor. There are numerous application adapters for ERPs (SAP, ERP Cloud, NetSuite, and JD Edwards), CX (oracle cloud service connectivity), HCM, e-commerce, and databases (Oracle DB, MySQL, MS SOL Server, IBM DB2). It also offers connectivity adapters for productivity, social, and Robotic Process Automation (RPA). Also, in order to connect to applications for which there is no specific adapter, the Oracle Integration Platform provides *Technology Adapters* to offer connectivity through standard technologies such as FTP, JMS, REST, and SOAP.

SAP provides a mechanism called remote function call (RFC) for interfacing communications between different SAP solutions (Mereddy, 2012). Each RFC involves an RFC client and an RFC server. The RFC server provides functional modules. RFC clients call one of the functional modules, pass on the data, and get a reply (value) back from the RFC server.

Electronic data interchange (EDI) is the automated, electronic exchange of business documents, such as purchase orders and invoices, in a standardized format between the software systems of trading partners (Cancilla, 2017). EDI is a communication technology that can be used as another type of integration. Common components of an EDI infrastructure include data translation and mapping software, communications, and specialized IT people (Arcesb, 2020). EDI can be implemented and maintained in-house or by using an EDI service provider. It is a well-proven standard method that can be used as an integration link between systems within a business as well. In an EDI integration framework, the sending system sends an EDI message to the receiving system, which receives and processes that message accurately. The messages can be sent automatically using pre-configured workflows. EDI might not be the newest technology, but it can serve well since it replaces paper-based processes and ensures both sender and recipient speak the same digital data language. This way many workflows and business operations can be integrated with ERP subsystems.

The Link Enabling/Electronic Data Interchange (ALE/EDI) capability provided by SAP is an EDI-based solution for SAP-to-SAP business data exchange (ALE) and SAP-to-other systems business data exchange (EDI) (Mereddy, 2012). The basis of this communication mechanism is the Intermediate Documents (IDOC). An IDOC acts as a data container facilitating the exchange of business information between SAP systems and non-SAP systems. IDOCs are generated using *message types*. Message types identify the usage of specific business data.

An Enterprise Service Bus (ESB) is a centralized middleware with a distributed messaging engine for managing the communication of heterogeneous systems throughout an organization (Hohpe & Woolf, 2004). It is considered the latest and greatest technology for enterprise application integration. In many cases, an ESB is the best choice to integrate an ERP into enterprise systems in a scalable, flexible, and future-proof way (Johnson, 2010). In an ESB, applications are connected asynchronously by a "communication medium" which is called Bus. Two systems can communicate with each other through "messages." The ESB provides capabilities for different individual systems to put each of their requests as a message. The ESB then "translates" that message into an acceptable format for the intended destination system. The receiving system can "hear" the message and understand its meaning.

An ESB can route messages between various systems when there are many systems in the environment. It will resolve any disagreement among those services related to particular messages. The ESB can handle data transformation, error and exception controls, queuing and sequencing, and enforce proper quality of messaging between systems. The advantage of doing integration this way is that other applications don't have to be modified when another component is added. The bus provides standard connectors and gateways to facilitate centralized communications. This is a more straightforward process than using custom applications or point-to-point integration.

There are several key benefits provided by ESB regarding ERP integration (Mulesoft, 2020; Hohpe & Woolf, 2004). Integration can begin by establishing the connections of some core applications. When a new application needs to be integrated with the systems, the only thing that must be done is to create a connection to the Bus infrastructure and configure its parameters. Moreover, ESB's modular design offers unique flexibility and allows for incremental adoption as resources become available. This guarantees that unexpected needs in the future will not prevent the return on investment. Furthermore, the individual components in an ESB offer separate features. This makes ESB integration much simpler and more cost-effective to ensure high availability and scalability for critical parts of the architecture. With an ESB, there is no need for coding integration solutions. Rather, we can configure the Bus to manage our communications with ERP provided that the software application has the standard capabilities required in the Bus (Johnson, 2010).

SAP Process Integration (SAP PI) is intended as a proprietary integration hub for all of the organization's information systems (Mereddy, 2012). PI includes several features with service-oriented architecture capabilities and is well-positioned to standardize and optimize all of the enterprise interface requirements. It avoids point-to-point interface connections and uses native integration capabilities between different SAP solutions, which helps reduce integration costs in a client's landscape. SAP PI provides SOA tools for facilitating organizations to build and consume enterprise services.

Despite all the benefits of ESB in an ERP integration, it is worth noticing that the ESB can set up a single point of failure bringing down all systems. ESBs are also quite complex and require a high degree of maintenance to keep the configurations operating at an optimal level. At this time, most ESB software is expensive and used primarily by large businesses with a high volume of communication to be integrated. Smaller and mid-sized businesses might not have the resources required to employ an ESB.

Most enterprise solutions today, including ERPs, offer a library of APIs (application programming interfaces). APIs are a set of clearly defined methods of communication with a software system at the programming level. A good API makes it easier to develop a computer program by providing all the necessary building blocks. Simply put, APIs define the way any software program can access and interact with an ERP system. An API will include data structures, specifications for methods and objects, and other components necessary to communicate with that system. The desired communications are made possible and enhanced when programmers develop programs to match the ERP system's API with an API of the other system that is to integrate with ERP. In this method, there is still a custom integration, but now the development of that integration is much simpler and we ensure that all the rules regarding the communications and data transfer with both systems are considered. Nowadays, many enterprise systems offer RESTful APIs which allow programmers to simply develop applications for data extraction and communication with the system. (Sapphireone, 2019).

8.2.4 Best Practices

Correct implementation of an ERP integration with the rest of the organization's system is the key to success. However, integration is increasingly challenging for today's organizations since they have many different applications and customize software from a variety of vendors. To overcome the challenges of ERP integration and ensure a successful implementation for the organization, the ERP participants must consider using the best practices in this area. Here we introduce some of the best practices and helpful methods that successful integration will benefit from (Johnson, 2010; Pierson, 2015; Hale, 2019; Rosencrance, 2019).

Implement integration points incrementally. Since the ERP integrations are complex and there might be little bandwidth in the organization, it is good to think scientifically and change one thing at a time, then observe the results. The possible issues should be removed and only when you can declare that integration is complete, move on to the next integration project. A business case should be built for integration. The ERP-project management needs to know what the integration will look like, where is the scope of integration and whether it's worth the effort. A comprehensive business case should identify who is going to be affected by an integration, how that integration is going to benefit the end user, and how much time/money/effort that integration is going to save each quarter.

Plan integration points define the desired outcome and set specific, measurable goals for each integration point. SMART goals should be a part of any project, but since you will be integrating as a series of integration projects, you should have goals for each one. For each integration point, you need to define the source (where the data is coming from), target (where the data is going), data direction (one-way, two-way), and the frequency of integration run (real-time, hourly, nightly, on-demand). Note that, a consistent integration process should be done over time. After the first couple of integrations, you should have an integration process that will be the framework for your ongoing integration projects. Create a balance between Fine-Grained and Coarse-Grained Adapters is also of paramount importance. It is very important that your selected ERP integration solution has the technology adapters needed to support your integration needs. This means in most cases much more than supporting connections to databases and web services. Look closely to see if the solution selected has support for communication protocols, file systems, encryption/decryption, networking, and other lower level more finely-grained technology that will allow you to assemble the needed integration without resorting to programming interfaces yourself for those technologies.

A loosely coupled architecture is suggested. The integration architecture should allow us to make flexible and easy changes to any one component without the need for making changes to many other dependent components. In addition, for ERP integration, it is important to maintain ERP sources and third-party destinations separately (and vice-versa). With a loosely coupled architecture, we can implement independent components that can operate together independently. A loosely coupled architecture lets us replace or modify components without having to make reflective changes to the other components. Using stateless and dynamic components is another essential factor. A stateless component is a software component that permits more than one instance of the component to be in use simultaneously and with separate states. As ERP systems need to be able to perform multiple simultaneous transactions at any point in time, using stateless components brings many benefits in terms of scalable ERP integration and is vital to a robust implementation of service-oriented architecture. Dynamic components allow us to modify and refresh their configuration to change the operation of any related subsystem in the target integrated environment. The use of dynamic components in our integration framework will bring flexibility and ease of configuration to the entire business environment.

8.3 MIDRP Integration

In this section, we discuss how the MIDRP system integration solution was implemented so that it can work as a unified ERP system and communicate effectively with the rest of the business operations of the organization. Integration practices in the MIDRP project can be discussed from two different perspectives: integration of MIDRP subsystems together (products and business processes) as well as integration of MIDRP subsystems with other operational systems in the organization.

8.3.1 Integration of MIDRP Subsystems

As mentioned in Chapter 3 (MIDRP) and Chapter 6 (analysis) the MIDRP system is a large process-oriented enterprise system which is more than a classic ERP system. It includes 13 Product groups (ERP Modules) with 36 products (as subsystems in the ERP modules). Each product can run a number of business processes that satisfy the requirements of a specific business area. It is natural that the business processes inside each product need to communicate with each other and share their data and information as necessary. On the other hand, the ERP system covers many business units throughout the MIDHCO holding and it is critical for it to span the business process automation of the whole organizational operations. Therefore, the different products and even different product groups may need to integrate to share their data and communicate their information in order to coordinate their functions and streamline business process automation across the whole organization. For example, when implementing a master production schedule in accompany, the Inventory and Warehouse Management (IWS) from SCM Module, Production Planning (PMP) from MFG Module, and Quality Control (QCS) from the QMS module need to cooperate and communicate effectively.

The integration of MIDRP subsystems has been basically implemented with a *process-oriented approach* using *messages and services*. It is devised mostly in the business and system analysis phase (Chapter 6). Integration in the system analysis is a two-way procedure. In order to achieve a good integration between two different products, it is imperative to align the analytic visions of the two product owners whose products need to communicate with each other. In any integration case, there should be a specific method that depends on the nature of the business processes and the software design issues. Obtaining good results depends on frequent joint meetings and analytical discussions. The FANAP approach to integration analysis of ERP modules dictates that in the business processes definition and modeling stage, the messages and information transferred between the business processes from different products be analyzed and incorporated into the BPMN processes models and recorded into the Document Content Management System (DCM) of the MIDRP project. Then, in order to finalize the integration cases in both products, a series of the meeting are held with the participation of associated product owners, the system analysis unit management (as the MIDRP integration supervisor), and a representative from the project management to examine and approve the details of integration method, communication points, the type of messages and their content, as well as the delivery schedule for the final documents. Eventually, the integration cases between each business process from a product and other business processes throughout the MIDRP system are described, discussed, and approved in the expertise meetings associated with the corresponding product with the participation of product owners in FANAP, the MIDHCO representatives, and an expert from POSCO ICT (as the project supervisor). Whenever a change in the ERP system integration was requested by the customer, the suggested changes are discussed in the expertise meetings and the decisions about the new integration cases are made.

The Big Pictures, which have been described in Chapter 6 (Business and System Analysis) have an important role in presenting a comprehensive vision of the integration points and mechanisms in the MIDRP system with different levels of detail. The Big Pictures can show the information and messages that are communicated among different processes, products, and modules within the MIDRP system. There are four views for depicting a Big Picture each of which focuses on a different integration level:

- The **satellite view** considers a high level of MIDRP system and shows the conceptual relationships between the product groups (ERP modules).
- The **bird's eye view** depicts the total integration of the MIDRP focusing on the product communications between different products (ERP module subsystems) throughout the whole MIDRP system.
- The **human view** is provided separately for each product and shows the integration points of the product with the rest of the system by displaying communications between the product and other products from within or outside its product group.
- The **magnified view** is provided separately for each product and displays the interactions of the business processes of the product with other business processes inside and outside of the product. Therefore, this view shows the integration points at the business process level.

As an example, to show the integration at the analysis phase, we present the integration of the *Manufacturing Management (MFG)* module in the MIDRP system. This module (product group) provides effective management of the organization's production processes, using comprehensive production system configuration, product production planning optimal machine scheduling, and production control. With the integration of the Manufacturing Execution System (MES) in the MFG with the process control system, real-time data from the Programmable Logic Controller (PLC) equipment of the production lines is exchanged between the two subsystems. Using this module, operating managers are always allowed to make decisions and issue orders to the production lines according to up-to-date information.

Fig. 8.1 shows the human view of the Manufacturing Engineering (MET) product in the MFG module. As can be seen, the Production Planning subsystem sends the information regarding the new product to the Manufacturing Engineering to build the new products. Fig. 8.2 shows more details of the business processes in the

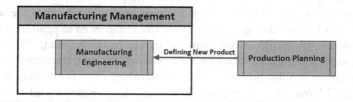

Figure 8.1   Human view of manufacturing engineering from MFG module.

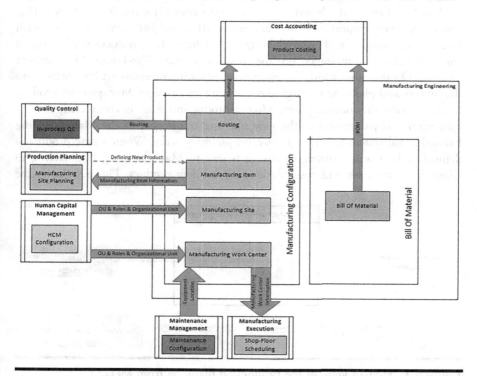

Figure 8.2   Magnified view of manufacturing engineering from MFG module.

Manufacturing of Engineering products using a magnified view. The communications and data exchanges between the business processes of this product with other business processes have been depicted. It can be seen that the relationship between Manufacturing Engineering and Production Planning subsystems is established by the two business processes respectively: *manufacturing items* and *manufacturing site planning*. When a new item is planned to be built in the Production Planning product or a new order comes from a customer, the Manufacturing site planning BP sends a manufacturing order to the manufacturing item BP as a new product definition. After the manufacturing engineers design the new item, the manufacturing item BP sends the information related to the item specifications to the Manufacturing site planning BP to plan for the production. The manufacturing work center BP in the Manufacturing Engineering product receives the service for the information about the equipment and machinery needed to produce a particular item from the maintenance configuration in the MTC product. After the work centers specifications are specified by the engineers, the manufacturing work center BP will send the specifications as a service to the Shop Floor Scheduling in the MES product the Manufacturing Engineering also exchanges necessary information with other products of the MIDRP system including Cost Accounting, Quality Control, Human Capital Management, and Maintenance Management.

Fig. 8.3 displays the human view of Production Planning inside MFG. This product is a very important subsystem in the MFG and has communications with several other products. The availability of the items for production planning is checked with the messages on the Inventory and Warehouse Management Product. On the other hand, the production planning needs to get information on the budget and planning through the Planning and Budget Management product to define new production plans. After a production plan is completed, the information and parameters of the new plan are transferred to the Manufacturing Execution subsystem as a new *production planning order*. When a new product is defined to be manufactured, a message is sent to Manufacturing Engineering to show the parameters and specifications of the new product. Fig. 8.4 shows the

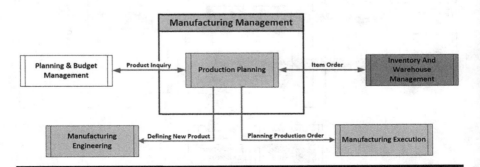

Figure 8.3 Human view of the production planning from MFG.

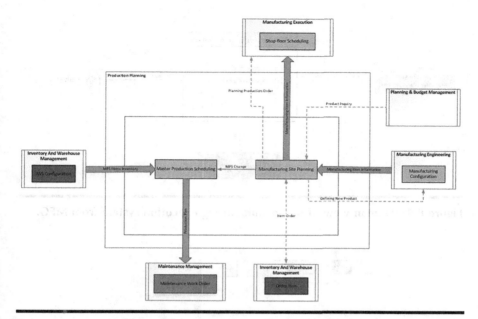

Figure 8.4 Magnified view of production planning from MFG.

details of the production planning integration with the rest of the MIDRP products with the focus on business processes that exchange the necessary information.

The manufacturing Execution System (MES) is one important product of MIDRP which provides many critical features for the manufacturing of the products in a plant. This subsystem issues a production schedule for each product and schedules, it separately for each operation per shift. It also reserves inventory automatically to order production based on the initial quantity required. Recording production performance and reporting various work centers, including information on production values, raw material consumption values, and energy carriers is another important feature of this product. Fig. 8.5 shows a human view big picture for MES and its communication with other products of the system. To provide the expected features, this product needs to communicate with Inventory and Warehouse Management, Production Planning, and Quality Control. Fig. 8.6 shows a human view big picture for MES and its communication with other products of the system. The business processes that exchange information and messages to provide the complete functionality of this product are depicted. A major part of communications is done by the *production control* business process because this process is responsible to control the production of the items, their quality, inventory, and scheduling as well as recording the production performance and creating many reports on the different aspects of the production.

As an integration scenario, we describe the message-based process-oriented integration mechanism between the subsystems of Manufacturing Management (MFG), Supply Chain Management (SCM), and Quality Management (QMS)

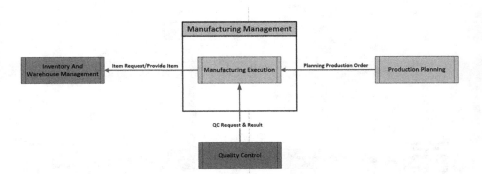

Figure 8.5 Human view of the manufacturing execution system from MFG.

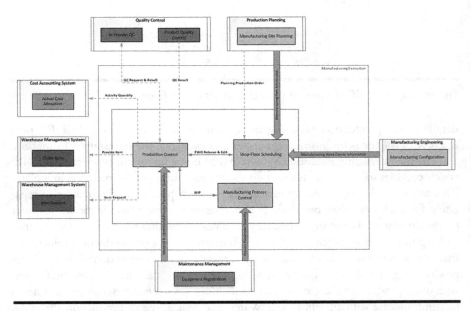

Figure 8.6 Magnified view of the manufacturing execution system from MFG.

modules. This integration is very important for Master Production Schedule in MIDHCO plants.

When creating a Master Production Schedule (MPS), the inventory of each item in the MPS at the beginning of the period is sent from the inventory and warehouse management (IWS) subsystem in SCM to the Production Planning (PMP) in MFG. As can be seen in Fig. 8.4, the *master production scheduling* business process receives such information from IWS. After the master production schedule is created for each company and the production plan is developed for each manufacturing site by the *manufacturing site planning* process, a "planned production order" is created in accordance with the amount of the planned production for each product at each site and for each time bucket. This order is sent to the *shop floor scheduling* process in the MES subsystem. In addition, information related to material requirements, operational parameters, utilized capacity of machinery, process parameters, and the specifications of the main products and by-products is sent to the MES. Concurrently, for each planned production order, a message is sent to IWS (the item order message) to increase the programmable item inventory in the associated warehouse at the end of the production time buckets with the same amount that has been determined in the planned production order.

As shown in Fig. 8.6, in the production control process inside the MES subsystem, the required materials for production are determined using the information received from the Maintenance Management (MTC), and a message is sent to the IWS to request needed items (item request). In the case that there is quality control during the process, after each operation in the manufacturing operation sequence, the information about the operation is recorded and a QC request is sent to the Quality Control Subsystem (QCS) to ask for in-process QC of the items. The results of the QC regarding the acceptance or rejection of the in-process items are sent back to production control. After the products for each shift, a message is sent to QCS to examine the quality of the complete product. The amounts of accepted products according to the results of the QC are sent to the IWS and will be recorded as the newly produced items in the associated warehouse.

As stated in Chapter 6 (Business and System Analysis), the Analysis Management System (AMS) is a powerful platform that has been designed by the FANAP implementation team to manage everything about the analysis activities throughout the MIDRP project. This system plays a significant role in managing the integration of business processes and products in the MIDRP. One important feature of the AMS is the ability to manage all aspects of BPs in a safe and standard manner. With the AMS the integration analyzers and developers could easily define standard messages for a particular BP in order to integrate it with other BPs in the system. Different aspects of a message, including type, data fields, receiver, sender, etc., are safely specified in the AMS so that no faulty message is created between two BPs. For example, if a certain process has not been defined in the system, the receiver of the message cannot be configured to be that process. Fig. 8.7 shows a sample message specification window from the AMS for a BP called "HSE inspection Management."

Another good feature of AMS is the ability to produce informative reports about the integration points between the products. The user can see all the messages that have been configured between two particular products in the "Products Integration Reports." Fig. 8.8 shows a sample report from the AMS about the integration of the products. In this report, we can see how a particular product has been connected with another product using a certain BP and a special message that contains the required information. The creation date of the integration method and the related bird view code is also presented for the tracking and reviewing activities.

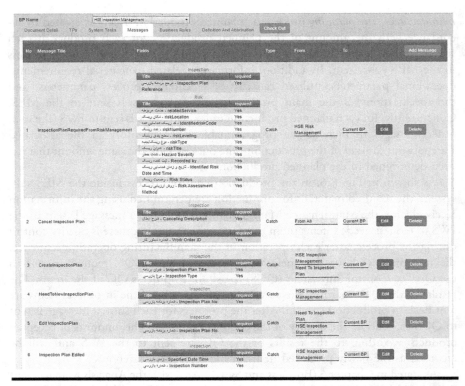

Figure 8.7 Specifying the elements of the message for a BP with the AMS platform.

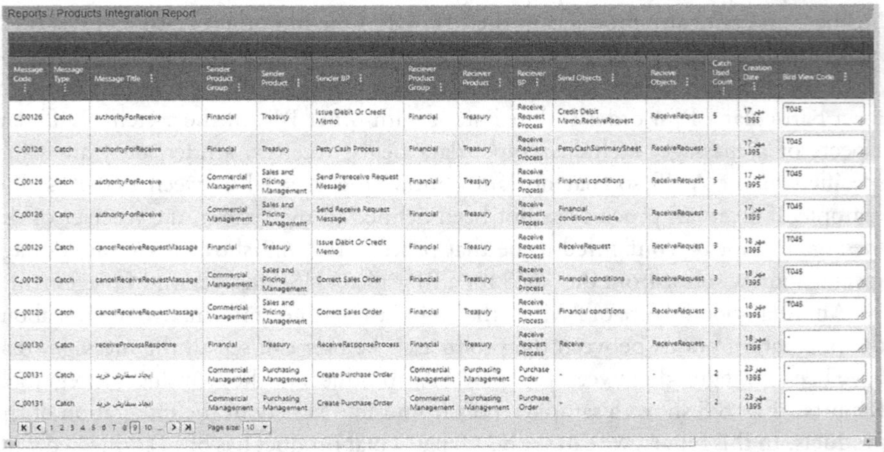

Figure 8.8 A sample piece of products integration report in the AMS.

8.3.2 Integration of MIDRP Subsystems with Other Operational Systems

MIDRP is a comprehensive software solution that organizes, coordinates, and automates all business processes in the organization and streamlines the operations of the production unit in different layers. In order to fully realize the benefits of such an ERP system, it should be integrated with the rest of the operating systems in the business environment. The significance of the ERP system is that it can integrate with all layers of automation in the organization and operation plants. According to the ISA-95 standard for enterprise control system integration, there are five levels of automation (ANSI/ISA, 2013):

- Level 0: Actual physical processes
- Level 1: Sensing and manipulating the physical processes
- Level 2: Monitoring and supervisory control of the physical processes
- Level 3: Manufacturing operations management
- Level 4: Business planning and logistics.

Fig. 8.9 depicts the hierarchy of automation in an organization. An ERP system works at level 4 as it is responsible for establishing a plant production schedule and logistics as well as operational management for different time frames from days to months. On the other hand, manufacturing operation management at level 3 plays

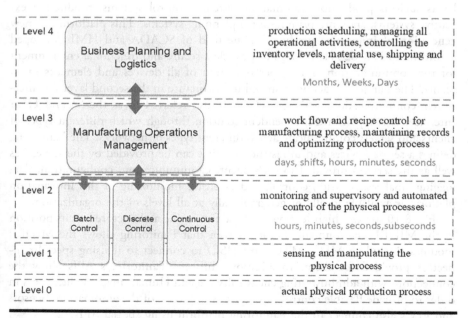

Figure 8.9   Hierarchy of automation solution for an operation plant.

an important role in controlling workflows and recipes to produce the desired end products. At this layer, a software solution is responsible for recording the used material, the facilities and machinery capacity, energy carriers, and optimizing the production process. This software solution is called Manufacturing Execution System (MES). At level 2, the focus of automation is on monitoring and supervisory control of the production process in short time frames from milliseconds up to hours. Usually, a Process Control System (PCS) works at this layer to perform these controlling tasks.

One of the critical things in ERP integration is to establish an efficient integration between the second, third, and fourth layers of the automation hierarchy (PCS, MES, and ERP). In order to fully implement the MIDRP system, it is necessary to establish system connections and information exchange between all automation levels. In the MIDRP system, the MES has been implemented as a subsystem in the Manufacturing Management (MFG) Module. This is a considerable feature of MIDRP since it creates most of the integration between levels 4 and 3 inside MIDRP. This integration provides significant flexibility in the business process automation and workflow coordination in the whole MIDHCO holding and its subsidiaries. In order to implement integration between the level 2 (PCS) and level 3 (MES) of automation a flexible and powerful platform called *Fanitoring* has been implemented by FANAP implementation.

The Fanitoring is an interface platform that can be used to create connections and information exchange between different enterprise applications in different layers such as production automation systems, control systems, production executive systems, and enterprise resource planning systems. This platform is a new generation of innovative products in the field of SCADA and HMI developed according to IEC 62541. It helps to provide a secure and functional environment for the communication and proper operation of all devices and elements in all plants. The Fanitoring defines a shared infrastructure in the second layer for intersystem-communication, which is why it is also referred to as the Second Layer Interface. It is a platform-independent solution through which different types of clients and servers communicate across different types of networks. The Fanitoring defines a set of services and infrastructures that can be provided by the servers, as well as the services provided to each client. Communication, configuration, data logging, analysis, security, control, and extensive monitoring of this information platform is available locally or geographically at all levels of the organization.

Fig. 8.10 shows a high-level view of the Fanitoring architecture and its position in the MIDRP environment. It can be seen that Fanitoring allows the MIDRP modules (including MFG, MTC, and HSE) to connect to it using special connectors provided for them. In addition, different Fanitoring's APIs allow the connections with administrating client software and Human-machine interfaces in order to provide flexible control mechanisms in level 2 of the automation. Sensors and PLCs also connect to the Fanitoring platform using special APIs.

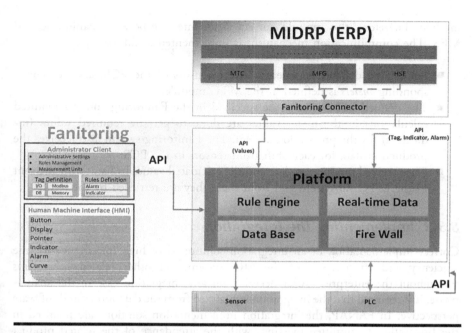

Figure 8.10   Fanitoring architecture.

One of the important cases of integration among the three layers of automation is recording and updating the operational parameters, inventory levels of different items, process parameters, and machinery capacity per production shift in the *production control* business process from MES. This activity is done when calculating the actual cost in the Cost Accounting (COA) subsystem from Financial Management (FIN), controlling the inventory levels of used materials and produced items in IWS, or calculating the discrepancies between the real values of different operational parameters with the expected values in the designed products by the MET. In order to record the right values in each working shift according to the sensors' data in the PCS, we need to retrieve the information from level 2 of automation (PCS) into the third level (MES).

> *"The production planning module of an ERP system works efficiently when the MES is connected to the sensors via PCS."*
>
> **—Ramin Amrbar**, *ICT Manager of MIDHCO Co.*

This is where Fanitoring comes into play. The Fanitoring's role is to establish connections between monitoring and supervisory systems installed in the MIDHCO plants with the MES subsystem. In the MIDRP project, all the machinery and their corresponding sensors have to be defined in the Maintenance Management (MTC) subsystem from the Maintenance Management (MTC) module. Therefore, this module can act as an interface between Fanitoring and MES. The communication mechanism is implemented as follows:

- For all the defined parameters in the sensors of the PCS, a set of corresponding *meters* is defined in the MTC module.
- The defined MTC meters are specified in the Fanitoring and the required calculations in the meter values are done to get the required values (indicators) for the production system. The Fanitoring system also receives the production data for each shift from sensors in the PCS.
- The received production data and the calculated values in Fanitoring are sent to the MTC subsystem and from there they are retrieved by the MES.

8.3.3 Implementing the Integration

Correct implementation of an integration solution is of high importance for the efficiency and effectiveness of the ERP system and other related subsystems throughout the enterprise. After deciding on any integration case in the analysis phase, it is required that the integration is analyzed from the data model and software perspective. In FANAP, the integration implementation solutions are finalized in the Integration Committee meetings with the attendance of the related product owners, technical leaders, the managers of the analysis unit and the development unit (as the integration supervisors), and the project management representative.

LESSON LEARNED 8.1

"The problems related to the development of an enterprise solution are intensified when encountering the integration stage. Although the accuracy of the integration among different products had been previously examined in the test environment, the business processes do not work properly in practice. The reason stemmed from the fact that users may execute a sort of issue that has not been taken into account when analyzing and developing the system. This implies the necessity of possessing an integration server during the test stage."

by Mohamad Hasan Masdar

In the integration meetings, the mechanism to implement the integration by the software components, the communication points, services, messages, and their contents as well as the data models are determined and approved. The required information for each message, including objects and data fields is determined. The use of services is very important in the integration mechanism since they can greatly enhance the flexibility and reusability of the integration architecture. Service is written in a standard structure and may be used in multiple integration cases. After implementing the integration, the receiver of the message or service needs to verify the correct functionality. The technical details of the implementation methods have been presented in Chapter 7 (design and development).

8.3.4 Integration Verification

In this chapter, we described the testing procedure for the developed software components of the MIDRP. One important step in the testing procedure is integration testing to verify the correctness of the integration solution of any developed product. The final verification of the integration is carried out in the deployment phase of the MIDRP project. When a developed component (business process or product) is tested in the integration and test servers, it is deployed on the customer premises and goes under operation after necessary training. The operational functionality of the MIDRP product and its integration with the rest of the subsystems is examined under real-world conditions according to the customer requirements. In the case of any failure or defect, the issues are reported to the implementation team to resolve and make appropriate modifications.

Integration plays an important role in increasing the usefulness of the MIDRP system and automating operations in the MIDHCO environment. Once the integration is implemented and verified for each product through vigorous testing, the product is ready to be deployed in the real working environment. In the next chapter, the deployment methodology of the MIDRP system in the MIDHCO business environment is presented and discussed.

References

ANSI/ISA. (2013). Enterprise control system integration Part 3: Activity models of manufacturing operations management. available at https://www.isa.org/store/ansi/isa-950003-2013-enterprise-control-system-integration-part-3-activity-models-of-manufacturing-operations-management/116782

Arcesb. (2018). Available at: https://www.arcesb.com/resources/edi/

Cancilla, C. E. (2017). *E*D*I - Electronic data interchange: An introduction*. EDI Education Series.

ERP Focus website. (2020). The most common systems for ERP integration. available at https://www.erpfocus.com/erp-integration-systems.html

Hale, Z. (2019). The benefits, challenges, and best practices associated with postmodern ERP integration. software advice website. available at https://www.softwareadvice.com/resources/erp-integration/

Hohpe, G., & Woolf, B. (2004). *Enterprise integration patterns: Designing, building, and deploying messaging solutions*. Boston: Pearson Education Inc.

IEC, OPC Unified Architecture - Part 100: Device Interface. available at https://webstore.iec.ch/publication/21987

Infor. (2018). Infor intelligent open network. available at https://webassets.infor.com/resources/Brochures/Infor-ION.pdf?noRedirect=1

Johnson, G. (2010). Enterprise Resource Planning (ERP) integration patterns and best practices. IT toolbox official website. available at https://it.toolbox.com/blogs/glennjohnson/enterprise-resource-planning-erp-integration-patterns-and-best-practices-072310

Jenkins, L. (2019). ERP integration: strategy, challenges, benefits, and key types. available at https://www.selecthub.com/enterprise-resource-planning/best-erp-software-integrations/

Linthicum, D. S. (2000). *Enterprise application integration.* Addison-Wesley Professional.

Mereddy, R. (2012). *ERP integration with other enterprise systems, in SAP basis administration handbook.* NetWeaver Edition, McGraw-Hill.

Miller, T. (2019). A beginner's guide to ERP integration. available at https://www.erpfocus.com/beginners-guide-to-erp-integration-1736.html

Mulesoft. (2020). ERP Integration - A united application architecture. available at https://www.mulesoft.com/resources/esb/erp-integration-application-architecture

Narayan, K. L. (2008). *Computer aided design and manufacturing.* New Delhi: Prentice Hall of India.

Oracle. (2020). Oracle integration platform – connectivity certification matrix. available at https://www.oracle.com/technetwork/adaptercertificationmatrix0217-3613709.pdf

Pierson, C. (2015). Best practices for ERP integration. ERP software blog. available at https://www.erpsoftwareblog.com/2015/01/best-practices-erp-integration/

Rosencrance, L. (2019). ERP integration strategy: 3 common approaches. available at https://searcherp.techtarget.com/tip/ERP-integration-strategy-3-common-approaches

Sapphireone. (2019). What are APIs and are you getting the most out of your ERP?. Sapphireone blog. available at https://blog.sapphireone.com/2019/10/apis-erp-application/

Srivatsan. (2019). A complete guide to ERP integration: Types, benefits and challenges. Cloras website blog. available at https://www.cloras.com/blog/erp-system-integration/

Stackpole, B. (2013). ERP system integration poses ongoing challenges. available at https://searcherp.techtarget.com/feature/ERP-system-integration-poses-ongoing-challenges

Chapter 9

Deployment Framework

"ERP deployment is an embodiment of businesses' inseparability from information technology. To get along such an inevitability, a successful deployment involves a clear purpose, delicate planning, agile trained team, and conscious employer."

—MIDRP Deployment Office of FANAP Co.

The story of MIDRP deployment is a showcase of achieving a resounding success by experiencing a dismal failure. This is, indeed, an acute step reflecting whether the previously adopted measures on the mission to accomplish MIDRP are going to pay off or fail. By unfolding this part of the story, it can be figured out that the MIDRP deployment will even lead to the implementation of a certain sub-project in the entire MIDHCO Holding. The current chapter narrates how the three main characters of the project, namely, MIDHCO, FANAP, and POSCO ICT interactively contribute toward installing the developed products in the real-work environment. In this regard, there are particular challenges such as conducting acculturation, and education for changing the mindset of users to putting aside the old system and getting used to the new one. In what follows, the underlying challenges of laying out the deployment framework and related remedies are explicated.

9.1 Overview

The deployment or post-implementation step is also called "the beginning of an end" (Maheshwari et al., 2010) referring to the fact that although the implementation of the ERP has ended, the final solution would bring a completely new life to another environment. This would certainly influence the way of working with users and

DOI: 10.1201/9781003369806-9

thereby could be accompanied by their resistance. MIDRP on the other hand was planned to be designed and developed to satisfy the users' requirements from the most basic ones to the most complicated by providing services such as real-time process and analysis and advanced reporting. Furthermore, post-implementation meant that MIDRP was going through the phase where the users' first impression of MIDRP was going to be created. An impression that affects the attitude of the users toward the solution and consequently leads to the acceptance of the new system or resistance against its deployment. Thus, needless to say, this fact created a huge demand for a comprehensive change management plan to start preparing the target environment for the changes to come.

Although the processes offered by MIDRP are designed with the aim of optimizing MIDHCO's As-Is processes leading to major changes in the organizational structure, the general framework of the integrated solution as a whole needs to be compatible with the overall policies and organizational structure of the organization. At some points, process optimization demanded changes in the organizational structure or the chart or even in the As-Is processes and procedure, while some users were going to be satisfied and others were expected to show resistance. This kind of issue should have been predicted and a practical solution should have been offered by the project team, specifically by the post-implementation team.

We can assume from what has been explained above that the major and perhaps the most critical issue MIDHCO users would have to encounter and deal with during the post-implementation phase is the number of changes they would be required to make in their jobs, as well as the endeavor they are expected to make so that they could eventually learn how to use the system smoothly. This indicates how critical, essential and significant it is for the post-implementation team members to support the users through this phase. Concerning the importance of the deployment, in the rest of the current chapter, the best practices are reviewed first. Section 9.3 narrates how the initial failure leads to significant success throughout the MIDRP deployment maturity process. Section 9.4 enumerates the remedies of the support process of MIDRP whereas Section 9.5 concludes the story.

9.2 Best Practices Review

Taking into consideration the role of pre-paredness in terms of both operation and the organization's culture, before the project goes live or what is termed here "deployment" makes it crystal clear that selecting the most effective methodology for this phase might be one of the most critical points. According to Welti (1999), there are three approaches for implementing an ERP project as a whole, i.e., step-by-step, big bang, and rollout. Taking into account the different ways the product(s) is going to be implemented in the employers' environment, these three approaches provide the project team with different choices so that the team could select the one which is most compatible with the employer's status. In the step-by-step approach, the modules of the whole product are implemented continuously in several steps, while according to the big bang approach all the modules are implemented simultaneously (Koch et al., 1999). Roll-out, on the other hand, "may be implemented as step-by-step or big bang" refers to the fact that a model of implementation is created at one site and rolls out to other sites as well (Al-Mudimigh et al., 2001). However, for some companies specifically small as well as the medium size companies it is not cost-effective "to spend years on a software project." To solve problems of this kind, rapid implementation approaches, e.g., Accelerated SAP (ASAP), were offered in order "to keep ERP system projects moving". ASAP is a standard SAP-related project preparation and systems implementation method. Despite all the benefits and vigor, the rapid implementation offers to employers, adopting them is limited to companies with the following characteristics (Holland & Light, 1999):

- Not planning to use the ERP implementation as an opportunity for reengineering.
- Not requiring heavy customization of the ERP software.
- Willing to bend to fit the software's definition of business processes.
- Willing to sacrifice large-group, consensus-driven decision-making and authorize a small, core team to make crucial decisions in a short timeframe.
- Understanding the enterprise's business processes well enough to prioritize exactly what functionality is required from the software.
- Not considering rapid implementation a means to save money, but having a strong, driving business need that requires them to complete the project by a specific date.

Although these rapid implementation approaches have been so common among the most reputable software companies such as SAP (introducing ASAP), Oracle (introducing FastTrack), and PeopleSoft (introducing Application Implementation method, AIM) (Benders et al., 2006), they do not seem to be sufficient for large-scale businesses for the above-mentioned reasons. Thus, focusing on the main benefits of implementing an ERP system, e.g., extensive customization, reengineering, etc., in order to have an organization with highly standardized business processes, large businesses still demand the conventional implementation methods. The go-live phase (also referred to as an installation) of these conventional approaches, however, might require the project team's special attention.

To be more specific, the go-live phase might be completed through a holistic approach, including all the necessary steps that not only include the go-live but also the post-implementation steps such as support. Defining a successful go-live in terms of a successful cutover phase, SAP provides a detailed methodology on how to achieve a successful cutover and consequently a successful go-live through a comprehensive rollout plan (Portougal & Sundaram, 2005). According to SAP terminology, going live may refer to the go-live of an upgraded version of SAP, "an enhancement service pack level," or "a greenfield implementation" with specified timetables for "dry runs and cutover activities." According to SAP methodology, two dry runs are recommended before the cutover in an attempt to avoid failure during the cutover. Basically, the cutover encapsulates the following activities (Williams et al., 2008):

- Final data migration
- Infrastructure readiness
- The final round of business acceptance for critical process
- Technical cutover (actual downtime or actual cutoff).

Furthermore, the full details of the major steps of cutover include:

- Pre-cutover activities
  - Creating the production environment
  - Preparing a cutover plan
  - Testing the cutover plan
  - Doing dry runs
  - Finalizing the cutover plan
- Cutover activities
  - Executing the cutover plan
  - Performing checks
  - Go No Go decision
- Post-go-live support
  - Transition to support team and issue management.

Table 9.1 shows the risk assessment criteria which are prepared with the cutover plan to help identify the critical areas and thus prevent issues from happening in those areas.

Another methodology that adopts a holistic approach to system go-live is called ERP institutionalization, which is concerned mainly with the post-implementation period. ERP institutionalization outlines the processes and mechanisms through which an ERP system evolves inside an organization and becomes institutionalized in it. Through institutionalization, an organization master changes, stabilizes technology, develops new competencies around technology and redefined processes, and develops complementary structures and norms (Maheshwari et al., 2010).

The institutionalization model driven by the analysis of multiple case studies includes three stages and four major events starting from the go-live and continuing to the future status of the system within the organization (Maheshwari et al., 2010). The following graph of Fig. 9.1 represents the three stages as well as the events triggering the initiation of the next stage.

Table 9.1   Risk Assessment Criteria in the Cutover Plan

Criteria	Risk Score
Site	High Impact
Technology	Medium
Training	Low
Data migration	High
Sustainability	Low
Functionality	Medium
Cutover planning	High
Tools	High
Resources availability	Medium

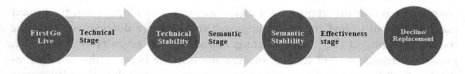

Figure 9.1   ERP institutionalization model.

The events demonstrated in the above graph are explained in detail below:

- **Initial go-live:** Referring to the first time when the ERP system is practically switched on and initiating the post-implementation stage, this event stands for the stage when the system implementation is ended while the system deployment at the vendor environment is started. Thus, depending on the scope of the ERP project every individual start to use the system in the actual operations. Of course, almost all of the users have been familiar with the system through the training sessions, but training is insufficient due to the fact that in most cases training is conducted through a "generic training configuration" and thus is significantly different from the one they will work with in go live.
- **Technical stability:** The fact that the user has just started working with the implemented ERP system and that in most cases the training sessions are not enough to help the users gain the required mastery to work with the system well enough. Consequently, at this stage issues left from the implementation phase, which have been either undetected or resolved inappropriately all emerge during the system deployment. At this point, the support team is actively engaged in settling these kinds of issues to avoid the inevitable slowdown

of the system, leading to the users' disappointment and dissatisfaction with the newly implemented ERP system. The purpose of this stage is to achieve the "technical stability" of the system which can be successfully achieved when the support team is able to resolve these problems and the remaining issues are reduced to an acceptable level and of low risk. Achieving such stability marks the beginning of the next stage, i.e., semantic stability.

■ **Semantic stability:** Despite the fact that technical stability is achieved in the previous stage, some disorder persists due to the lack of understanding and confusion about using and supporting the system. Thus, this stage is aimed at the flawless functioning of the new system which is achieved when an understanding of the new system is developed across the organization. This is actually the point where the system's effectiveness is at work.

■ **Decline/Replacement:** This stage is mainly concerned with the future status of the ERP system within the organization when the stable and effective ERP no longer meets the new requirements of the company and may be gradually replaced by the new system.

Despite the diversity of approaches that can be adopted for the post-implementation phase, there is only one approach for each organization to adopt. Thus, the project team is required to find the proper approach considering a different aspect of the specific ERP project they are conducting. Aspects such as organizational structure, resources, attitude toward change, or even the distance between the various production facilities impact the team's macro-level decision regarding the ERP system implementation as well as its post-implementation method.

At a later stage, deployment is about taking the main steps which are essential for the system to go live in the environment of the user. This stage includes almost all the main activities related to education, adjustment, data migration, pilot, and go-live. Thus, we can infer that the project has reached a crucial stage where all the work conducted by the project team was going to be practically used by the actual end-users. The detailed steps taken throughout this stage are listed below:

■ Providing the users with the required education in the following three steps:
  • Teaching the managers as well as the key users the business processes
  • Teaching the end-users, the general and basic concepts
  • Teaching the technical experts, the setting of the configuration
■ Making the required adjustment through the following steps:
  • Identifying the unsystematic processes
  • Preparing the documents of each process which has been customized for each BU as well as the approval procedures
  • Controlling and checking the deployment activities
  • Adjusting the systematic roles to the organizational chart
  • Providing solutions for the processes which belong to the next phases and are not planned to be prepared at this phase

- Preparing the adjustment report
- Receiving the employer approval for the adjustment report
- Receiving the deployment committee's approval for the adjustment report
- Specifying the location as well as the features of the software workstation
- Identifying and creating unofficial OUs
- Defining the users and assigning the roles to specify the access level
- Providing or modifying the instructions required for using the system and manual work
- Sending a letter to MIDHCO requesting supplying the required hardware
■ Data migration
  - Specifying the configuration data list and determining their prerequisites
  - Receiving the new data, refining and adding them to the pre-deployment database
  - Preparing and converting the data for data entry
  - Transferring the configuration data provided during pre-deployment
  - Testing the transferred data and approving them by the supervisor
  - Providing and presenting the data migration report (master and configuration data entry)
  - Receiving the supervisor's approval for the data migration report
  - Receiving the deployment committee approval for the data migration report
  - Preparing the data migration template
  - Preparing the scenario for data migration from the previous systems
■ Pilot
  - Arranging the document transfer or the existing system output for the parallel system operation
  - Setting up the hardware systems and the software solutions
  - Executing the pilot by the FANAP deployment team and MIDHCO operation team
  - Preparing the reports and printable forms required for operation
  - Preparing a comparative report of previous systems and MIDRP solution
  - Preparing a report of the users' ideas after one-month examination in the operating environment
  - Granting access to the users
■ Proposing the start of go-live
  - Demonstration and temporary system delivery
  - Receiving the supervisor and employer approval for the system delivery
  - Conducting the migration of the previous transactions.

9.3 Toward Maturing MIDRP Deployment Framework

After investigating best practices in the context of ERP deployment, it is appropriate to assess the maturity of MIDRP in this regard. This framework follows the proposed deployment process which is also highlighted by Figs. 9.2 and 9.3. To narrate the story, Section 9.3.1 has been devoted to the initial trial for the pilot deployment of MIDRR. That event can be denoted as the story climax. It seriously undermined the preceding rising actions and thereby breaks the onset of maturity in the deployment framework as well as the entire methodology. Section 9.3.2 describes the sub-steps of the framework while Section 9.3.3 focuses on the second trial for the pilot deployment.

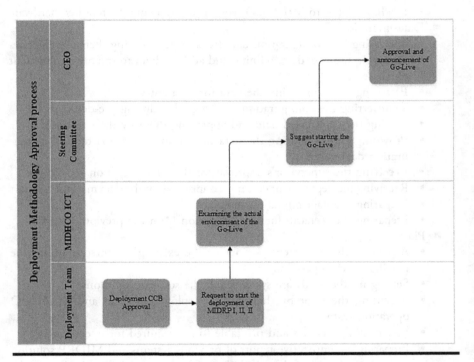

Figure 9.2   Approval process of deployment methodology.

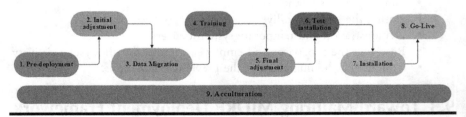

Figure 9.3   Generic methodology of MIDRP deployment.

9.3.1 Challenges of the First Pilot Deployment

To initialize the deployment step, a pilot choice is needed and among the others, Zarand Co., MIDHCO's largest subsidiary with various products, has been adopted. The reason behind choosing this subsidiary was that the company is the largest and subsequently the most complicated procedures and processes exist there and this can have a vital role in evaluating how MIDRP would react to these complexities. Almost all of the specialists in FANAP were dispatched to Kerman for the deployment in Zarand concentrate BU. Long working hours, in some cases 14 hours of work per day, the lengthy commute they had from Kerman to Zarand, all the pressures to resolve minor issues on time so that a user could perform his/her task satisfactorily. This means that a lot of time and energy has been spent on deployment, regardless of the amount of money invested at this stage of the project. However, the inherently unique nature of the project and lack of maturity lead to the disappointing result of the pilot case.

Actually, the unsuccessful attempt to deploy the first package in Zarand became evident to the employer during a site visit to Zarand when MIDHCO's CEO accompanied by a number of officials, including his MIDRP consultant as well as MIDHCO ICT manager, tried to ensure that the system is actually working well and is fulfilling the users' requirements satisfactorily. On the contrary, what they witnessed as a result of MIDRP deployment was simply the system fails to work properly and satisfy the users' needs. In fact, regardless of the users' dilemma in getting along with the corresponding package, there were other key issues such as the slowness of the system and in many cases the bugs the users encountered during their tasks. Actually, the nature of their job entails a real-time operating system with an expected rate of speed to which MIDRP at this stage could not be very accountable. Disappointed at what they witnessed in reality and concerned about the consequences of these delays and the operations which used to work before MIDRP and stopped now, the CEO decided to stop the deployment in Zarand and officially announced the failure of the first deployment attempt.

The official announcement made by MIDHCO's leading managers was shocking not only for FANAP but also for the whole project team, including MIDHCO ICT as the mediator between the employer and FANAP as well as POSCO ICT as the project consultant. The crisis posed key questions about the root cause for all the individuals who were involved with the project. Questions such as: What did the dismal failure mean? Why did we fail in our first attempt to deploy the project's first phase? Was the first pilot chosen wrongly? Should the pilot, which was going to create the first impression on the user have been chosen more carefully? Who was responsible for that? Was it only one person who should have taken the blame? Is it reasonable to blame one person only? Could we find any trace of the butterfly effect in this unsuccessful attempt?

The first problem identified was that as mentioned earlier MIDRP package could satisfy only some parts of the operations, providing the users with an output that must have been used as an input to the systems other than MIDRP which have been in operation in the company before MIDRP package was delivered. In other words, MIDRP output from the weighing system was going to be used as an input in another finance solution which was unacceptable to users. Second, although the large-scale size of Zarand was supposed to be helpful in the optimization and maturity of the system, choosing it as the pilot was not the best decision for many reasons. First, as the meaning of the "pilot" implies the scope of the pilot needs to be small just to make sure that the system or the product under test works successfully which is the main purpose of the pilot. Second, the large number of positions in Zarand on the one hand, and the limitation of recruiting only local people of Kerman, on the other hand, led to the fact that many users of MIDRP were not qualified experts, and sometimes they could not totally grasp the business processes. So FANAP specialists had to teach them the business process and how it is supposed to work through the MIDRP system which was really time-consuming for FANAP.

Third, and most importantly, the initial products which were supposed to be deployed were not fully covering all of the steps of the steel-making chain. A chain that includes MIDHCO's main activities from A to Z from the moment the weighing is done to the last step when the accounting voucher is created. FANAP specialists somehow did know that their MIDRP package might not fully cover the whole processes in this chain so they preferred the other solutions to be operating alongside MIDRP so that if MIDRP fails to work there is no risk of data loss. This, although rejected by the MIDRP project managers, indicated the lack of confidence, and the insufficient understanding of the systems and processes they have analyzed and developed to such an extent that they were not sure about the functionality of their own systems. This might indicate the minor role of the system test which had in this project. Although the system test was officially included in the system development steps, the results of these system tests were not taken seriously by the project team.

LESSON LEARNED 9.1

"The worthiest lesson learned associated with the pilot deployment in Zarand Company could be attributed to figuring out the critical position of the financial module in the context of the enterprise solution. Indeed, the financial module must be included in the initial package of an ERP when it gets to the deployment phase."

by Mohammad Reza Najminezhad

Another critical problem identified by the project team as a contributory factor in the failure of Zarand deployment was the lack of integration between the processes and systems at work. As mentioned earlier, as the comprehensiveness and integration of a software package increases, so does the complexity of its analysis and development. At the beginning of the project, when the scope review was performed, the processes were analyzed and designed in such a way that all the communications they needed were considered. But in a large-scale project like MIDRP, it may be impossible to identify all the potential connections in advance. For this reason, in the first deployment, many of the problems were due to this lack of integration and incomplete communication between processes. Naturally, when one process fails to obtain the data needed to perform the operation from another process, its function is disrupted. So, this great lesson was learned for the people involved in this project that the deployment will not be successful until the products and their integration have reached full maturity.

As the main feature of UI which greatly affects the first impression of the users, the attractiveness has an undeniable role in shaping either the users' desire or on the contrary their reluctance to work with the system. On the first deployment, MIDRP UI was not attractive enough for the users. In fact, most of the issues, the users were complaining about were related to the way the UI looked and how undesirable it is to work with a system that has such an unattractive UI. Furthermore, the lack of a significant number of trained employees in the support team besides the different criteria in labeling the goods across the business units could be denoted as the other challenges.

LESSON LEARNED 9.2

"The absence of the end-users in the coordination committees for detecting the system's requirements as well as demo presentations of a product could exacerbate the challenges of the deployment step. When end-users are not asked to play a role during the system analysis process, their significant comments for promoting the performance of the system may be missed."

by Sedigheh Bahmanyar

Dealing with a system suffering from faults such as the ones mentioned above for almost one month led to serious disturbance to the users and consequently aroused growing dissatisfaction among Zarand's users. This dissatisfaction led to the users' unwillingness to ignore the system's faults anymore and was crystal clear to MIDHCO CEO as well as the officials who accompanied him during the aforementioned site visit. The scene of a large number of dissatisfied employees who have been operating the business of MIDHCO left the CEO with no choice but to declare officially the failure of the first MIDRP deployment. Therefore, this paves the way for the employees to proceed with their job using their previous systems which have been shut down the day MIDRP started operating.

LESSON LEARNED 9.3

"The challenging condition of the first trial of product deployment in Zarand Company advocates that the initial system analysis has followed an impractical logic. This experience emphasizes that the system analysts should be in close relationship with the deployment office in order to inject the practical terms of the business into the analysis."

by Farbod Mosadeghi

9.3.2 Deployment Measures

Now, the involved parties need to considerably utilize the lessons learned from the Zarand case and adopt the necessary measures in the context of the following substeps of the MIDRP framework. These measures work as a number of well-developed templates that would guarantee a much smoother path toward deploying the MIDRP in the next attempts. In fact, after the implementation phase, the mature and fully tested products are ready to be installed on the MIDHCO sites by respecting the below measures.

9.3.2.1 Pre-Deployment

Here, initial steps are taken to deploy MIDRP. One of the most crucial actions is the management and planning of the deployment process in which the delivery schedule of products that can be installed on the server at different sites is determined. As the name suggests and as it is explained above MIDRP predeployment included all the work which needs to be conducted before the system go-live. For example, the first step of education, i.e., the standardization of terminology, is taken in pre-deployment so that everyone involved in the project uses a common language to implement the solution. Moreover, data migration preparatory steps, listed below, are also taken at this stage.

LESSON LEARNED 9.4

"The pre-deployment practice of MIDRP implies a noteworthy hint about the extent of an enterprise solution. In the contractual terms of an ERP implementation, the vendor should be conscious that an enterprise solution is not just the story of developing the business processes and embedding them together. Sometimes, the working condition enforces the vendor to carry out a specific sub-project that is significantly different from the expected scope of an ERP. The huge sub-project of standardization can be categorized in the context of a peripheral yet necessary activity within MIDRP accomplishment. Accordingly, it is prudent for ERP vendors to predict the consequences of such sub-projects in terms of financial and time-based setting within the content of the contract."

by Mahdiyeh Mirzady

- Sending the deployment requirements letter to MIDHCO
- Identifying the hardware and physical requirements
- Preparing the "identification" document related to the pre-deployment
- Identifying the type of connections to the hardware as well as their prerequisites
- Identifying the documentation format as well as the printable forms
- Receiving the master as well as the configuration data and refining them
- Identifying the existing solutions in MIDHCO's factories and companies

Obviously, preparation for deployment meant that both parties of the project, the contractor as well as the employer, cooperate with each other so that all the steps which are essential to achieve the deployment of such a project would be conducted in the best possible way. This fact demonstrates that MIDHCO as the project employer had to be aware of its professional responsibilities toward MIDRP. Actually, among all the professional, technical, and managerial responsibilities of MIDHCO, providing a desirable working environment for the FANAP team is critical so that operational team members could proceed toward a completely successful MIDRP deployment. In order to achieve this, some steps were specified for MIDHCO to be fulfilled during pre-deployment which are as follows:

- Fulfilling the deployment requirements
- Equipping the workshop

- Providing permanent space for education
- Providing appropriate space for FANAP's deployment team
■ Holding an introductory session in order to provide the users with the basic information about the project deployment
■ Providing or updating the instructions
■ Providing FANAP with the master and configuration data
■ Preparing the required hardware
  - Providing the users with an appropriate system or upgrading the existing ones
  - Preparing and installing the required hardware.

9.3.2.2 Initial Adjustment

In order to have a better understanding of MIDRP adjustment, we should bear in mind that there are two types of processes at work. On one hand, we have MIDHCO processes that have been in practice, then while on the other hand, we have the MIDRP processes which are expected to replace those processes. As a result, not only are these MIDRP processes expected to fulfill all the user requirements covered by the previous processes but also, they are supposed to optimize the way these processes work. Thus, it is possible to conclude that the processes designed in MIDRP should be adjusted to the processes actually in practice at MIDHCO subsidiaries. As a main step in the deployment process, adjustment was planned to be conducted in each individual subsidiary plant, BU, and company.

In this regard, questionnaire-like forms are designed by each product owner in an attempt to address their concerns and find solutions to them. As a matter of fact, these forms were considered a kind of data-gathering practice. For example, each PO could find out whether there is currently any system in the subsidiaries per specific domain of activities such as maintenance or supply chain.

Then, the software programs which used by the users were identified mainly for data migration purposes. In other words, each PO had to understand the existing system to identify the data. Identifying the hardware, on the other hand, meant ensuring that the minimum hardware requirements for MIDRP implementation would be met as well as identifying the places where these minimum hardware requirements would not be fulfilled so that the employer would be notified of the existing lack of hardware.

Furthermore, as mentioned earlier, the MIDRP system was implemented in different phases. This means that these processes would be done manually until their automatic counterpart in MIDRP is implemented. In other words, in this step, a list of the processes which are supposed to be done manually in each system was prepared. In fact, this list of unsystematic activities used to be updated whenever a new process was implemented. Notably, the BPMN diagram for each BP must be modified and applied to the process-oriented execution engine of each BU. In this respect, the codes related to the executor roles of each component of the process have to be updated. The hierarchy of approvals in each organization is needed to be completed. A description of how to implement that component of the process is also required. For this purpose, a form will be completed by the analysis team and provided to the development team, to customize the relevant processes.

Besides, mapping the systematic roles onto the official and unofficial organizational units should be taken into account. This mapping means considering the role of the process component with the equivalent activities in the current Bus. The accuracy of the role considered in the process diagram and the role of its executor in the customer organization should be checked; Maps should be redefined in the customer organization if necessary. Therefore, documentation, including the organizational architecture structure associated with each system should be prepared and attached to the process implementation plan.

Although users can also be considered as part of the basic information about the system, it is necessary to be systematically addressed and defined separately as one of the major steps. In this way, alternative processes for the next phases according to the process integration form must be set. By alternative processes, we mean those processes which were set as a temporary solution and used as alternatives to the processes or systems which were not ready for deployment yet. These alternative processes were explained in the process integration document. Another practice embraces gathering and configuring data. Along this step, all the configuration data, including the master data as well as the data related to the individual plants were identified. The required data was gathered in Access or Excel file and delivered to MIDHCO users so that they could fill out the files with the required data. Then FANAP would receive the data and conduct the data entry in two ways: whether manually, this method was used for cases with a small amount of data, or through scripts which are used when there is a large amount of data.

For queuing processes that run in the operating environment, it is necessary to lay out the workstations in order to provide a proposed physical location for the workstations and to identify and provide the relevant equipment and hardware for it. Additionally, in accordance with the data migration plan, e.g., previous transactions, a scenario must be developed with the agreement of the expert team. The scenario should respond to the following questions. Which part of the information can be used operationally? Which part of it can be transferred only for reporting? And which part of the information will remain only in past systems? This process is the responsibility of the deployment team.

9.3.2.3 Data Gathering and Migration

Here, basic information is updated and the latest information used in the organization's work processes is collected and entered into the MIDRP system. Data immigration, which includes Master Data and Configuration Data, is done based on the information received from the standardization team for Document, Equipment Structure, and Item and for other data, based on the information received from the companies and approved and standardized by the expertise team. Data immigration is done with the purpose of product configuration for operation.

Data immigration in pilot deployment is done in three steps. First, part of the data is migrated with the aim of system operation in a test environment, and the training is done based on this data. Then, the second step is taken before the initial operation with the purpose of implementing MIDRP parallel with the previous software. The third step will be done before operation and with the aim of the final operation of MIDRP. While considering all the business principles and validation in the data-gathering step and implementation of BPs, data migration is done automatically and with no intervention from the user by an engine. Using this engine accelerates data gathering and data entry in the shortest time possible.

Data immigration in the next deployments (other than the pilot one) will be done in two steps. First, part of the data is migrated with the aim of system operation in a test environment, and the training is done based on this data, and then the second step is taken before the operation with the aim of the final operation of MIDRP. According to the methodology, migration documents will be published and provided for the supervisor and the employer to be controlled. Due to the different architecture of island systems compared with that of MIDRP and other fundamental differences, previous transactions of the old systems will not be migrated. In exceptional situations, the previous transactions will be migrated provided that the mapping between the old and new data is done by the users of previous systems. These cases will be planned with MIDHCO ICT's approval under specific scenarios.

Data standardization is another task which is done by the project's participants. For Item, equipment structure, and document standardization, a sub-project is defined in MIDHCO. Other master data and Configuration Data will be standardized in the expertise team of every business. The standardization plan is based on the MIDRP deployment plan. If the standardization is not prepared based on deployment scheduling, the standardization team will also announce the mapping between the data entered and the new data.

9.3.2.4 Training

Issues related to the training of all personnel in connection with the MIDRP system should be conducted here. In this stage, all users are taught how to use the solution properly and efficiently. After that, the training is evaluated, and a certificate is issued to the admitted employees. Generally, the training approach in the MIDRP project includes simultaneous training and culture building. This is done with the aim of increasing productivity by developing people's knowledge and skills. The project training committee is responsible for planning, monitoring the implementation, and evaluation of project training activities, as well as ensuring the establishment and effectiveness of measures taken in the field of training. This committee is composed of joint members of MIDHCO and FANAP, to make training policy and facilitate training solutions. In this step, by identifying target users, detailed planning of system training will be done during the project phases. The training committee also determines the requirements of the education system and, after approval by the Project Steering Committee, notifies the executive units.

There are three types of training in the MIDRP deployment phase:

- **Primary:** Includes theoretical discussion on introducing MIDRP Project
- **Professional:** Includes the presentation of business rules and structure of application forms
- **General:** Includes the first task of application forms.

It should be noted that the training plan includes specialized and general training for managers, end-users, and system administrators.

LESSON LEARNED 9.5

"Generally, the deployment step is a manpower-oriented practice. The MIDRP project has experienced certain occasions in which the skilled staff of the deployment team vacated their job even during the sensitive periods of the Go-live stage. It was, in fact, an undeniable Achilles' heel of the project, where both practical and scholarly sides of the team were dramatically fallen. There was an immediate necessity to devise a special program for succession planning and staff development. As a remedy, the deployment office started forming the pedagogical requirement matrix for the staff who was active in user, process, and technical support teams. This matrix was converted to the elementary, intermediate, and advanced courses that leads to honing the deployment skill of the corresponding staff. Doing so, the necessary knowledge and experience have been injected into the body of the deployment team again."

by Mansour Shiani

Additionally, a learning management system has been designed to provide a user-friendly basis for an efficient training structure. Therein, in addition to the downloadable booklets, one can also access the educational videos as well.

LESSON LEARNED 9.6

"The experiences of the MIDRP deployment practice have shown that the golden time for the system's users to undergo the training courses is three weeks before starting the Go-live event of a product. By considering such an interval, users have enough time to get along with the system on one hand and not forget the instructions for using it on the other hand. Furthermore, a workable curriculum is to provide a subjective perception regarding the accurate procedure of interacting with the system at the beginning of the course. Then, it gets to describe per field of the forms, their associated functionalities, and the way of communicating with other processes. Finally, the biggest and most significant chunk of training must be devoted to workshops that bring about practical guidance for the users."

by Sima Yazdanpanah

9.3.2.5 Secondary Adjustment

Necessary steps are taken to prepare the MIDRP system for launch and start using it. The secondary adjustment is to remove the prospective problems of the initial one as MIDHCO's employees are getting more familiar with the system functionality. Notably, this familiarity is the outcome of the training process in the previous sub-step. At this stage, the final tests on the performance, security, and integration are performed and the issues are sent to the CCB committee along with the changes. If changes are required, the implementation team will re-develop the software and apply the changes, and this process will continue until the CCB committee makes the final approval. If approved, we will enter the deployment phase of the solution.

9.3.2.6 Trial Installation

MIDRP system is set up on the test server so that end-users in a test interval, in real-time (in real conditions with real data) work with the system and provide their feedback. In order to install the software, in the first stage, the servers are transferred to the client site and the required operating systems and databases must be installed on them; then the software version of each product will be installed on the server. Since the hardware requirements have been reviewed in the previous steps, the hardware installation should also be followed up at this stage. Hardware can include PC, printers, barcode readers, tablets, RFID readers, and more.

Trial installation of each product will be performed in the pilot deployment to achieve the necessary stability of the system and in subsequent deployments, there will be no need for this installation. At this stage, the end-users perform the UAT system deployment. If changes are needed, the implementation team will consider the change cycle and this process will continue until the CCB Committee gives final approval. During the trial period, the tasks will be gradually transferred to the users, in order to ensure the users' capabilities before the go-live stage.

9.3.2.7 Installation

After the end of the trial use, the MIDRP system will be launched on the main server for the operational use of users. One of the most important actions at this stage is the weighing maneuver. Three days before the go-live date, all configurations of the purchasing, selling, warehousing, and weighing systems must be entered on the main server. In a systematic process, the test server syncs with the main server. The next day (two days before the go-live date) all input and output weights of the factory (s) must be executed on the test server in one working day without any problems.

9.3.2.8 Go-Live

After the trial period and confirmation of the system performance based on the approved reports, the trial period ends and the final go-live begins. At this stage, if the servers are separate, it may be necessary to re-transfer information and trans-actions and be approved by the client. Here, with the request of the deployment team to start the go-live of the solution and then review the MIDHCO ICT regarding the necessary conditions for go-live of the system, with the approval of the CEO, the official go-live will begin. The go-live process is not going to be ended immediately. In fact, it is a milestone that depends on the MIDHCO confirmation to be terminated and this thereby enters the project into the support stage. Notably, the go-live event is a key period in which the initial feedback of both users and deployment officers on the proposed solution could be captured and the appropriate improvements could be made.

LESSON LEARNED 9.7

"Towards taking the acquired feedback during the pilot deploy-ment, several barriers in terms of the streamlined performance of the Health, Safety, Environment, and Community (HSEC) product have been detected. Indeed, the system needs a number of basic input data to provide the necessary outputs for users. To resolve this issue in the other business units, it has asked the employer to complete the information about standardizing the hazards as well as hazards' consequences and origins. It also has been notified that assigning the law-based requirements to the hazards demands further clarification while evaluating the re-assignment of the self-protective equipment to the hazards seems crucial."

by Vahid Hajipour

9.3.2.9 Acculturation

As discussed in the challenges section of Chapter 1, ERP needs to be customized from region to region based on cultural terms and MIDRP has been significantly adapted to the regional condition of MIDHCO. In fact, as the deployment step gets highlighted, the cultural measures to capture the users' resistance to the changes reach the heart of the story. Precisely, Culture building continues from the beginning to the end of the deployment phase, and all necessary measures are taken to prepare the company and factories of MIDHCO culturally for the successful launch and go-live of the MIDRP system. The objectives of Acculturation include:

■ Introducing MIDRP project
■ Understanding the advantages of the MIDRP project
■ Highlighting the impact of the MIDRP project on individual occupation (change management)
■ Enhancing professional skills of involved individuals by acquiring MIDRP project knowledge.

To do so, different sorts of measures have been considered to promote the attitude of users toward working by MIDRP. For instance, incentive bonuses have been offered to the nominated users that acquire high scores in the pedagogical courses. There were also some users that lacked sufficient concentration during courses. To cope with this, the top-level manager of MIDHCO emphasized the importance of MIDRP in terms of boosting their future working conditions. Notably, MIDHCO has considerably aided the executive character in activating such measures which leads to promising deployment results. Furthermore, the deployment is not only a matter of methodology and technical facts.

LESSON LEARNED 9.8

"One of the most important issues that can be attributed to the cultural terms is associated with the personal traits of the staff in the deployment team. The staff is supposed to work in a stressful environment where the users are constantly complaining about probable system imperfections at the Go-live stage. Training such staff on the appropriate way of capturing the tense atmosphere of the working condition and providing tranquility for the users would significantly lessen the difficulties of the deployment."

by Amirhossein Ahadian

9.3.3 Second Pilot Deployment

Regardless of the reasons, the failure of the first deployment was officially announced by the employer and this was considered the turning point of the whole project which led to the establishment of a new procedure. FANAP was given another chance to prove the functionality of the MIDRP system. Being aware of the functional weaknesses of the solution, FANAP decided to change its model to a new one. Noteworthy, the FANAP team focused on designing a model which could achieve the integrated functionality of all parts including, accounting, purchasing, sale, warehouse treasury, etc. It ranges from the first step where the supplier is getting involved to the final step where the financial voucher is generated by the system. Adopting this new approach led the project team to make substantial changes to the project management framework in all its parts and design a new model which these changes are mentioned in previous chapters. So, when the model was completely prepared to support the core business of a steel company and even various processes in its subsidiaries it was time to start the go-live once again. Bearing in mind the previous failed attempt and being more mature, this time the project team decided to choose a smaller subsidiary company, i.e., Pabdana with almost fewer challenges in an attempt to deploy MIDRP processes as a pilot successfully.

According to the new model, integration as the main critical issue of the previous deployment needed to be thoroughly fulfilled. Thus, a document of all the processes which were going to be deployed in phase I was prepared, and the connections each process should have with other systems are specified in detail. For each process, a separate flowchart of the relationship between that specific process and the processes of other systems was drawn providing a vivid map-like picture for the project team to develop these connections. The document was supposed to be updated before each deployment. Take for example the purchasing request process which belongs to the purchasing system and requires going through various steps in order to be completed. To take these various steps the purchasing system requires to be connected to other systems such as finance, treasury as well as inventory, and warehouse.

Eventually, the countdown to the day when the new model's feasibility and system functionality were going to be tested for the second time began. Of course, this time because of the previous failure experience the stress level of the project team was much more and their self-confidence was now vulnerable. Saturday, November 10, 2018, was the due day and all the systems operating in Pabdana were going to be shut down and the new system, i.e., MIDRP I was going to operate instead. However, on the due day, some product owners insisted that shutting down the previous systems is a great risk. Accordingly, some of Pabdana's previous solutions should be operating in parallel with the new system in an attempt to eliminate the risk of data loss or validate the functionality of the system. Despite their insistence, their suggestion was rejected and MIDRP I was in operation on the due day while all the previous systems were shut down. On the first day of MIDRP I operation, the first weighing was registered into the system at 12:00 which means 4 hours of delay. Regardless of all the problems, shortcomings, and pressures that existed at this stage, MIDRP was finally successfully established and fortunately started working. It is noteworthy that the deployment of MIDRP products is not limited to one organization and is based on 15 factories, five companies, and two headquarters, which indicates the complexity of the process.

Although the second pilot was successful, it had its own problems and challenges. While the system integration was fulfilled this time, the system functionality was the most challenging perspective. In order to manage the challenges encountered by the project team, this time FANAP project management developed a methodology for tracking the issue status. Besides the system integration, having a procedure to track the issues which for any reason were affecting the system functionality adversely made sharp distinctions between ZARAND deployment on the one hand and PABDANA deployment on the other hand.

9.4 Support Mechanism

As the final action in the post-implementation phase of MIDRP, support for enterprise solutions is one of the main stages of its life cycle and ensures a stable relationship with customers or end-users. The purpose of the support is to provide the necessary platform for the efficient use of software solutions and features for customers. In the support system, in addition to providing services to users on existing products, with various updates, any functional changes are applied in the new update. Then, the support team is accompanied by the system's users to easily grasp these changes. One of the most important features of the MIDRP solution is the continuous support of system users. The main kinds of support services that are provided in the MIDRP solution include:

- Delivery of the latest version of the products along with the release notes
- Provide complementary training and consultation for efficient use of users

- Create a bridge between users and system developers to fix system bugs and add or modify functional features
- Schedule product launches and updates
- Provide the fastest and easiest ways to communicate with users.

But providing such services to users will not be possible unless there is a systematic approach. In the following, we will get acquainted with how this approach was formed in the MIDRP project. In its initial stages, the system support started right after the deployment in Zarand, however, it was not systematically organized and was simply based on communication through social media instead of accurate documentation.

LESSON LEARNED 9.9

"At the early stages of the development phase, every oral request issued by the representatives of the employer was resolved for the sake of their satisfaction. After a while and in certain cases, dissatisfactions aroused when the corresponding resolved items were undermined by the representatives who already asked for changes. In fact, they had forgotten their previous request due to the absence of an organized documentation procedure. In this respect, preparing even a simple minutes-of-meeting could handle such misunderstandings during the project accomplishment."

by Abdolhossein Pourjafari

As the project proceeded and especially after the failure in Zarand, the project team grasped the full significance of an organized and systematic approach to the management of the users' issues. For this purpose, the project team decided to dedicate a systematic tool to registering and tracing the users' issues whose steps should acquire status indicating the current conditions of the issues. Such a tracing tool is helpful for the project team not only in tracing the issues' status but also in producing any kind of reports about the issues as fast as possible. Thus, it has enabled the management team to identify the critical points and the root causes. Finding the root cause so fast is a great advantage for project management because needless to say, time matters a lot in supporting a system that is already being used by the users. Apart from the data loss the system errors might cause for the company, it can cause disappointment among the users leading to less motivated personnel at MIDHCO's subsidiaries.

Taking all of the above-mentioned factors into consideration, the project team came to the conclusion that a project management system, including an issue tracking tool, is a must when the go-live stats. FAMS was the name of the candidate online tool for MIDRP issue management. MIDRP users could register their issues in a form and fill in all the required information such as the issue title, the related product, the informer, the related company, explanation, etc., after the issue is registered a notification is sent to the corresponding individual. Also, the deployment team, on the other hand, can register issues in FAMS. In fact, on the task list board, they can add a new issue which turns into a new task for FANAP's different teams depending on the nature of the issue. As for the issues which were ambiguous, the deployment team was in charge of providing clarifying explanations by contacting the informer of the issues. The rest of the issues would be assigned to one of FANAP's teams, i.e., the user support team, business support team, or the platform and network team by the deployment team member in charge.

LESSON LEARNED 9.10

"Subsequent to the Go-live period, on one hand, the support team should handle the new requirements of the customer at the earliest time for the sake of its satisfaction. On the other hand, one should notify whether such a new requirement is covered by the contract terms or not. If it goes beyond the underlying commitments of the contract, the support team needs to announce the terms to the higher managerial level to acquire the necessary permits. As the number of requirements increases, the aforementioned terms have to be managed and expedited in a systematic manner. In MIDRP, FAMS has been, indeed, a perfect embodiment for fulfilling such cases."

by Mohammad Ganji

The FAMS solution is used to register needs, bugs, errors, or any problems expressed by users in the system, and at the same time, face-to-face support is on the agenda of the deployment points. Initially, immature solutions, especially face-to-face support, had become the Achilles heel of the support sector, reducing the quality of support and user satisfaction from an acceptable range. Hence, new approaches were put on the agenda of the support team. In fact, in this methodology, the same policies and mechanisms should be used that are used in development and implementation. The approach was designed to minimize face-to-face support and provide services as a Service Desk and Ticketing methods. In fact, the approach of the Ticketing and Service Desk is to create a mechanism based on telecommunication and computer systems. It aims to reduce a large amount of daily work, through a framework to register, categorize and prioritize tickets. These features are included in the FAMS system and minimize the need for users for face-to-face support. The main features of this system are efficient and user-friendly methods for tracking issues, correct scheduling of review and troubleshooting, creating update solutions for sending messages, notifications, warnings, etc., and finally efficient management reports.

One of the most important issues in the ticketing method is to create a solution to ensure that the support team agents adhere to the problem-solving schedules. If a ticket is not closed within the deadline, the necessary reports will be referred to senior support managers through alarms and reports. With a ticketing system, however, users can have extensive scientific resources. Therefore, users will be able to easily find the information they need in the form of frequently asked questions (FAQ) or troubleshooting solutions without the need for the support team. This method along with the knowledge management system will cause an increasing reduction in the number of registered tickets. In addition to this system, the use of a Service Desk or Help Desk has also been able to achieve user satisfaction, quality improvement, and troubleshooting in the shortest possible time. One of the most important advantages of this method is the use of remote-work staff in both Ticketing and Service Desk systems.

9.4.1 Issue Management in MIDRP Project

Unexpected problems and challenges will almost always arise in all projects, especially in large-scale software projects. When these issues arise, we need to have a solution for them because they can potentially affect the outcome of the project. In fact, the issues are unexpected in nature and should be responded to quickly. Therefore, we have to have a plan and a strategy to deal with them in advance. Issue management is the process of identifying and resolving issues. Technical problems and non-compliances are the most important issues in software projects. If the issues are not resolved, it will cause delays or even failure to produce and deliver the products.

One of the most important and complex concepts in the programming world is the concept of software defects which is so-called software bugs. Therefore, discovering bugs and fixing them in the software is essential and software production organizations use various methods and tools to register, track, and fix bugs. On the other hand, in software development, especially products that are highly complex and at the same time their scope includes most of the processes of organizations when the system is deployed or even when the system is fully operational in the organization, there are requests from users, the source of which is the maturity of the organization processes and also the technology advancement. These issues may not be seen in the initial production of any system, and software developers should consider requests and needs from users and apply mechanisms to create these in the product life cycle. In today's competitive world, companies will be successful if they identify customer needs and satisfy them as quickly as possible.

In the MIDRP project, the issues appeared from the beginning of the project development. Maybe the most important reason is that this project is managed in an agile method, that is, product testing is done at the same time as product development. In this case, the team does not have to wait for the release of the full version and testing request. In fact, it's a great way for developers and testers to cooperate to solve the issues. This prevents the accumulation of issues and ultimately leads to less time and complexity for solving software system problems.

Therefore, in the MIDRP project, a systematic mechanism was created to register, track and fix issues. The key point is that the management of issues begins from the go-live date and continues until the end of the customer support process. Issues submitted by the employer, deployment experts, and analyst persons are registered on the main, test, and integration servers in the system, and can be tracked until reviewed and resolved. Due to the fact that in software projects, identifying and fixing bugs is one of the costs of rework, in order to reduce costs, these items should be identified in the production and testing part. Fig. 9.4 shows the importance of quality costs in software projects. Following an optimal guideline for registering and tracking bugs, quality costs in this area can be reduced as much as possible.

According to Spillner et al. (2014), a bug is defined as a type of error or mistake in running the software that causes the wrong results or non-execution of the software. These cases occur due to defects in the software. Software bugs are created when the software is developed or modified, and only become visible when the software is running, and failure is visible. The ISTQB[1] standard uses the classes to show the severity of bug failure: (1) **Fatal:** the system is severely disrupted and will likely be associated with data loss. The system cannot run under these conditions. (2) **Very serious:** a major breakdown that results in significant damage to many stakeholders; requirements have not been met or incorrectly implemented; the system can only be used with severe restrictions. (3) **Serious:** deviation or functional limitation (natural failure) has occurred; requirements are incorrectly or only partially implemented; the system can be used with restrictions. (4) **Moderate:** partial deviation or small damage injuries to a small number of stakeholders. The system can be used without

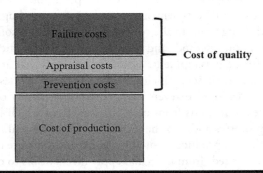

Figure 9.4 Cost of quality in software projects.

restriction. (5) **Mild**: slight damage to a small number of stakeholders, the system can be used without restriction (e.g., typos).

Given the importance of registering, reviewing, and tracking issues declared by the customer and ensuring that these items are fully traceable, a systematic framework needs to be used to manage them. The solution used in the MIDRP project is a web-based solution called FAMS, which we get familiar with it in the task management section in Chapter 4. As mentioned, FAMS is used to manage the task in the MIDRP project. Using this application, pre-defined people can specify operations such as defining members, assigning tasks to the members, scheduling each task, and tracking its progress.

 # LESSON LEARNED 9.11

"The staff of the deployment team has the closest connections to the end-users and can significantly digest the gist of their requirements. Nevertheless, the lack of a representative associated with the corresponding team within the expertise meetings was the constant yet prudent complaint of the deployment office. To fill this gap and enhance the related contribution, a specific mechanism has been designed, composed of the support and business layers. The individuals of the support layer are called agents and are supposed to do their best in solving the problem at the site of the customer. If it could not be realized, the problem is transmitted to the business layer. Concerning each product, there is at least one representative of the deployment team at the business layer. The participants of this layer are in close coordination with the development and system analysis team and thereby can properly convey the exact problem of the customer with the system."

by Mohammad Hamidi

9.4.2 Issue logging

The first step in issue management is to log it. When an issue report is created, a tool is provided to report and articulate what happened in connection with the project. This causes the issue to be raised and then examined and resolved. The logging of issues makes this issue to be considered by the corresponding team. It also provides the ability to track, assign to the person to act, analyze and prioritize issues, create a history of resolutions for future reference, and monitor the proper functioning of the entire system.

The logging of an issue must include all the necessary details. The type of issue has to be specified first, including technical bugs, requests, or proposals. A technical bug means that there is a problem with running the software. In general, if a particular feature is incorrectly implemented and it is the cause of the failure observed in the software, it is a bug. On the other hand, request means that changes are needed to run the program better or more accurately. These changes either did not exist in the analysis documents from the beginning or did not exist in the current version. In this case, the user must be assured that this issue will be addressed in future versions. Additionally, the proposal is a sort of request that has no direct effect on the user's performance, and users do not claim to need to implement it on the system. In other words, the proposal is a request that is not contractually binding, or its non-implementation will not have a negative impact on project's progress. These items will be placed in the backlog only if approved by the product owner and will be implemented to improve future versions of the system if there are resources and possible time.

In detail, the impact and severity of issues are required to be signaled. In other words, software bugs have a separate degree of importance, so in the terminology of this project, the defects are divided into four categories.

- **Fire Fighting:** A bug in the software that completely disrupts user operations and makes it impossible for processes to progress; the error is in the part of the system where the key stakeholders are facing, and a large number of stakeholders are having trouble with it. This type should only be used when an issue has been viewed on the main server, and this issue must be fixed to continue working with the product. For example error messages when users log in, not being able to use the processes, disrupting to run of the process, and not displaying data in the search window.

- **Critical:** A bug in the software that causes computational problems and provides invalid output from the software; the requirements have not been met or have not been properly implemented; in this bug, a large number of stakeholders are affected and in the short term, it also affects key stakeholders. All issues that are registered on the Integration Server and must be fixed to release the registered version of the issue are of this type. Also, all the issues that are very important and need to be fixed as soon as possible will have this type. For example, problems with key calculations and erroneous output, excessive slowness of a process, the incorrect performance of a process, and problems with basic system capabilities.

- **Necessary:** A bug in the software that displays conditions that are not expected by the user. In this case, a part of a product is damaged. In this situation, the functional needs of the user are met, but it has created failures for the user, which has reduced the reliability of the system. In this case, a small number of system users suffer minor damage in their operation with the software. For example, the repetition of a record (with moderate sensitivity), the problem in displaying form information, and the error of the bundle. In fact, there are issues that do not affect the customer's business in the short term, but by not fixing them shortly, they will become critical bugs. This bug can be registered on all three servers.

- **Important:** It is a bug that has caused a minor deviation in the system. The system can be used without restriction. This bug can be registered on all servers, e.g., spelling errors or incorrect pages, minor visual errors, and no display of information in non-mandatory and low-usage fields.

It is also crucial to set the identifier. The identifier is the individual who registered and identified the issue. Besides, the server on which the issue is observed should be indicated, i.e., main, integration, or test server). The same needs to be considered to highlight the underlying business process associated with the issue. In the meantime, the first step in reviewing is to assign the registered issue to the relevant team. From now on, this team or person will be responsible for reviewing, fixing, or trouble-shooting the issue and delivering the request. Furthermore, to declare the site of the issue, the corresponding field should be reported. The actions taken by the relevant team are also notified to the user. The feature of timing can be used if it takes a certain amount of time to check and fix an issue. Moreover, specific monitoring is required for detecting the status of an issue. After registration, the issue is delivered to the product responsible (PR). PRs review the issue and change its status. (1) Approved: at this stage, PR informs the technical leasers (TL) to follow up and resolve. (2) Approved with low priority: this means that despite the approval, it will be done in a longer period. (3) Unconfirmed: in this case, the PR rejects the issue while stating the technical reasons for the non-acceptance of the registered issue.

After an issue is logged, it is assigned to the intended person for action and resolution. In fact, a certain person is responsible for taking care of and resolving this issue. They can then monitor the status of the process. After completing the issue resolution process, the PR is required to confirm it, and if this issue is approved, it is terminated. The entire process of logging the issue by a user to fixing it by the implementation team is shown in Fig. 9.5.

LESSON LEARNED 9.12

"The active engagement of the support team in the debugging practice is of paramount importance. Indeed, the staff of the support/deployment team is among the first individuals who face a new system bug. If they have the necessary knowledge in analyzing that error, the ideal debugging result will be yielded in a much more efficient manner. Playing a very passive role in dealing with a bug and just passing it to the technical individuals would naturally lengthen the issue management interval. In the

MIDRP project, the true practice for the support staff is to control the product reports, oversee the status of the error in Yama, and double-check the issue within the test server. By following these simple maneuvers, almost 50% of bugs would be immediately resolved and the support staff gains the necessary knowledge in handling the upcoming issues."

by Reza Mohammadi Gisaki

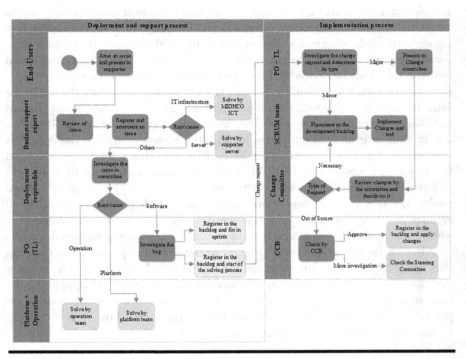

Figure 9.5 Issue-solving procedure.

9.5 Conclusion

This chapter is devoted to discussing the very challenging issue of deployment of the MIDRP solution and describes in detail the various aspects of its implementation. In the meantime, concerning a long-sighted perspective on the aforementioned story, there may be some doubtful issues that also need to be explored in the final discussion. Primarily, had the involved parties predicted that the readiness level of MIDRP was not suitable for undergoing the pilot deployment process? In case of a positive response, why has it happened despite the prospective prediction? Actually, the involved experts were aware that both readiness levels of the FANAP product and the MIDHCO environment were not acceptable for a perfect deployment. Meanwhile, that attempt for deployment with a partial level of readiness could be attributed to the gist idea behind the foundation of FANAP and MIDHCO by the Pasargad Financial Group. This idea is grasped by considering the following quotation.

> *"Progress is the outcome of movement, even at a snail's pace. By standing motionless, you are supposed to get off the bike, otherwise, you'll be falling off."*
>
> —**Majid Ghassemi**, *CEO of Pasargad Financial Group*

At that time, MIDRP managers insisted on starting the deployment stage to realize the progress and prevent getting stuck in the implementation step. Additionally, it is also required to be mentioned why the initially designed deployment procedure has remained almost intact during the maturity period. Certainly, the survival of the framework is dependent on the significant role of POSCO ICT. In fact, the supporting character of the story could propose an applied framework based on the best practices that have removed the necessity of being fundamentally changed throughout the deployment. Nevertheless, why was not such an applied framework successfully worked during the initial pilot trial? Probably, it originated from the lack of tangible experience of FANAP and MIDHCO in toughing dilemmas of the operational environment out. Initially, both parties had not clearly grasped the necessity of adopting the appropriate measures in light of fulfilling the sub-steps of deployment though it had been implied in the framework of deployment. In other words, they did not have a tangible sense of the fact that missing a simple item in the test environment could be exacerbated in practice. This has brought about the initial unsuccessful experience despite the true functionality of the proposed deployment framework.

All in all, the involved parties could pass the climax of MIDRP and surmount the challenges by significantly putting the lessons learned from the initial failure into practice.

Note

1. International Software Testing Qualifications Board.

References

Al-Mudimigh, A., Zairi, M., & Al-Mashari, M. (2001). ERP software implementation: An integrative framework. *European Journal of Information Systems, 10*(4), 216–226.

Benders, J., Batenburg, R., & Van der Blonk, H. (2006). Sticking to standards; technical and other isomorphic pressures in deploying ERP-systems. *Information & Management, 43*(2), 194–203.

Holland, C. R., & Light, B. (1999). A critical success factors model for ERP implementation. *IEEE Software, 16*(3), 30–36.

Koch, C., Slater, D., & Baatz, E. (1999). The ABCs of ERP. *CIO Magazine, 22*.

Maheshwari, B., Kumar, V., & Kumar, U. (2010). Delineating the ERP institutionalization process: Go-live to effectiveness. *Business Process Management Journal, 16*(4), 744–771.

Nagpal, S., Khatri, S. K., & Kumar, A. (2015). Comparative study of ERP implementation strategies. *Long island systems, applications, and technology* (pp. 1–9). IEEE.

Portougal, V., & Sundaram, D. (2005). *Business processes: operational solutions for SAP implementation: operational solutions for SAP implementation*. IGI Global.

Spillner, A., Linz, T., & Schaefer, H. (2014). *Software testing foundations: A study guide for the certified tester exam*. Rocky Nook, Inc.

Welti, N. (1999). *Successful SAP R/3 implementation: Practical management of ERP projects*. Addison-Wesley Longman Publishing Co., Inc.

Williams, G. C., Ainsworth, D., & Jones, K. (2008). *Implementing SAP ERP sales & distribution*. McGraw-Hill.

Chapter 10

The Intelligent Future

> *"Not only does MIDRP automate the business processes of MIDHCO, but also aims at employing the industry 4.0 model even at the sensor level using Internet of Things"*
>
> —**Shahab Javanmardi**, *C.E.O of FANAP Co.*

So far, we have gone on a journey to the unique practice of building a flexible enterprise solution from scratch, called MIDRP. The uninterrupted attempts of the main characters of the story have been described in full detail throughout the chapters in this book, from the initial planning steps up to the complete deployment. When the deployment phase is completed, the end users are able to benefit from the full functionality of the system to automate their business processes and improve workflows. The performance will increase and there will be a considerable reduction in the costs and time for making business processes. Although this significantly conducts MIDHCO toward reaching its ambitious target which has been illustrated at the onset of the story, the MIDRP mission is not accomplished yet. Despite all the achievements and innovations, there is still a lot to do in order to improve the system and provide outstanding services for business process management throughout the MIDHCO holding. The final puzzle of the story embodies the way of injecting intelligence and state-of-the-art technologies into the body of MIDRP that is going to be discussed here.

10.1 Toward System Advancement

As an ERP implementation matures in an enterprise, there are always new needs and expectations as a result of technological advancement and the change in

DOI: 10.1201/9781003369806-10

working conditions and business requirements. Companies gradually need to provide more capabilities for their enterprise solutions to support the business requirements in the ever-changing competitive market. Since MIDHCO's slogan is "move toward world-class," it opens to globalization as a way of looking to the future and taking advantage of new business opportunities. More specifically, the company is planning to realize a *digital transformation*. Digital transformation is defined as the set of organization actions to use new digital technologies and exploit their benefits (Matt et al., 2015). With the emergence of the digital revolution and Industry 4.0, the accelerated technological developments and their numerous applications in various business environments is gradually changing the industry landscape and will bring new needs and expectations for company stakeholders in order to stay in the competitive markets. Nowadays, the range of companies seeking digitalization is very wide. From mechanical engineering companies that use predictive maintenance systems to automotive companies that use Big Data to improve traffic safety, as well as retailers that improve the performance of their physical stores using digital channels. Whatever they use in their companies, their common goal is to promote their business through smart networking and new ideas. Hence, in order to achieve its goals, MIDHCO is eagerly pursuing these transformational approaches, which MIDRP can be a suitable bridge for their digital transformation. As a result, it is often necessary to add new features and capabilities to the enterprise software systems and products to meet new requirements or maximize customers' satisfaction.

FANAP executives believed that MIDHCO's requirements could not be fully met without considering the developments of the digital era. They need a comprehensive and integrated set of applications, a data-driven platform, and a set of technologies such as artificial intelligence (AI) to deliver a perfect package to orchestrate the processes of MIDHCO. Hence, in addition to meeting the various needs of a specific industry, the MIDRP system has also evolved in line with technological developments adding new tools and capabilities to its functionality. To be more specific, FANAP has attempted to embrace innovative technologies such as AI, big data analytics, the Internet of things (IoT), cloud computing, and blockchain. The application of these technologies for improving the MIDRP performance is a great concern of the FANAP management as stated in the specifications of the last phase of the MIDRP project. The correct implementation of digital technologies will bring system intelligence, improved performance, and advanced capabilities to MIDHCO so that it can survive and succeed in the digital transformation age.

As one of the leaders in the information technology industry in the region, FANAP provides many tools for organizations to achieve digital transformation. Analyzing, developing, and continuously monitoring novel technologies and business trends is the main concern of any IT company. These trends may be so significant that ignoring any of them can lead to the disintegration of some parts or all of the organization's business and the loss of competitive markets. As a result,

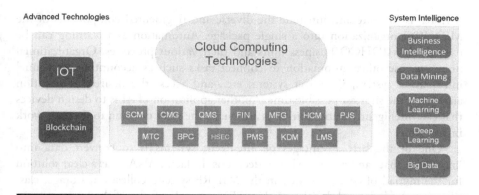

Figure 10.1 MIDRP future perspective, Intelligence, and technologies.

with the aim of developing intelligent and digital platforms in various organizations, including MIDHCO, FANAP is progressively trying to introduce and deploy technological applications in different industries. FANAP also sought to provide novelty in various processes of its products, according to the policy it had established from the outset to develop the MIDRP solution.

Although the description of MIDRP III and the various novel features offered to the system is a long story and may need another book to be fairly covered, in this chapter, we introduce, in a nutshell, some of the most important technologies that are adopted in the MIDRP new phase. Fig. 10.1 shows a general perspective of the MIDRP future landscape with the new features and capabilities. Our focus is on two related categories: *system intelligence* and *advanced technologies*. By using innovative capabilities offered by new technologies such as AI, Big Data Analytics, Cloud Computing, and IoT, FANAP is going to make the system more competitive and bring a high level of intelligence and automation so that it can perform as a powerful enterprise system and meet the requirements of the customer in the new digital era. In addition, using novel technologies and applications, FANAP can create a well-prepared environment to bring innovations to the industry.

10.2 System Intelligence

One of the most important aspects of today's business requirements is to create some level of intelligence in the business operations, processes and workflows as well as in customer and partner relationships. The intelligence brings more automation to the enterprise system operations and enhances its learning abilities to gain knowledge of what is happening in the enterprise so that better tactical and strategic decisions can be made by the management. Simply put, an effective and configured ERP can greatly help organizations in the strategic advancement of digital maturity (Ustundag & Cevikcan, 2017). As stated before, the goal of

MIDRP is to unite and integrate the diverse and fragmented components of the MIDHCO organization into a single package. Automation and learning can be used in all MIDHCO business units and their various processes. Organizational units can use office automation to connect tasks such as accounting, personnel information system, timesheet system, etc., and access the desired information analysis in the shortest possible time. Another application of AI is to design devices that can intelligently learn their tasks and make the right decision to do their work in real-time.

One of the best advantages of intelligent systems is to convert data into knowledge that can help make better decisions. In fact, FANAP has a clear solution for the myriad of data generated in the MIDRP system: collection, storage, classification, analysis, and decision-making. For example, if one of the business units has to decide what products (or services) to offer next month based on customer information, this can be achieved easily by using smart approaches such as business intelligence and predictive analytics.

Therefore, the system intelligence can now be effective in achieving the new MIDHCO goals in the digital age, by creating more efficient processes and making the organization smarter and more accurate in decisions making processes. In this section, we elaborate more on system intelligence, according to *the AI* and *big data analytics* capabilities.

10.2.1 Artificial Intelligence

AI is introduced as a branch of computer science that deals with the generation of intelligent behaviors. In general, the term *AI* is used to describe systems that aim to use machines to mimic and simulate human intelligence and related behaviors (Nilsson, 2014). This goal may sometimes be achieved using simple algorithms and pre-defined patterns, but sometimes it requires extremely complex algorithms. There are various tools and methods for using AI in the real world. The basis of all these methods is "machine learning" which is defined as a system that turns experience into knowledge (Russell & Norvig, 2020). This process gives the system the ability to identify patterns and rules at an ever-increasing rate. Thanks to the rapid expansion of neural networks for machine learning and the creation of more complex systems with new layers, novel and powerful methods such as *deep learning* have emerged (Goodfellow et al., 2016), which can be easily changed and adapted to many applications.

AI tools are used in detecting, identifying, and classifying objects and people in photos and videos. The use of chatbots in the customer service department is increasing day by day. These text-based assistants do their job by identifying keywords in the customer request and responding appropriately. In addition to predicting the outcome of elections in the world of politics, opinion analysis is also used in marketing and many other fields. Opinion Mining, also known as "Sentiment Analysis" is used to search the internet for emotional ideas and expressions (Liu, 2015). Using these methods, polls can be conducted anonymously. Search algorithms, like those used by Google, are naturally highly confidential. The methods of calculating, ranking, and displaying search results are largely based on mechanisms that use machine learning (Bahrammirzaee, 2010). AI tools can predict the future with great accuracy, and we are still at the beginning of understanding its great potential (Mitchell et al., 2013).

Organizations around the world are increasingly looking to automate activities that were previously performed by human resources. This has created a fundamental change in the labor market and manpower. Today, dangerous and time-consuming activities in factories are performed by robotic arms. Automation has even penetrated organizational services such as factory customers, and many companies now use automated systems that receive basic questions and feedback from customers. One of the areas that are highly affected by AI is enterprise solutions, like the MIDRP system. The MIDRP system can benefit from AI in many of its functional modules to enhance system performance and improve business processes throughout the organization. The effects of AI tools can manifest themselves in the following various domains:

- **Production management:** For production planning, the life cycle of the organization's products and inventories from the moment of supply until delivery to the customer is one of the most important and challenging points. Determining how much inventory is required and where to store it is one of the most difficult activities that involve different parts of the organization. AI algorithms help the inventory management module efficiently control and manage inventory under the MIDRP system by predicting product flow based on supply and demand modeling.
- **Automation:** Today, with the help of AI, robots can even talk to humans and react to their behavior. This application can save tremendous labor time and power. Most of the time in business processes, MIDHCO's employees follow pre-defined rules when working with MIDRP. These rules can be easily taught and applied by an AI-powered system. In fact, instead of wasting human energy doing something, we leave it to the AI capabilities of MIDRP and use the workforce elsewhere. This greatly affects MIDHCO's productivity.
- **Finance:** Many data mining and machine learning methods can be applied to MIDHCO's financial data, to predict the financial future of the company. Other things like payroll, compensation distribution, and other complex financial aspects that are important to companies of all sizes can also be done with the help of AI. In addition, appropriate AI tools can be used for fraud detection and abnormal behavior identification in companies. Finance is one of the most vital parts of any organization like MIDHCO where human error must be kept to a minimum. AI can give this valuable feature to the financial module of MIDRP.

- **Human capital management:** The intelligence in the Recruitment Management System helps to automatically identify the most suitable candidates for a specific job requirement, leading to the optimization of the candidate selection process. Recruiters can have in-depth information about job-seeking candidates. This feature helps the recruiter or hiring manager and reduces the time and cost of selecting candidates. AI tools for the RCS product use machine learning algorithms to identify and rank candidates and applicants who meet the requirements of a particular job.
- **Sales:** The integration of customer profiles with sales information through AI capabilities leads to the addition of important information about customer behaviors. Recommender systems optimize sales performance by providing automated offers (Jannach et al., 2010). These offers are based on past sales information, sales steps and trends, and customer behavior analysis. Also, Market Basket Analysis (MBA) (Kaur & Kang, 2016), offers good information about customers' buying habits, by receiving and analyzing business invoices and discovering buying patterns in transaction data.
- **Supply chain:** The MIDRP system's intelligent capability for supplier selection allows automated classification and ranking of suppliers based on various factors. This is achieved by combining supplier information, purchase orders, invoices, payables demand, and other details with the company's external data sources. The AI-powered tools in the SCM module constantly monitor the results and implement various models on it to optimize every decision the system makes. The intelligent development of this MIDRP feature covers a variety of areas, including negotiating the best discounts available to ensure compliance with purchasing policies.
- **Manufacturing:** Production planning and scheduling as well as manufacturing engineering is among the most significant functions of ERP systems. The sheer volume of data and the over-complexity of real-world problems, make traditional methods incapable of calculating correct or optimal solutions. Intelligent optimization methods can solve these problems and improve the accuracy of results. Inventory management, transportation planning, and maintenance scheduling are other major challenges that require optimal decisions. AI now acts as a powerful engine, receiving data from various MIDRP processes and providing appropriate output to each of them.

With the correct implementation of AI tools and capabilities in the MIDRP system functional modules, we can gain many advantages including the following. In fact, with the learning and optimization algorithms used in various business problems, end users and managers can get closer to optimal decisions. AI can also do many things that were previously done by humans and were accompanied by error, and therefore creates optimization and efficiency in time, cost, and use of organizational resources. In light of increasing customer satisfaction, sometimes end users of the system have requirements that can be customized with the help of AI capabilities.

10.2.2 Big Data Analytics

Big data usually refers to a set of data that is too large and complex to be retrieved, refined, managed, and processed in a reasonable amount of time with standard software (Snijders et al., 2012). In the digital world with social networks, multimedia tools, and automated processes, more and more data is generated every day and creating a huge volume of data in the form of text, images, audio, and videos in organizations. A large-scale enterprise system like MIDRP may as well generate a huge amount of data as a result of a broad set of business processes that are done in the holding every day. Big data can be used as a valuable source for all important business operations, from accounting to human resources, to gain unparalleled insight into your organization's performance. There are various methods and tools to analyze big data and gain beneficial insight from them. By using NoSQL databases, such as MongoDB, ArrangoDB, and ElasticSearch, in the database layer system architecture, the big data is well incorporated and managed by the MIDRP system. Machine learning and deep learning methods are capable of absorbing the invisible insight of big data and transforming it into useful knowledge with minimal human contribution. But what capabilities will this feature give to the MIDRP system:

- **Future Prediction:** Big data analytics can make a forecast of the market or the company's future accurately by analyzing the company's past data and identifying its current and upcoming trends. The trends can be used to predict the future in the long and short term. MIDRP solution provides a complete picture of the operations within a company, and the large amount of data contained in them makes it a complete platform for data mining and predictive analytics to perform the necessary analysis. By minimizing speculation in forecasting seasonal demand, supply and financial performance, forecasting with the MIDRP solution gives MIDHCO a more accurate and in-depth insight into the current and future of the organization.
- **Improved scheduling:** By using Big Data tools, the MIDRP software can analyze more data in less time, offering deeper, more precise insight into operational inefficiencies. This allows different business units to schedule processes more effectively and reallocate resources into areas with more urgency. For example, the integration of big data with business processes can be really helpful in the manufacturing management module. The timely delivery of products relies on correct production schedules. When ERP software integrates data points from across the organization, users can review the status of a given job, make adjustments on the fly, and ensure optimal utilization of people and machinery.
- **SCM optimization:** Big data processing tools can also help to optimize manufacturing supply chains. Effective supply chain management requires thorough and constant analysis of manufacturing processes and their numerous interdependent moving parts. Large volumes of data created through

each stage of the supply chain, from raw materials procurement to distribution, can give visibility to the managers about the workings of the chain and the possible inefficiencies in each part system. With real-time monitoring of the data at hand, MIDHCO's business units can optimize all the routes involved in the flow of products and their movement in the supply chain cycle. GIS information processing can be really helpful in the distribution stage, where businesses depend on fleet management and route optimization to efficiently deliver goods and services.

■ **CRM improvement:** The customer relationship management (CRM) module in an ERP system is a great place to benefit from customers' Big Data analytics. The MIDRP software's CRM component offers deeper insight into customer-related activity with the analysis of historical trends, social network activities, and individual buying habits. Currently, a large number of businesses are benefiting from social networking sites for understanding customer preferences. The use of big data and predictive analytics offers more accurate buyer perspectives and a better view of the loyalty and satisfaction of each group of customers.

■ **Providing Business Insights:** A large amount of data is generated every day in MIDHCO holding as a result of business process execution. The MIDRP modules are able to receive a semi-structured type of data from the sensor networks and operational devices in the production environment. Most of the data generated in business processes can be collected in a structured manner using big data tools. The analysis of this data helps business units to gain insights regarding inventory, supply chain management, manufacturing, health, and safety processes in an efficient manner. The data can be used in a Business Intelligence (BI) framework to generate dashboards and informative reports about the company's performance. In addition, the insights obtained from the big data enable managers to make better and more precise decisions that can be beneficial to the organization. Using big data with ERP can bring about the development of new and innovative strategies for the growth of the business.

10.3 Advanced Technologies

MIDRP has expanded its capabilities to embrace the digital age and prepare MIDHCO to start a digital transformation. In this section, we describe some of the most important technologies that FANAP is incorporating into MIDRP to extend its functionality in the digital revolution era.

10.3.1 Cloud Computing

Cloud computing is a technology that uses the internet and decentralized services to store and use data and offer computing resources (Xu, 2012). Cloud computing and its widespread use not only facilitated the collection of information but also increased the capacity of companies and organizations to improve performance. This technology resolves the needs of companies, of any size and capacity, for costly IT infrastructures and high maintenance costs (Velte et al., 2009). The cost-effectiveness of cloud computing has led to its recognition as a service system that has enabled small companies to access reliable computing resources. Amazon, Google, and Microsoft Web Services are some of the largest and most well-known companies in the field of cloud computing.

Cloud computing has been able to make a significant impact on one of the most challenging ERP issues, namely inflexibility. Table 10.1 shows some of the most significant differences between the cloud system and the On-Premise systems.

According to the provided features, the MIDRP system has been developed based on a hybrid cloud platform. This means that some parts of the system are cloud-based and the other parts are on-premise. In this case, companies sometimes store some of their data and information on their servers for security or techno-logical limitations and send the rest of the information to cloud servers. This allows users to access the system from anywhere and allows organizations to control their vital information. Software as a service (SaaS) is currently one of the most common types of cloud computing services. MIDRP also uses SaaS, enabling MIHDCO to have access to special software for financial management to gain higher efficiency and better accessibility.

Advanced reporting through business intelligence dashboards in MIDHCO requires huge databases because a lot of information is available and recordable in the subsidiary organizations. On the other hand, this holding has several branches of factories and business units. High-performance access to information systems is possible through the cloud computing infrastructure. Due to the use of big data and cloud computing features, the necessary infrastructure for implementing business intelligence on the cloud platform will also be provided. According to the MIDRP cloud solution, administrators can send their requests in the cloud computing space with the aim of receiving various complex reports. This approach reduces costs and allows managers and employees to access the professional reports they need at any time and place with appropriate speed and quality. Moreover, the issue of guaranteeing security and updating the business intelligence system has been resolved to an appropriate extent, and all support services will be performed in one place in a centralized way, on the servers of the cloud.

10.3.2 Internet of Things

The IoT refers to an interconnected system of computer equipment, mechanical and digital machines, objects, or individuals identified by unique identifiers (UIDs) capable of transmitting data over a network without the need for human-to-human or human-to-computer interaction (Gubbi et al., 2013; Ashton, 2009). The Shrinking of sensors has changed the way the data is gathered in businesses and supply chains around the world, making it easier to gather large amounts of

Table 10.1   Benefits (+) and Disadvantages (–) of Cloud ERP vs. On-Premise ERP Systems

	Cloud ERP	*On-Premise ERP*
Cost	■ Costs identified over time ■ Inexpensive preliminary investment ■ Limited investment in hardware (e.g., server infrastructure) ■ High property costs over the entire system lifecycle	■ High risk of primary investment ■ Reduced initial system risk
Security	■ Data is stored on vendor servers, and security is usually in the vendor's hand. ■ Prospect of continuing stability resulting in regular updates from the vendor as little customization is necessary. ■ While data security is in the hand of vendors, security is not fully guaranteed. In addition, prospects may not go well in some organizations.	■ Providing the organization with data security may keep the data secure. ■ The runtime may be a function of customization. ■ The data is stored on the customer's server, and security is usually provided by the organization.
Customization	■ Facilitation of customization for its flexibility. ■ There are a few customization options.	■ Customization may lead to problems after a software update by the vendor. ■ Facilitation of customization
Implementation	■ Lower implementation time is needed. ■ Shorter implementation time may be a function of lower customization options.	■ The implementation time sometimes lasts longer than usual. ■ The enterprise exerts a higher level of control.

information and create more organized systems. Industries such as manufacturing and retailing have equipped trucks and factories with IoT equipment and other smart devices to make it easier to collect information on a large scale. The Industrial Internet of Things (IIoT) has become a specialized field, and companies can use this technology to gather complete information about their machines and tools, and then use machine learning and AI to analyze information. These systems can make the workplace safer for employees and even identify areas that have additional costs. The more workplaces are equipped with IoT technology, the more analytical tools will be developed, and companies will find new ways to improve their services (Lee & Lee, 2015).

One of the main purposes of MIDRP systems for MIDHCO is to provide usable data and information for managers of organizations. However, gathering the right information is a constant challenge for them. The IoT has the potential to dramatically increase data accessibility and accuracy. This has important implications for customer service, forecasting, inventory management, and business intelligence. In order for businesses to take full advantage of the potential use of IoT, companies and manufacturers need to equip their products with the sensors and tools they need to fully integrate them into production operations.

Thanks to the IoT, communicating directly with the end-user has become a key feature of the MIDRP system. Previously, the CRM module was updated with the information registered for the product serial number for each customer, both at the time of shipment and afterward. Therefore, when the manufacturer contacts the customer directly, all consumer information is accessible in the ERP system. However, when a product is sold to a customer through an intermediary, getting end-user information is always a challenge. The IoT has solved this problem by making it possible for the manufacturer and the customer to communicate from the moment the device starts working. This has created more stability in the sales process and has become a treasure of information for service operations and product engineering for the manufacturer.

The process of predicting the required inventory for products in an organization from past patterns is very complex. Using the capabilities of IoT, MIDRP facilitates this process in the organization. In connection with product customization, the IoT also provides the organization with tremendous information about the desired product specifications that customers want. In other words, the IoT makes it possible to easily understand which products and with what specifications have attracted the attention of which group of customers.

Since the semantic web is considered to be an effective method for achieving the integration among systems, integrating MIDRP and IoT is implemented with semantic web and Cloud MIDRP APIs. Fig. 10.2 depicts the integration model. The semantic web acts as a middleware between the IOT services that are offered by the IoT devices and the MIDRP cloud APIs. The APIs get meaningful information about the devices (such as products, operating devices, or monitoring sensors) using the semantic web and the MIDRP modules can use this information

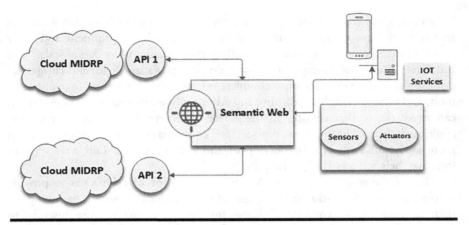

Figure 10.2 IoT and cloud MIDRP integration model.

to perform their tasks. This integration model has many benefits, including the
following:

- Some key points of time such as re-orders, replenishment, out-of-stock inventories, and missed deliveries could be informed automatically via
  Internet-connected sensors and devices.
- IoT makes it possible to send notifications and warnings to the producers for
  informing them. For example, some of their products require additional
  attention or some machines are down. However, such a functionality is
  provided only when the business processes adapt to this new model.
- IoT provides a considerable amount of data that needs to be gathered,
  processed, and analyzed appropriately to gain the maximum benefits from
  IoT-based MIDRP. Nevertheless, the robustness of this solution is a real
  concern and is required to handle the vast flow of data from various devices
  and goods. Thus, a lot of pre-preparation is demanded of the manufacturing
  companies while they need to take into account the size of their current
  MIDRP and whether it is capable of connecting to IoT.
- Real-time information is a prerequisite for an efficient solution. The integration of MIDRP and IoT paves the way for real-time data and immediate
  solutions at the same time; this is possible through MIDRP, which provides
  a clear understanding of the situation while IoT offers potential solutions. In
  fact, IoT will create valuable information that can be extracted through
  MIDRP in an attempt to improve the business.
- In the supply chain, IoT enables goods or equipment to be monitored as
  they are transported from one point to the next and, as a result, provides
  information in real-time. Subsequently, real-time data is fed into the
  MIDRP system, providing all those involved in the supply chain with a

feature that enables them to monitor the interconnections between the product life cycle and the material flow.

Providing a safe and practical platform for communication and proper operation of all devices and elements in factories and industries is the basis of the *fourth industrial revolution*, which is also called the future *smart factories*. The Fanitoring platform developed by FANAP provides the required services in the field of industrial automation, SCADA, and monitoring. As stated in Chapter 8, Fanitoring defines a shared infrastructure in the second layer for inter-system-communication, which is why it is also referred to as the Second Layer Interface. It is platform-independent through which different types of clients and servers communicate across different types of networks. Thanks to the support of modern technologies in the world, this monitoring platform has made it possible to manage and store data in a large volume and with high security, based on the needs of different industries. Fig. 10.3 shows the position of Fanitoring in the automation levels of the MIDHCO organization. Fanitoring has significantly increased efficiency, quality, and flexibility for users and engineers. An intuitive configuration environment in Fanitoring facilitates the working process on large and complex projects. Also, in this platform, data recording, analysis, security, control, and monitoring of information are widely available. Due to its comprehensive and flexible type of architecture, it can also be presented in a modular way.

In addition to supporting standard protocols, Fanitoring can connect to all devices that have the ability to connect to the Internet via the FANAP's IoT cloud, thus facilitating data exchange at all levels of the system.

IoT connects tools and employees over the Internet, in which case data generation is rising exponentially. Now, let us consider a large steel-making holding with several business units and 20 plants that are supposed to exchange information on a MIDRP solution. This large amount of data makes analysis very complicated, but it does provide a more reliable forecast. In reality, companies may use analytical tools to design a stronger approach to their business strategy. The noticeable amount of data captured by IoT is highly valuable. Several physical objects existing in the different IoT applications are in charge of creating such big data. Thus, the large amount of data generated by physical devices must be analyzed online to acquire useful knowledge.

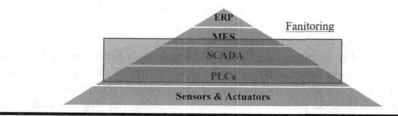

Figure 10.3   Fanitoring position and role in the automation levels.

10.3.3 Blockchain

Blockchain is a new technology in the field of secure computing. This technology can transform the digital world by using the "distributed ledger" feature for any online transaction in such a way that digital assets can be identified and trusted in the future. It has penetrated into almost every industry due to its wide variety of features. Blockchain was introduced in 2008 as part of the cryptocurrency industry and later became known as a pioneering technology in the financial industry. For more than five years, banks and financial institutions have been using this technology in everything from smart contracts to simplifying loan forms. In recent years, many companies have begun researching the impact of blockchain, concluding that the technology has had a huge impact on supply chains. Large retailers such as Walmart and successful companies such as McDonald's now use blockchain to supply resources and raw materials (Banerjee, 2018).

Although the term "blockchain" has become widely known with cryptocurrency, its connection to corporate systems and production environments goes beyond "Bitcoin." Today, with the support of technological tools, a wide range of data that can be recorded at different locations on a string of "blocks" can be connected in a timely and irreversible manner. Since changes in network data are permanent and observable, blockchain technology provides a validated record that can be used by all participants at the same time. Blockchain technology has shown a variety of capabilities that have led to the creation of new application domains in the field of ERPs (Parikh, 2018).

In the sense of organizations, the ERP solution and Blockchain technology should complement each other in all facets of the business functions, enhancing efficiency, competitiveness, and cost reduction. Therefore, with a forward-looking vision, FANAP has begun to add this new technology to its MIDRP system. In order to go in the right direction, FANAP conducted all the necessary research to find the best way to enjoy the benefits of this technology in order to better serve their customers, especially MIDHCO. Herein, some of the capabilities for empowering MIDRP that can be brought about by blockchain technology are described.

Under the blockchain framework, proper visibility at every stage of the supply chain increases transparency. Blockchain in the MIDRP system can provide MIDHCO with the highest level of visibility in any part of the process. Usually, the supply chain tends to be a long and fragmented process. In addition, tracking all stages or how the product works at each stage becomes relatively difficult. That's why using blockchain can really solve supply chain issues in MIDRP by tracking processes in real-time. In addition, real-time reports on product location, temperature, or quality can be received.

With the ability to create a standard and reliable form for recording historical data by blockchain in the MIDRP solution, the efficiency of the organization will also increase. For example, the transfer of products in a supply chain typically involves several different business partners and processes, including shipping, invoicing, and keeping inventory records. Naturally, this will create different approaches, as each organization may work with different systems or applications. Blockchain technology, on the other hand, will provide a greater understanding of the data for each business operation. This in turn encourages organizations to trade with partners and suppliers who can have the ability to create and share data in a secure, traceable and reliable manner, ultimately creating closer collaboration between buyers and suppliers. With blockchain technology, constant access to accurate and reliable information, which is one of the primary goals of supply chains, will be achieved. Gaining the trust of all supply chain partners is achieved in such a way that everything is visible and transparent to them and ensures that there is no trouble or corruption in the system.

Another application that blockchain technology offered in the MIDRP solution is the execution of smart contracts to automate processes and payments. A smart contract is a protocol encoded in the blockchain to automate transactions (Blockchainhub, 2019). Smart contracts are being used gradually in the supply chain industry, specifically in manufacturing and distribution. Since smart contracts are electronic agreements that are automatically executed as per contractual terms and business logic, they are ideal for integrating in ERP applications to automate transactional processes. For instance, an ERP system can trigger purchase orders when stocks fall to baseline levels. The business unit in MIDHCO can also verify credible transactions without any third-party intervention. With smart contracts, companies can easily confirm the agreement with their suppliers. Also, in process automation, the contract can be started automatically, and the transactions can be processed as soon as the pre-defined rules of the contract are observed.

Furthermore, blockchain can provide a high level of real-time data security and privacy. In fact, the integration of this technology with MIDRP is able to prevent any data leaks and security threats and detect unauthorized activities immediately. Blockchain can define access validation for businesses and create privacy for information that should not be made public. Because of the sensitivity of corporate information, access to privacy-based information can help maintain in-company policies and avoid vulnerabilities in employee interactions. Ensuring the security of digital transactions is one of the biggest benefits of this technology. In fact, blockchain provides processing of P2P transactions in a completely efficient and fast way. Thanks to the high security provided by this technology, it is impossible for hackers to manipulate MIDRP subsystems.

10.4 Final Word

MIDRP system is a powerful enterprise solution with many useful features that provide great functionalities to automate the business processes and increase performance throughout MIDHCO holding. MIDHCO Holding needs a set of perfect tools to achieve a 4.2 million tonnes spike in annual production. In addition to human capital, technological advancements have always been a priority for managers. The vision statement of the organization's IT strategy utters that

"MIDHCO and its subsidiaries will become a developed company in the use of ICT and e-business to provide superior services and products with greater productivity through the optimal management of organizational resources." The use of IT in line with organizational goals is achieved only when the various applications of modern technologies are recognized and the culture of using these technologies is accepted by all members of the organization, especially the managers. In order to achieve this objective and in an attempt to prepare for digital transformation, the managers of MIDHCO and FANAP, have taken another step toward advancing their achievements by incorporating the latest technological developments in the context of the MIDRP project in the final phase.

With a bold move to the edge of technology, FANAP has made it possible to implement the latest technological advances in various industries such as steelmaking, helping them to embrace the digital age. The MIDRP system is a comprehensive enterprise solution for MIDHCO to create a digital organization. Therefore, after the full implementation of the MIDRP system, which covered all the basic and urgent needs of MIDHCO, the addition of important features such as system intelligence and digital technological tools could make it a complete and powerful package. Cloud computing makes it possible to use computing platforms without the need for local servers and at a lower cost. Collecting and sending data from various devices and analyzing them in real-time was an achievement of the IoT. The huge volume of data in all MIDHCO factories and how to control, manage, and analyze them was an important step that is done with the help of big data analytics. In addition, advanced reporting and analysis, smart dashboards, and optimal decision-making are the biggest achievements that AI offers to this solution. Furthermore, data security and data transport in a secure environment will also be achieved with the help of blockchain technology.

The future and its technological advances never end and keep going. The winner of this competition is the one who has a better knowledge of the future. FANAP, as a solution provider that develops these technologies, and MIDHCO, as the industries that are expected to benefit from these technologies, should both take advantage of the ahead opportunities to enrich the enterprise systems and help create an innovative environment to better increase productivity, reduce costs, and enhance customer satisfaction.

With a description of the advanced technologies and system intelligence, we come to the conclusion of this book. The story of MIDRP implementation has now come to an end. The opening of the story, in fact, narrated the ambitious target of the leading character, namely MIDHCO, in terms of a significant spike in the annual production rate. Considering enterprise resource planning as the best way of meeting such a target, several concerns were risen, e.g., taking the lack of similar applied experience in the target geographical region into the account, who should implement that solution and how should it be designed? Throughout this book, the issues, challenges, and remedies to such concerns were revealed one by one under the presence of the executive and supportive characters of FANAP and

POSCO ICT companies, respectively. The requirement of the leading character has been called MIDRP. MIDRP methodology sheds light on the project roadmap on its rocky accomplishment path. With a special focus on business process management and automation, the core concepts inside the MIDRP were formed over business processes and all the analysis activities were conducted to plan, identify and model the business processes that are required to satisfy the customer's business requirements.

A well-designed "Analysis Management System" helped to integrate and co-ordinate the analysis activities and ensure the consistency of defined elements throughout the system. The specified business processes along with all the classification and hierarchy in the product structure were transferred into software components in the design and development phase. For developing an efficient enterprise system, it is imperative to design a robust and flexible architecture with state-of-the-art technologies. The architecture of the MIDRP system was fully described and the innovative points in its style and components were introduced. In the development phase, a wide variety of innovative tools and techniques were used to optimize the software products and facilitate the development process. Most of the platforms, tools, and techniques were built as in-house modules by FANAP engineers. This infrastructure will be a great legacy for other projects specifically in similar enterprise solutions. By using rigorous testing procedures and version issuance policies that were established by the quality control unit in FANAP, the developed products were integrated and deployed on the customer's premises.

The MIDRP project was full of valuable experiences and learned lessons that might be helpful for other enterprise solution experts and ERP professionals. Regardless of the principles and guidelines that must be carefully followed in the enterprise solution implementation and software engineering, one should notice that every enterprise solution has its challenges and pitfalls. Each year, a considerable number of enterprise solution implementation projects fail due to a lack of understanding and prediction of the challenges and problems that might appear during the project for different organizational, technical, and cultural reasons. Learning about the experiences of each successful enterprise project may be helpful to reduce the cost of the implementation and avoid serious mistakes.

Enterprise solutions play an important role in facilitating and optimizing business processes and workflows in an organization. In the future, more companies will decide to implement some sort of ERP or similar systems in their business environment. We hope that by sharing our experiences in the MIDRP project for designing and implementing this complex and extensive system, we have been able to provide a beacon for researchers and professionals interested in implementing large organizational projects and provide useful insights for the ERP research and professional communities for tackling their own problems. Indeed, the happy ending of the story, in spite of formidable challenges, advocates that MIDRP can be regarded as a perfect practice for future reference in the era of enterprise solutions.

References

Ashton, K. (2009). That 'internet of things' thing. *RFID Journal, 22*(7), 97–114.

Bahrammirzaee, A. (2010). A comparative survey of artificial intelligence applications in finance: Artificial neural networks, expert system and hybrid intelligent systems. *Neural Computing and Applications, 19*(8), 1165–1195.

Banerjee, A. (2018). Blockchain technology: Supply chain insights from ERP. In *Advances in computers* (Vol. 111, pp. 69–98). Elsevier.

BlockchainHub. (2019). Available at: http://blockchainhub.net/smart-contracts/.

Goodfellow, I., Bengio, Y., Courville, A., & Bengio, Y. (2016). *Deep learning* (Vol. 1). Cambridge: MIT Press.

Gubbi, J., Buyya, R., Marusic, S., & Palaniswami, M. (2013). Internet of Things (IoT): A vision, architectural elements, and future directions. *Future Generation Computer Systems, 29*(7), 1645–1660.

Jannach, D., Zanker, M., Felfernig, A., & Friedrich, G. (2010). *Recommender systems: An introduction.* Cambridge University Press.

Kaur, M., & Kang, S. (2016). Market Basket Analysis: Identify the changing trends of market data using association rule mining. *Procedia Computer Science, 85*(Cms), 78–85.

Lee, I., & Lee, K. (2015). The Internet of Things (IoT): Applications, investments, and challenges for enterprises. *Business Horizons, 58*(4), 431–440.

Liu, B. (2015). *Sentiment analysis: Mining opinions, sentiments, and emotions.* Cambridge University Press.

Matt, C., Hess, T., & Benlian, A. (2015). Digital transformation strategies. *Business & Information Systems Engineering, 57*(5), 339–343.

Mitchell, R. S., Michalski, J. G., & Carbonell, T. M. (2013). *An artificial intelligence approach.* Berlin: Springer.

Nilsson, N. J. (2014). *Principles of artificial intelligence.* Morgan Kaufmann.

Parikh, T. (2018). The ERP of the future: Blockchain of things. *International Journal of Innovative Research in Science, 4*(1), 1341–1348.

Russell, S., & Norvig, P. (2020). *Artificial intelligence: A modern approach.* Englewood Cliffs. Prentice Hall.

Snijders, C., Matzat, U., & Reips, U. D. (2012). "Big Data": big gaps of knowledge in the field of internet science. *International Journal of Internet Science, 7*(1), 1–5.

Ustundag, A., & Cevikcan, E. (2017). *Industry 4.0: Managing the digital transformation.* Springer.

Velte, T., Velte, A., & Elsenpeter, R. (2009). *Cloud computing, a practical approach.* McGraw-Hill, Inc.

Xu, X. (2012). From cloud computing to cloud manufacturing. *Robotics and Computer-Integrated Manufacturing, 28*(1), 75–86.

Index

Printed in the United States
by Baker & Taylor Publisher Services

Printed in the United States
by Baker & Taylor Publisher Services